GLIMPSES OF INDUSTRIAL INDIA

GLIMPSES OF INDUSTRIAL INDIA

A Collection of Speeches of

Dr Bharat Ram

1963–1994

MANOHAR

ISBN 81–7304–057–5

First Published 1994

Price: Rs 295

Published by
Ajay Kumar Jain
Manohar Publishers & Distributors
2/6 Ansari Road, Daryaganj
New Delhi 110 002

Typeset at
Tulika Print Communication Services Pvt. Ltd.
R–271 (Lower Ground Floor), Greater Kailash I
New Delhi 110 048

Printed at
Pauls Press
E44/11 Okhla Industrial Area II
New Delhi 110 020

CONTENTS

FOREWORD

My introduction to the Shri Ram family came in 1953 when I was invited to lunch as a member of the International Monetary Fund Mission by Lalaji at his residence on Curzon Road. In itself, there was nothing unusual about this event. Visits by economists from abroad were rare then; and it was in the nature of things for the doyen of Indian industry in the north to entertain a Fund team to lunch at his home. What remains etched in my memory, however, are two things. Lalaji was preoccupied throughout with the arrival of his new, and I think, first, grand-daughter-in-law, whom he kept by his side all through, and whom he was determined to train in the family tradition of effortless hospitality. Equally significant for me was the fact that he gave me—a young Indian economist just cutting his teeth at economic policy—as much attention as he did to our distinguished leader, Dr E.M. Bernstein.

After that, it was no surprise that some ten years later, about the time the speeches in this volume begin, my wife and I, who were striving to settle down in Delhi to a new life, found ourselves sucked into a similar warm cocoon at the Lal Kothi on Sardar Patel Road where Bharatji had already established himself as the ruling patriarch. Once drawn into this magic circle, there was no turning back. Over the years, Lal Kothi became a home away from home, my wife a daughter of the family; even I graduated from the ambivalence of a promising bureaucrat to the security of a member of the family, and Bharatji became an elder and a friend at the same time. This, if you like, is a declaration of interest on my part to forewarn the readers of this foreword.

There are, I am sure, several Indian industrialists who have made greater fortunes since Independence than Bharatji—and one or two, like J.R.D., may have made a greater impact on the public mind. But about no one I know can I say truthfully what I can say about Bharatji: that he instinctively inspired both love and respect among all those he came in close contact with. The chemistry of this particular combination may not be unique. But it is certainly rare. In Bharatji's case, many things come to mind: his openness and spontaneity with not a touch of guile or deception; his seriousness about things without taking himself at all seriously; his elusive charm that invites without intruding; his small frame, soft words and slow gait gently gliding around you without grating or colliding; that touch of carelessness even in the midst of unmistakable sartorial and tonsoril elegance; the same effortless warmth and hospitality you witnessed at Curzon road; an almost adolescent joy in some of the simplest pleasures of life such as watching Wimbledon every summer in London, or on television if need be; and above all, his constant concern for the well-being of the nation and the urge to argue all points of view with everyone in search for the right path. There is never any condescension or affectation in anything he says or does; and if he assumes no airs, there is never anything light-hearted or flippant either about what he does or says.

It is difficult not to think of the man first and his ideas later in reading this collection of his speeches and articles. The very first piece, a tribute to Panditji, is as perceptive about the 'maker of modern India' as it is revelatory about the author of the tribute itself. It is difficult to avoid the impression that Bharatji is thinking of himself and his aspirations when he ruminates about Nehru. The piece is not at all structured and is even rambling. But it is straight from the heart, a song of the soul set in the mood and music of adoration. His description of the relationship between Panditji and the Mahatma is perhaps reminiscent of Bharatji's relationship with his own father. 'Although I did not agree with him on many things,' reads a quotation from Nehru, 'I never refused to obey his wishes.' In Bharatji's own case, I am sure none of his children and grandchildren—or his daughters-in-law and grand-daughters-in-law, for that matter—ever even dream of disobeying him, although, I am equally sure, they all argue with him vigorously on many occasions. To those who love and respect the man, I recommend two articles from this selection, and their last few paragraphs in particular—the one on Nehru and the one on agriculture.

Most of the other articles deal with Bharatji's views on Indian economic policy and on industrial policy in particular. Much of what he has to say is what you would expect from a man of his experience and perception. It is not surprising that he should emphasize the perversity of controls, regulations and licensing and their complexity and contradictions, or that he should extol the virtues of competition and family pride as the two pillars of sound management. He rightly reserves his severest criticism for the antipathy towards large houses and that peculiarly Indian contribution to demonology in the form of a concept of concentration of economic power in the aggregate as distinct from control over a particular sector or industry through monopolistic practices. As early as 1989, he was pleading for privatization. And he anticipates much in modern development theory when he puts the development of human resources at the top of the art of management.

Bharatji is a man of his own thinking, not just an echo of current thinking among Indian industrialists. Businessmen in India are not staunch advocates of financial prudence and the avoidance of inflation. Bharatji is forthright in his condemnation of inflation as the most inequitous of taxes. Poverty or unemployment, for him, are not just residual or incidental phenomena to be remedied by ad hoc measures. They are central to his view of our developmental challenge. Nor is he half-hearted in his advocacy of import liberalization. Once the process started, he wished it more speed and pleaded for more imports as well as exports—not just of goods, but of services, capital and technology as well. He is not afraid of taking a bold and unpopular stand on some of the most sensitive issues.

Where I think he differs most from the younger generation of strident liberals is in that his criticism of controls or regulations and of the public sector and the government's own monopolistic and restrictive practices is muted and subdued, as if he is fighting with one hand tied to the back. In this, he is typical of the generation that grew up during the time when giants like the Mahatma, Nehru and the Sardar dominated the Indian scene. That generation of enlightened businessmen were nationalists first and businessmen later. Like everyone else, their ambitions for the country were great and varied and they were in a hurry, impressed as they were by the complexity and contradictions of the Indian predicament. That is why the emphasis on harmony and cooperation among all—business and labour, business and government, business and business, business and the common man, the private and the public sectors, industry and agriculture, large industry and medium, small and cottage industry, the north and the south, the Hindu and the Muslim. Such varied and noble dreams, the craving for harmony and order in the midst of much discord and complexity, do not permit stridency of any sort.

I have often wondered why the Swatantra Party did not take root and find lasting support from Indian business. The instinct for survival had certainly much to do with it—you did not pit yourself against those who have the power to make or mar you. But I think that awkward but ardent nationalism born out of the actual struggle for Independence also had something to do with it.

What would a man with this background be wishing for India as he approaches his eightieth birthday? Let Bharatji speak for himself: 'A feeling is abroad that what has been achieved is meagre. This is true. Instead of making good the shortfalls, there is a reckless tendency to adopt new life-styles that are vulgar. Quick money must somehow be made, and the means are not important. The levers of power are indiscriminately used. . . . Human resource development is no more and no less than individual growth. Such growth consists in living a healthy life physically, learning all the time, inspired by the faith that individually one can do something about making the lives of others better and happier, and above all, association with a larger cause than eking out a mere living, however profitable, thus adding to one's own stature. . . . There is no rational ground for despair. India has too long a history to feel frustrated. Creative manners, creative words and creative actions have to arise sooner or later. The power of balanced judgment is bound to come.'

We all speak of creativity, of creative words and creative actions. But how many of us would even think of 'creative manners' and put that at the top of the list? The manners here relate to the mode of living, the very heart and soul of all cultures and civilizations. But a doubt persists. Can creation ever be well-mannered and orderly? Is it not messy and bloody, as with human beings, and full of thunder and lightning, fire and brimstone, as with the cosmos? Perhaps we will never be sure of the springs of creation. But preservation, sustenance, security and sanity have a distinct genetic code which we call our common heritage. No wonder, in the Hindu pantheon, Brahma is seldom remembered and Shankar arrests with his awesome ferocity. Only Vishnu, with his pranks and high philosophy, is both loved and worshipped.

4 August 1994 I.G. PATEL
Baroda

Acknowledgement

I am grateful to Mr P. Chentsal Rao,
Dr Meenakshi Nayar,
Mr R.R. Prasad,
and Mr Manjit Singh
for their help in
compiling this book.

A TRIBUTE TO THE MAKER OF MODERN INDIA : JAWAHARLAL NEHRU

A TRIBUTE TO THE MAKER OF MODERN INDIA : JAWAHARLAL NEHRU

Human beings are not all of a piece. In each one, indeed, different and even incompatible traits exist. Yet, they yield a rough harmony and some kind of a working philosophy, made out of shreds and patches, maybe. Pandit Jawaharlal Nehru displayed attractive and bewitching contrasts. These meshed to bring about a luminous and pleasing personality, a complete man, who appealed to children, men and women, the masses and the classes. A handsome man with a handsome mind. No one has brought out better than Panditji himself the portrait of his own mind in the many books and letters that he wrote, in the many speeches that he made. They make one feel as if Jawaharlal and Nehru were ever, if not in conflict, in pursuit of the truth from different angles.

While Jawaharlal was like a force of nature, like a tumultuous river overflowing its banks, Nehru was a sober judge of the multifariousness of life, its confusions and cross-purposes, and of the remoteness of causes that result in significant effects. In neither is there a trace of intellectual pettifogging or trivial passion.

Like father, like son. Father Motilal Nehru was an aristocrat to the fingertips. When confronted with vulgarity, his nose would virtually flare. Far from averse to the refinements of life, he also had the strength to accept monastic asceticism. His powerful intellect would restrain the waywardness of a restless heart. No decision was ever taken by him in a precipitate manner. He always led, but he never gave the impression that he sought obedience, much less servility. When the situation so arose that he was to become a follower of the Mahatma, it was a great moment for him. Yet his full-bloodied personality could not in any way be diminished. It was the impetuous Jawaharlal who converted the father. Nehru followed the father in his footsteps.

Both Jawaharlal and Nehru abounded with vitality, alternating between poet and social scientist. Jawaharlal and Nehru kept each other company, the one supplementing the other. This is all too evident in all that has gone into print, as in workaday life. The following passage, written from Ahmednagar Fort, reveals the union of Jawaharlal and

Nehru and a smooth flow of commingled concepts.

> The moon, ever a companion to me in prison, has grown more friendly with closer acquaintance, a reminder of the loveliness of this world, of the waxing and waning of life, of light following darkness, of death and resurrection following each other in interminable succession. Ever changing, yet ever the same, I have watched it in its different phases and its many moods in the evening, as the shadows lenghen, in the still hours of the night, and when the breath and whisper of dawn bring promise of the coming day. How helpful is the moon in counting the days and the months, for the size and shape of the moon, when it is visible, indicate the day of the month with a fair measure of exactitude. It is an easy calendar (though it must be adjusted from time to time), and for the peasant in the field the most convenient one to indicate the passage of the days and the gradual changing of the season.

The poet talks of the moods of the moon, a shimmering crescent, and the social scientist sees in the waxing and waning of the moon 'an easy calendar' for the peasant.

Jawaharlal Nehru developed into a superb craftsman as a writer, because he was born to it, and bore out the dictum that the style is the man. As he was imprisoned by the British rulers for long stretches of time he read prodigiously, thought intensely, and wrote exquisitely. An instance of good coming out of evil. Would he have retired voluntarily to solitude to devote himself to writing a history of the world and a picture of India in his day that was struggling to gain political independence? This is an 'if' of history.

Analysing himself, he wrote, 'I have become a queer mixture of the East and the West, out of place everywhere, at home nowhere.' Actually, Jawaharlal belonged to the hoary India; Nehru to the modern world. Witness his last will and testament. The words are those of Jawaharlal:

> I am proud of that great inheritance that has been and is ours, and am conscious that I, too, like all of us, am a link in the unbroken chain which goes back to the dawn of history in the immemorial past of India. That chain I would not break, for I treasure it and seek inspiration from it. And as a witness of this desire of my mind and as my last homage to India's cultural inheritance, I am making this request that a handful of my ashes be thrown into the Ganga at Allahabad to be carried to the great ocean that washes India's shores.
>
> The major portion of my ashes should, however, be disposed of

> otherwise. I want these to be carried high up into the air in an aeroplane and scattered from that height over the fields where the peasants of India toil so that they might mingle with the dust and soil of India and become an indistinguishable part of India.

Jawaharlal, the freedom fighter, laid down his burden in his famous Tryst with Destiny address to the Constituent Assembly on 14 August 1947. 'Long years ago,' he said, 'we made a tryst with destiny, and now the time comes when we shall redeem our pledge, not wholly or in full measure, but very substantially. At the stroke of the midnight-hour, when the world sleeps, India will awake to life and freedom.' And the burden was picked up by Nehru who, in his first broadcast to the nation as Prime Minister, proclaimed, 'Production is the first priority.'

Jawaharlal it was, who went farther than the aspirations of the early Indian nationalists to secure self-government within the British Empire. He declared at the Lahore Congress in 1929 that independence meant complete freedom from British domination and British imperialism. Even at Lahore, Nehru declared: 'Having attained our freedom I have no doubt that India will welcome all attempts at world co-operation and federation and will even agree to give up part of her independence to a larger group of which she is an equal member—India could never be an equal member of the Commonwealth unless imperialism and all that it implies is discarded.' And Nehru, the Prime Minister, was more than a little responsible for India becoming a member of the Commonwealth and turning this Club of Whites into a multi-racial one. The United Nations had in him an ardent supporter.

In one sense the career of Jawaharlal Nehru was haphazard: at the same time, it was replete with success as if it were planned in advance. His mind was of a composite build: English by education, Muslim by culture, and Hindu by birth. Even his dress spoke of this blend—the 'Jawahar' coat, a short sleeveless one, the *achkan* that flaunted a rose, and an immaculate turnout in either was a pleasing synthesis. Jawaharlal admitted that he was not cut out for the legal profession and found law dry. But Nehru, the Prime Minister, had to grapple with Constitution-making, institution-building and resource mobilization. If Jawaharlal would see a black marketeer hung by the nearest lamp-post, Nehru had to contend with the problem of bringing tax-evaded money into the official mainstream. Jawaharlal thought that 'confiscation is the basis and life-breath of the present system' and a clash of class interests 'seems inevitable'. But Nehru, with his humanist liberal tradition, resorted to economic planning within the framework of democracy. This was one of his precious contributions to socio-political thinking and practice. Planning ceased to be the preserve of socialist countries. Democracies, too, Nehru demonstrated, could undertake the planning exercise; planning and individual liberty were not antithetical.

Even before the National Planning Commission was constituted in 1950, Nehru was keen to articulate government policy in the industrial field. This was embodied in the Industrial Policy Resolution of 6 April 1948. Emphasizing the importance to the economy of securing a continuous increase in production and its equitable distribution, the Resolution set out as its credo that the state must play a progressively active role in the development of industries. On this basis the development and establishment of some key industries became the exclusive monopoly of the central government. The rest of the industrial field was left to private enterprise with the caveat that it should be 'properly directed and regulated'. Eight years later, in 1956, taking note of the many important changes and developments in India—the enactment of the Constitution, the recently completed first five-year plan, the acceptance by Parliament of the socialist pattern of society as the objective of social and economic policy—a fresh Industrial Policy Statement was issued. This spelt out in greater detail the content of the earlier Resolution. Since then, some changes have been effected off and on, but without altering the basic structure.

In retrospect, it must be conceded that the formulation of the concepts and their realization are two different things. The best of concepts can misfire and produce unintended results as, indeed, has happened with the regulatory aspect taking precedence over the development of private enterprise, and with the public sector enterprises, in the main, failing to fulfil the originally envisioned expectations. In this hard world, the most exquisite sensibilities, the noblest expressions of fine feeling, and even the profoundest insights into goodness may go awry at the level of implementation. But the pursuit of political and social ideals will suffer if the visionaries, too, fall back on the comfortable philosophy, 'I see the better, and approve of it; the worse is what I pursue.'

The relationship between Jawaharlal Nehru and Mahatma Gandhi, between the disciple and the master, defies ordinary reasoning. Jawaharlal rebelled, Nehru acquiesced, and he had gone on record to say, 'Although I did not agree with him on many problems, I never refused to obey his wishes.' Jawaharlal resolutely spoke out his objections, and Gandhiji in his turn was most unwilling to say anything that might even remotely hurt Jawaharlal.

The mystique of the Mahatma intrigued and baffled Jawaharlal and Nehru alike. What is the 'inner voice' that the leader spoke of and which prompted him to suspend the Civil Disobedience movement to wrest freedom from the alien rulers? To the Mahatma, God did not rule the world from some remote heaven, but by his intimate omnipresence, not an absentee, foreign and external government, but in every finite working of every revealed will, knowledge and action. Jawaharlal was prepared to accept an infinite force at work, and his impetuous nature was rather inclined somehow to set right wrongs instead of being thwarted by vague notions of sin and redemption. On the other hand, the well-read Nehru was aware of the grip of custom on human behaviour. Man is somewhat superstitious by nature and he will worship some god or the other. However, he would not concede that this scripture or that alone provided the eternal truth. Truth expresses itself in time and through the mind of man. Every scripture must necessarily contain two elements, one temporary, belonging to the ideas of the period and country in which it was produced, the other eternal and imperishable and applicable in all ages and all countries.

Fixed doctrines can be discarded. However, the problems of life cannot be evaded. So a joint solution was found by Jawaharlal and Nehru in the following terms, a 'living philosophy' that deliberately eschewed metaphysical speculation:

> The real problems for me remain problems of individual and social life, of harmonious living, of a proper balancing of an individual's inner and outer life, of an adjustment of the relations between individuals and between groups, of a continuous becoming something better and higher, of social development, of the ceaseless adventure of man. In the solution of these problems the way of observation and precise knowledge and deliberate reasoning, according to the method of science, must be followed. This method may not always be applicable in our quest of truth, for art and poetry and certain psychic experiences seem to belong to a different order of things and to elude the objective methods of science. Let us, therefore, not rule out intuition and other methods of sensing truth and reality. They are necessary even for the purpose of science. But always we must hold our anchor of precise objective knowledge tested by reason, and even more so by experiment and practice, and always we must beware of losing ourselves in a sea of speculation unconnected with the day-to-day problems of life and the needs of men and women. A living philosophy must answer the problems of today.

'He is an extraordinary paradox', said Jawaharlal of the Mahatma. Jawaharlal could not, for dear life, accept Gandhiji's theory of trusteeship', his plea for 'almost a self-sufficient village', his insistence on 'village industries', an extension of the khadi programme, the 'stress on sexual abstinence, on the giving up of drink, smoking, etc.' How could the capitalist be invited to regard himself as a trustee for those on whom he depended for the making, the retention and the increase of his capital, asked Jawaharlal. It was clear to him that it was next to impossible to go back to the pre-industrial era and a quaint old religious outlook to resolve the many problems facing India. He was firm in his conviction about the urgency to have a highly developed industrial system. It was left to Nehru to combine the old and the new, to build 'modern temples' in the form of huge dams and large public-sector enterprises, and to inject new life into rural India so as to increase agricultural production, revive ancient crafts and arts, and launch upon an official programme of family planning, the first of its kind. He sought to improve agriculture and rural prosperity through industrialization. To him it was axiomatic that an aggregate industrial complex was necessary to support agriculture: an increase in food supply was not possible without the engineering and chemical industries to provide tractors, agricultural machinery and fertilizers; bridges, roads and houses could not be built without steel and cement; power could not be made available without generating equipment; and so on. On a practical basis, the concept of a simple and yet prosperous village life vanishes as a dream when one awakens.

Jawaharlal was all for making the state the prime energizer and developer of the economy. If this entailed controls and high taxes, have them, he said. However, Nehru was cautious about going in for nationalization. He advised Parliament to curb political enthusiasm for socializing private economic projects.

> It is talk with which one naturally tends to agree—but one has always to remember that the primary function of a growing society is to produce more wealth; otherwise it will not grow, and you will have nothing to distribute. If in the process of your fixation of ceiling or in any other process, you stop this process of growth and wealth accumulation, you fail in your objective.
>
> I have no shadow of doubt that if we say 'lop off the private sector', we cannot replace it adequately. We have not got resources to replace it. . . . Let the State go on building up its plants and industries so far as its resources permit. Why should we fritter away our energy in pushing out somebody who is doing it in the private sector?. . . It is foolish to take charge of the whole field when you are really incapable of using that huge area yourself. Therefore, you must not only permit the private sector, but I say encourage it in its own field.

In the area of foreign policy adumbrated by him, there are two streams of thought. Nehru was wont to explain the policy of non-alignment 'as essential to the fulfilment of India's economic revolution, for it maintains a free access to the technical skills and capital of all the great industrial powers'. India's policy was 'a friendly approach, a patient approach and a humble approach', and there was no desire 'to sit on a perch and to moralize to anybody because we are conscious of our own failings in our own country'. But Jawaharlal was impelled to remind his own countrymen and the world, 'We are free because we take decisions independently of any pressure of threat or temptation.' Furthermore:

> India's pivotal position between Western Asia, South-East Asia and the Far East made it the crossroads of that part of the world. India is the central point of the Asian picture. . . . India's role of leadership may not be so welcome to others although it may satisfy our vanity. But it is something which we cannot escape. We cannot escape the various responsibilities that arise out of our geography and history.

Indeed, Nehru succinctly brought out the content of independence when he told the Constituent Assembly in 1948:

> What does independence consist of? It consists fundamentally and basically of foreign relations. That is the test of independence. All else is local autonomy. Once foreign relations go out of your hand into the charge of somebody else, to that extent and in that measure, we are not independent.

The revolution in China impressed Jawaharlal, as did the revolution earlier in Russia. Nehru, however, viewed the goings-on in China with caution. He felt that revolutions had a way of 'spilling over'. Little did he anticipate that China would transgress the boundaries of India. This was something of a spiritual Waterloo for him, and it told on his health as well. In the end, he was a saddened man, but his faith in the Indian people and the future of India did not falter.

This faith led him to believe that the performance of the public sector, though not up to expectations, would improve once the teething troubles were overcome; that the drawbacks of the regulatory system, which was called the licence-raj by uncompromising critics, were outweighed by the socio-economic objectives the system sought to attain and did attain in some measure; that the burgeoning corruption in administration and politics should be traced to the flux of change, from a wholly rural to an emerging industrial society with uncertain norms. It must be said to the credit of Jawaharlal Nehru that he never swerved to the last in his objective: to make India prosperous, to secure distributive justice, and to keep alive creativity, vigour, vitality and the joy of life in individuals.

The Nehru era is important for India. Major transformations were initiated without violence. The princely states were amalgamated into the Indian Union. Many laws were passed to protect and promote the interests of the underprivileged. People were stimulated to be alive to the larger issues, to the design for growth and the design for living. The atmosphere gave ample opportunities to every section of society to air views and question beliefs with a view to arriving at a consensus.

Today, we have distanced ourselves from both Mahatma Gandhi and Jawaharlal Nehru. No doubt, over a period of time, old images tend to disappear and new ones emerge. But time is not the only reason. A feeling is abroad that what has been achieved is meagre. This is true. Instead of making good the shortfalls, there is a reckless tendency to adopt new life-styles that are vulgar. Quick money must somehow be made, and the means are not important. The levers of power are indiscriminately used. If the Mahatma and Jawaharlal Nehru differed, which they did on many issues, they were united in the thought that human resources development is no more and no less than individual growth. Such growth consists in living a healthy life physically, learning all the time, inspired by the faith that individually one can do something about making the lives of others better and happier, and, above all, association with a larger cause than eking out a mere living, however profitable, thus adding to one's own stature.

The cycle of rise and fall goes on. It cannot come to a halt merely because we are passing through a distressing and distrustful phase. There is no rational ground for despair. India has too long a history to feel frustrated. Creative manners, creative words and creative actions have to arise sooner or later. The power of balanced judgement is bound to come.

Article published in Jawaharlal Nehru Centenary Volume, Implementation Committee for the Commemoration of the Jawaharlal Nehru Centenary, 1989.

DIMENSIONS OF DEVELOPMENT : THE ECONOMY

WHITHER ARE WE BOUND?

I am happy that I have been given an opportunity to address this distinguished gathering. 'Whither are we bound?' is the title of my talk. In a sense, this question has been with us almost throughout history. It is a question that can receive different answers from different people under different circumstances, inasmuch as it involves the mixed elements of intelligent anticipation and individual predilection. Given the fast-changing national and international scenes, I should be cautious, for otherwise I would either be accused of being rash or of indulging in our national pastime of reading the stars.

One's view of the future would naturally be correlated to one's experience of the past. If one limits oneself to the economic and business aspects of our national life, there are some objective guidelines that may be followed. Thus, one can view the trends in population, national income, production, etc., assess the trends in each of these basic economic factors and then attempt some predictions regarding the immediate and not so immediate future. Developments in a vast country like India, however, cannot be judged merely by statistical indices; there is something of an overall climate which is the result of not only mutually inter-related but even contrary events and situations. This evening, I propose to give an indication of my overall impressions first, and then to go on to a somewhat detailed examination of the individual areas of economic performance in order to assess the future.

Let me at the outset say that my overall judgement is optimistic though it is restrained and qualified. This is inevitable against the record of progress on the one hand, and on the other, the setbacks and disappointments which we have had almost continuously since the initiation of the third five-year plan. The economic development of out country, perhaps more than any other, is directed by some factors over which we have some control and by others over which we have very limited or no control. Among the factors over which we do have or should have some control are the basic policies of economic administration as well as the management of economic and business institutions, both public and private. The factors in which we have very limited say are international markets, as also the climate in India. A bad monsoon may result in poor agricultural production and low commodity prices may reduce the net availability of foreign exchange resources.

Thus, it becomes all the more necessary to have in-built reserves and stabilizers, if only to reduce the imbalances arising out of areas over which we have no direct control. In this context, I feel that our competence in various fields—the management of economic affairs, administration and the like—must be substantially improved so that what is humanly possible to be done is done at the right time and in the right way. Of equal importance is our reaction to the emergence of potentially favourable factors. We have a tendency to assume that what is feasible and desirable has already been accomplished, with the result that we relax in our efforts as well as vigilance. In essence, therefore, our basic attitudes require reorientation to enhance our possible progress and to mitigate our possible failures.

I shall now turn to the specific sectors of our economy and begin with agriculture in which the largest shortfalls in production targets have been seen over the past two seasons. The plan expected an increase of 30 per cent in the production of foodgrains over the five-year period. Production in the present season is expected to be higher than in the last year. This is not merely a matter influenced by the vagaries of the monsoon. There has been a decline or insufficient increase in the production potential of agriculture. Where the production potential already exists, there may not be full utilization, particularly in the case of irrigation.

The use and distribution of fertilizers as well as better seeds are far from optimal. This is so because of faulty distribution methods and inadequate subsidiary services. There has been no systematic nationwide effort to disseminate knowledge of the advantages of newer methods of production to the Indian farmer who is fairly receptive. He wants, naturally enough, to see for himself the positive results. It is not also unnatural if he expects to be persuaded before he effects a changeover. It is in these areas that we require to concentrate our attention.

Productivity is usually a term associated with industrial production. The concept has to be transferred to, adopted by and executed in agriculture. In the recent past, we realized how a shortfall in agricultural production can seriously hamper our efforts to increase industrial output or to augment our export earnings abroad.

As for industry, the rate of increase in production seems to be a little higher than in 1962–63. However, here, too, there has been a lack of balance inasmuch as there has been larger growth in producer and basic industries as compared with the general index, while the output increase in consumer industries has been comparatively small. As far as industries in the private sector are concerned, the main obstructing factor has been the shortage of foreign exchange which has become more severe since the beginning of the third plan. While this general shortage is a chronic factor which will be with us for a long time to come, the recent constriction has had a particularly crippling effect on industry both with regard to current output as well as proposed increases in capacity or installation of new capacity.

Exports has always been a pet theme with me and I would like to discuss it a little more. We have had enough slogans like 'export or perish' and exhortations galore. There can be hardly any difference of opinion on the need to augment our total export earnings. The fact of the matter is that our capacity and ability to export must be attuned to the needs and requirements of foreign consumers. Basically, our exports, whether emerging from the field or the factory, must be on a scale and of a quality to compete in international markets. In other words, production itself must be large enough to enjoy economies of scale; also, it must be large enough to yield substantial surpluses for exports on a regular basis. The problem of export earnings, or more generally speaking, the question of balance of payments has now to be more closely linked with the overall strategy of long-term planning than hitherto. A distinct reorientation has to be made not only in terms of export incentive schemes or refinements of import policy but also in the patterns of investment. This readjustment has to be effected in investments in agriculture as well as industry. With simultaneous efforts to assist export promotion and to increase import substitution, we must remedy the low utilization of available foreign resources and assistance, which is at present being examined by a special committee under the chairmanship of Shri V.K.R.V. Rao. I have no doubt in my mind that the Rao Committee will remove such misunderstandings as there might be on the subject in the public mind and also outline appropriate courses of action. I trust the implementation of the Committee's recommendations will be prompt.

In meeting the general deficiency of our foreign resources we have had necessarily to depend on assistance from friendly countries and the inflow of private foreign investment. There is a view, to which I do not at all subscribe, that our country is far too heavily committed in terms of repayment of obligations and therefore should go slow in the matter of obtaining private foreign capital. Let us not forget that we invite foreign investment only in areas where it is needed most. Consequently, its role is a valuable one. I am happy to note that the Finance Minister, Shri T.T. Krishnamachari recently expressed himself in favour of permitting greater flow of private foreign capital. This acquisition of monetary resources and technical know-how will increasingly stimulate and foster our overall industrial growth. At the same time, we must clearly recognize that foreign private investment will be attracted to India only if the conditions here are not only better than in its own country, but also in the countries competing for foreign capital. It is in this light that this subject should be handled officially, privately and administratively. As far as I can gather, apart from political stability, foreign capital attaches great importance to stability in tax policy and simplicity in tax structure and other procedures. So far as administrative procedures are concerned, the interim recommendations of the Swaminathan Committee have been formally accepted by government. This is, indeed, good. The results have yet to unfold. In regard to taxation policy, I would earnestly recommend that at least during a plan period there are no fundamental changes. This should apply equally to the tax structure. If swift and basic changes are effected, then the entire calculation of the entrepreneur, whether foreign or domestic, will be completely upset. Business confidence, whether anyone likes it or not, is closely linked to the balance-sheet.

We businessmen are interested in the processes and methods of economic planning. We are proud of the fact that our plan efforts are within the framework of democracy. No doubt, the Planning Commission has consultations with a fairly wide section of public opinion and specialized agencies. Nevertheless, there is a feeling that the thinking is restricted to small official groups and institutions close to the government. It must be confessed that the plans so far have not livened up economic thinking in the country as a whole in any distinct manner. I would, therefore, suggest that this important matter should be looked into so that, besides others, industrial and business organizations feel involved, emotionally and otherwise, in the charting of the country's economic future. There is another point. How are we to formulate targets? Are they to be easily attainable or set at points for which greater effort is required? It stands to reason that the second course must be followed. The important issue, however, is that a good deal of thought and greater effort must go into computing each individual target. If the targets are not reached for any reason there is public disappointment at the planning mechanism and loss of confidence in those who fail to reach the targets.

We have to accept the criticism that while India has about the best planning machinery in the underdeveloped world, it also has about the lowest standard of living and continues to have about the lowest rate of increase in per capita income. There are many factors responsible for this and some of them are intractable in the short run. The tremendous, inexorable increase in our population continues. As Eugene Black has said, 'The business of having babies is certainly the largest private enterprise in the world.' As a result, no visible dent is being made into the serious unemployment and underemployment existing in our economy. Planning as well as the general increased pace of economic activity have increased the availability of certain goods to the ordinary population, particularly in the cities and industrial areas. There is, however, a considerable lag in the provision of social services which make life easier and richer. In this, education may be regarded as one of the main sufferers. It is frequently seen that education is the first item to sustain a cut when economy measures in government expenditure are contemplated. Even when resources are available, the overall lack of uniform thinking in educational policies has resulted in the supply of educated personnel who are uneven both in quality and quantity. A fair degree of thought is now being devoted to studying and planning manpower for future development plans. There is much ground to be covered here; it is also essential that quick decisions are taken so that the wastage of university graduates is checked. Agricultural education should receive very high priority. Short-term courses in technical fields have to be increased and improved so that those who are already dependent on agriculture and who are likely to continue in it find attractive and promising results.

Socialism is a topic that has been very much in the news during the past weeks. This has been in a sense an assessment of the progress made so far in the policies and implementation of measures meant to induce greater equality both in income as well as economic opportunities. As must have been observed during the discussions which have been going on, a definition of socialism which is acceptable is yet to emerge. In the nature of things such a definition is not possible. What is now clearly apparent is the dissatisfaction felt in various quarters concerning the specific steps undertaken so far in our economic management. Thus, there is a view that reducing disparities in income, which should be regarded as an inherent aspect of socialism, has not been carried out to a sufficiently drastic extent. There is also a view that control of the commanding heights in the economy has not been sufficiently exhaustive. In all this, we may tend to forget what should really constitute the essential ingredients of a policy to redress and remove poverty. I would suggest that discussions, even if they might begin from somewhat vague theories and sentiments, would be useful if they soon get down to studying specific issues. It is when we are more specific about the economic content of socialism that one realizes the basic limitations of our economic structure. I am not suggesting here that poverty is inevitable or that it is something one is born with and has to live with.

I am, however, of the view that we should attempt to solve the problems of our low standards of living by looking at them from the point of view of production as well as of distribution or redistribution. Greater production is the only key to better distribution.

We must consider that the way to break out of the vicious circle of low income, low savings and low investment, is to undertake policies which lead to increased production of goods according to realistic priorities. Our production and business apparatuses have a history and a momentum and these should not be interfered with without an eye on the consequences. The history of our productive institutions and agencies shows that production is induced by the possibilities of profit. Profits are inevitably connected with the concept of a mixed economy, which alone provides the widest possible base for individual economic pursuit. Profits must be a feature of both public and private sector undertakings if they are to develop. It is, therefore, necessary that when attempting to achieve the end of socialism one does not attack concepts like profit as inherently evil, for they form an essential part of all economic activity, whether socialized or not.

I would, therefore, suggest that we look more closely at the material content of socialism in terms of goods and services. We should look at it in terms of whether the development of the economy has benefited the poorer sections of the community since the advent of independence and planned economic progress. An increase in the per capita availability of those commodities and services which enter the ordinary citizen's budget should indicate that his standard of living has improved. Under such items, one can include the production and import of commodities such as foodgrains, cloth and sugar, and services like education, health and rural electrification. One can arrive at comparatively reliable conclusions about the general availability of these items. For instance, we may note that whereas the growth of population in the past ten years or so has been less than 25 per cent, the net availability of foodgrains through production and imports was higher by 45 per cent. During the same period, the production of cloth rose by over 60 per cent, of sugar by 140 per cent and of vanaspati by 110 per cent. There was also larger consumption of wheat and rice as against millets. The number of children going to school increased by 85 per cent and the number of hospital beds by 65 per cent. Thus, the process of development has undoubtedly brought about better living standards in terms of the quantity as well as quality of available goods and services. It would be wrong to lose sight of these distinct and definite gains when considering the overall poverty and generally low income of the country. There is still great poverty, malnutrition and lack of educational and cultural opportunities. Their persistence is a fact. At the same time, when one feels unhappy about this situation and impatient about the pace of social improvement, one should realize that we started out from much lower levels of consumption.

When expressing dissatisfaction at the low rate of increase in incomes, it would be next to useless to blame any one section. If there has been a failure in the developmental process, it is not the exclusive responsibility of a single section of the society. Almost everyone is responsible for it in some measure or the other. It is facile to isolate one section and to give vent to frustration by condemning it. This is neither fair nor constructive. It is even likely to be damaging inasmuch as it may harm the morale of the hard-working administrator or ordinary businessman, neither of whom presents a *prima facie* example of minor dictators or scheming exploiters respectively. In examining closely the causes of our low rate of development, each of us should, both in our individual as well as representative capacity, look inwards and find out how much less we have given of ourselves to promote the general progress of the country.

I propose to conclude with a few remarks on the matter of incentives not only for the businessman or the agriculturist but for all sections of the society. It is easy to suggest that improvements in economic structure and in the functioning of the economy can be brought about by legislative measures and sanctions. Here, one can refer to the remark of Barbara Ward, 'What India needs to avoid at all costs is an economy in which neither incentives nor sanctions work.' The basic credo of a democratic socialistic society excludes the extremes of limitless incentives or exhaustive sanctions which would end up in *laissez faire* or totalitarian control of society. Neither of these would work in India because both would result in chaos.

I have covered a wide range of circumstances and situations, and in so doing I trust I have avoided over-simplification of issues and facile panaceas to cure our ills. My attempt has been to suggest some pattern for the future on the basis of available aggregate data pertaining to our economy. We are still on the path of progress despite setbacks here and there. This progress will be neither easy nor automatic. Our economy will not soar on a self-sustained flight and our people will not have satisfactory standards of living, unless we learn to work hard and to work together.

Address at a meeting organized by the Commerce Graduates Association and the Democratic Group of the Indian Merchants' Chamber, Bombay, 29 January 1964.

EXPLOITATION OF OUR RESOURCES

I have pleasure in welcoming you all to the Thirty-seventh Annual Session of the Federation. Since we met last, about a year ago, the international scene has been darkened by the tragic assassination of President Kennedy. The world has lost a brave man, who deeply concerned himself with the welfare of underdeveloped nations and underprivileged people. His desire for world peace was indeed infectious. No better homage could be rendered to him than the one by his successor, President Johnson, who declared in his State of the Union Message to the US Congress: 'Let us carry forward the plans and programmes of John Fitzgerald Kennedy—not because of our sorrow or sympathy—but because they are right.'

At this time last year, our memories were painfully fresh of the blatant and perfidious aggression on our territory by the Chinese regime. A part of our territory is still occupied. We have not only to be vigilant, but have to do all that is in our power to adequately equip ourselves to protect the national boundaries. It is through strengthening our industrial and agricultural base that we can preserve national freedom and dignity. Economic development, therefore, is essential both for improving the standard of living of the people and for augmenting the defence potential.

It is in this context, I feel, that the mid-term appraisal of the third plan must be viewed. The Planning Commission has frankly admitted serious lags—national income has grown only at half the rate expected during the plan period; industrial output has increased at a slower rate; agricultural production has remained almost stationary. The Economic Survey for 1963–64 presented by the Finance Minister, Shri T.T. Krishnamachari, to Parliament has highlighted the problems facing accelerated economic growth, and admits, among other things, that the need was felt for improvements in the implementation of agricultural programmes, in the execution and working of many of the public sector industrial undertakings, in the revival of the capital market, and in the stimulation of investment and output. The question naturally arises whether the approach to the solution of our problems is right as well as dynamic. Many times government spokesmen have restated the general principles underlying economic policy and have re-emphasized the importance of increasing production. But if a large part of the economic field is brought within the domain of politics, then the pragmatic approach to economic issues gets weakened, as also the thrust towards greater production.

In my view, the basic problem is one of exploitation of our resources. In regard to natural resources, India is better placed than quite a few of the industrially advanced countries. Our mineral wealth of coal, iron, limestone is ample; so also our water resources for generation of power and for irrigating the land. While the overall potential is enormous, absolutely as well as relatively, the area of development is also large. It is not as if our effort needs to be only marginal. So much has got to be done, and that too speedily. But somehow a psychology of scarce resources has come to dominate official thinking. This has been a great handicap to faster growth, and is an important factor responsible for the setback in the results of our planning effort. Also, there is a feeling that we cannot afford to go too fast. For instance, it was suggested some time back that the licensing of new industrial undertakings in the private sector could possibly be slowed down because there were shortages in rail transport and power. One should have thought that instead of slowing down the rate of development in any one sector, greater effort would be made to hasten the composite growth of all sectors. I would like to reiterate what the Federation has been urging all along, that the solution does not lie in withholding industrial progress, which in fact will be tantamount to avoiding the problem itself, but in accelerating the progress of those economic sectors which have fallen behind. At the same time, we have to avoid a situation which, while leading to fulfilment of targets and outlays in the public sector, will result in a corresponding slower rate in the private sector.

I am not to be misunderstood as belittling the part government has to play in the economic affairs of the nation. After World War II particularly, it has come to be generally accepted everywhere that governmental intervention at certain key points and in certain circumstances may be necessary. But it is also held that when regulatory measures are adopted, they should be minimal and essentially elastic. In this view of things, controls become necessary only in conditions of extreme scarcity, but the policy itself must be forward-looking. Short-term considerations should not vitiate the view about the future, or the prospects for larger production. There has been, I think, growing recognition of these factors. From November 1963, there has been some liberalization of credit which, apart from signalling the commencement of the busy season, is symptomatic of a change in outlook. The Finance Minister had even assured that further measures would have to be devised to make credit more freely available. There was also decontrol of prices of sixteen commodities in December last. I am glad that this matter is further engaging the government's attention. In my view, such controls as have been prevailing in some of the most important industries like iron and steel, cement, coal and fertilizers, contributed to the shortfalls in production in these specific industries, and hindered the fulfilment even of the overall plan targets. So, controls have to be removed or rationalized to make investment attractive. Whether for the private or for the public sector, investment is regulated by business considerations. Otherwise, it will encourage wasteful use of our resources. If our economy is caught in conflicting currents, it is mainly because the policy has become uncertain. Only stability creates confidence. It is in long-term projections that both administrative and business decisions can be taken. Of course, rigidity should not be mistaken for stability. In a dynamic world, there is bound to be fuller adaptation of policies to situations; but the basic concepts and values—the rules of the game—should be predictable.

Even so, the very nature of private enterprise has generated competition and Indian businessmen can claim with pride that they have fulfilled the prime function expected of them. Private enterprise has brought about a rapid expansion of industries, that is in the fields where it is allowed to operate. During the last decade, the output of private industries has doubled; over 188 new major products were manufactured for the first time in the last five years; the quality of products has been continually improving. These are clear indications that private enterprise has taken the economy to higher levels of production, borne the risks of pioneering into new fields, bringing within the reach of the people more goods and services, and promoting higher consumption.

Yet, the view is propagated that private enterprise in industry and trade has somehow failed; newer agencies are assiduously recommended to replace it. The popular sentiment that more could have been accomplished during the last thirteen years of planning cannot be confounded, speaking bluntly, by seeking to make a scapegoat of private enterprise. Nor can disappointment be assuaged by proclaiming that there is lack of ideology. We already have the Directive Principles of our Constitution. The 'socialistic pattern of society' which was accepted at the Avadi Session of the Indian National Congress was not deficient in content or in force. It was not less socialistic than the Bhubaneshwar Resolution which has now adopted 'democratic socialism'. If at all, the only difference, I find, is that the latest Resolution has raised a chorus for nationalization and establishment of cooperatives in respect of all conceivable economic activities—from banks to rice mills and wholesale and retail trade. So much so, we find the strange phenomenon of the demand for nationalization of banks being made even by ministers at the state and central levels. The strength of credit institutions lies not only in the public confidence reposed in them, but also in the public assessment of government policies that govern their operations and their future. If these institutions are treated in an almost cavalier fashion in public discussions, irreparable harm will be done to them as well as to the economy as a whole.

It is most unfortunate that there is a tendency to ignore the achievements of private enterprise and to chastise, with reckless confidence and without acquaintance with facts, all actions of businessmen. A new superstition is growing, that the competence and resources of governmental organizations are infinite. Maybe, we can somehow contrive to have an endless supply of salaried persons and salaries for them too. This is not an answer to the problems of greater production. Democracy, whether socialistic or otherwise, which curbs individual effort stifles itself. Nationalization *per se* will not secure the objective of increased welfare of the masses. We are not likely to maximize the common welfare by merely changing the agency, from private to public, or vice versa.

I have great regard for our administrative machinery, which has been called upon to undertake new tasks. It is by no means easy for a bureaucracy, however efficient, to grapple with the staggering size, variety and complexity of our problems, made more so because of outmoded, weird and weary governmental procedures. It is no wonder that the administrative machinery at all levels has not been working efficiently and expeditiously. There are too many instances of delay at each step. This has created a sense of frustration among the people in all spheres and even encouraged undesirable practices. The government itself is fighting back to remove them. The Federation had occasion to impress upon the government that a qualitative difference in the administrative set-up can be secured only if the burden on the administration is reduced and procedures simplified. However, it is also incumbent upon businessmen, who in a controlled economy are perforce compelled to have greater contact with the administration at different points, to do nothing that will give the impression that they are taking unfair advantage of such contacts. I know that if files move quickly, no one would want to pursue them. We have to function, let us realize, in a very sensitive area; and no precaution can be too great to guard against possible misinterpretation of steps we take.

I have dealt with the economic setting to refer to some specific economic indicators. During the year under review, agricultural production declined and industrial production increased at a slow rate, which together pushed up the level of prices. Although in the past agricultural production increased on an average at about 3 per cent per year, in the last two years there have been considerable setbacks which have accentuated the rigour of the agricultural problem. In 1961–62 production increased by 1.2 per cent, while in 1962–63 there was an actual decline of 3.3 per cent. The shortfall in production was particularly marked in the case of rice and wheat, groundnut and sugarcane. The shortage of foodgrains was partly made good by larger releases from government stocks. Imports of foodgrains in 1963 were of the order of 4.6 million tons, about a million higher than in 1962. But on the whole the per capita availability of foodgrains was slightly lower than in the previous year. There is no lack of conferences and meetings to discuss agricultural problems. Purely in terms of the number of authorities looking after agriculture, the set-up is impressive. But it seems to me that there are too many authorities without any apparent coordination of functions. The problems of agriculture are well known; so also the solutions. What is required is administration at all levels. Also, responsibility must be clearly specified, infringement punished and performance rewarded. Let us not forget for a moment that our progress in other fields of activity is largely governed by the development of agriculture. Besides depending upon agriculture for food supply, our major consumer industries like tea, sugar, cotton and jute textiles too draw their main raw materials from the land. While our agriculture-based export industries account for over 60 per cent of our total exports, the raw material content is between 40 per cent and 60 per cent of the cost of production. These figures represent the quantitative importance of agriculture and its influence on the general price level, industry and exports.

Over the past year, there has been more widespread realization that questions relating to balance of payments, export promotion and import substitution must be regarded in their entirety and with reference to their inter-relation with the total economic performance and planning. The development of export-oriented industries has to be brought closer to other major plans for industrial development. There has been an increase of nearly Rs 100 crore in our exports in 1963 as compared to 1962. The year is also marked by a slight contraction in imports. But this is not necessarily due to successful import substitution. We still continue to regulate the import of the much needed capital goods and raw materials, inhibiting the development of industry, its expansion, modernization and operation to the fullest capacity. We have, therefore, to keep before us the view that we must plan for a substantial increase in exports in the next five years. On this basis, exports must be geared to meet the anticipated increase in the import bill.

I hope that the deliberations of the UN Conference on Trade and Development will lead to the adoption of helpful policies by the developed countries, and we will be able to gain better access to the markets of developed countries. Raising the standards of living of the people in developing countries is a major concern of our times. The process lies in expansion of domestic and international trade and investment. Harmonious development of the world economy will be possible only if the developed countries effect the requisite coordination in their aid and trade policies. Although trade expansion may not by itself lift a country to the point from which self-generating growth may be possible, that point will certainly not be reached unless the possibilities of enrichment through trade are utilized to the fullest extent.

The benefit of economic development to the individual depends primarily upon the size of the population. The rate of population increase, which was around 2 per cent per annum in the fifties, is now about 2.3 per cent. In a decade's time, from 1951 to 1961, our population increased by as much as 80 million, nearly eight times the population of Australia. This growth in numbers, if unabated, will necessarily absorb a large part of the investment merely to equip the labour force to produce to keep up the constant flow of per capita production. The population 'explosion' has already accentuated unemployment and shortages of food. Had the birth rate been halved in the first plan itself, the per capita income over the first two plans would have been higher by 21 per cent as compared to the 18 per cent actually achieved. These differences would be more marked at the end of the third and fourth plans. I cannot overemphasize the need for taking immediate measures to control population growth. Placed as we are, we cannot offer gainful employment opportunities to all those who seek them. Non-agricultural employment, in industry and other tertiary occupations, it is estimated, would grow only at an annual rate of 3 per cent. However, we have to reckon with the backlog of unemployment of over 21 million, as also transfer of population from land-based to non-agricultural occupations.

One of the most important indicators that reflects the health of the economy is the level of prices. This showed an increase during the current year. But it was more prominent in the agricultural sector, and reflected the scarcities which took place in specific branches of production. While the index numbers of wholesale prices of manufactures increased last year from 128 to 131, the index for food articles increased from 123 to 138. The only permanent solution to price rise is to avoid conditions in which prices rise. To increase production should be the objective, and any means which leads to it in the shortest time must be considered to be of the highest importance.

Stimulus to production, whether in agriculture or in industry, comes from profitability. Even fully controlled economies plan for profit. In our country, while the need for larger investment of capital and the use of advanced modern technology are stressed, the conditions for the growth of savings and investment continue to be uneven. In August last, the Federation organized a seminar on the problems confronting public and private sector industrial undertakings. The discussions at the seminar showed that there are many problems peculiar to each and common to both. Of the common problems, an outstanding one centres around retention of profits for further development. The size of such funds itself depends upon the rate and quantum of profits. It is of utmost importance to undertakings in both the private and public sectors that they earn an adequate return and that they are allowed to do so. If the available resources are dissipated by way of current expenditures, the problem becomes more acute. I have in mind the increases in the wage bill unrelated to production and productivity. Seemingly, the workers will be better off; but the increased demand that will be generated without reduction in costs or increase in production will inflate prices. Worse, our strength to increase production will reduce, and that will not help the consuming public either now or in the future.

I will now take up some of the major points in the budget speech of the Finance Minister while presenting his proposals for 1964–65. As he did seven years back, in 1957, so also now Shri T.T. Krishnamachari has laid down criteria for taxation policy after taking into account the changed circumstances and the new accent on social values. During this period, tax payers have been left in no doubt that in order to produce revenues government may resort to extreme measures in taxation, extreme in magnitude as well as in form. It is heartening to find that the Finance Minister has set out as one of the cardinal principles of the taxation policy that it should also be geared to the paramount task of promoting growth. However, I am afraid some of his proposals are at cross-purposes with this objective. The Committee of the Federation has given its reactions in a press statement, and I will restrict myself to the administrative techniques which the Finance Minister proposes to adopt in his search for revenues. As it is, the discretionary power in the hands of the executive is ominously large. It is to be further widened, especially in computing deductible expenditure for purposes of business. Because the Finance Minister feels that 'unduly large amounts are spent'—a moot point, and because, according to him, it is not practicable to spell out all the restrictions in detail in the Act, government will assume the powers to make rules in this behalf. In effect, it would mean that the assessees would be required to submit to the prejudices and predilections of individual officers. With the onus of having to prove their *bonafides*, the position of the assessees has become more perilous.

The five steps which the Finance Minister has proposed for checking evasion will expose even the honest assessee to unprecedented embarrassment and even harassment. I do not see how the government expects that the combined effect of all these will give a fair deal to the honest tax payer. The proposed removal of the secrecy provision from the Income Tax Act and other similar enactments may well result in character assassination, but without any benefit to the exchequer.

The Finance Minister has also announced the government's intention to set up a commission 'to enquire into monopolies and the concentration of economic power in the Indian economy'. For a variety of motives, these two concepts—monopoly and concentration—have been off and on thrown up in public discussion, despite the fact that in our country, the development of industries has taken place on a diversified basis. If there has been growth of some companies, it is more a reflection of the changing pattern of economic development rather than monopoly. The Industrial Licensing Policy even now takes care of this aspect, and the Prime Minister in a statement to Parliament in April 1963 observed that this policy contained *inter alia* safeguards for avoiding the concentration of industrial capacity in a few hands. The Finance Minister too has said in his budget speech that the biggest industrial plants in the country today belong, in terms of ownership, much more to the people at large than to the original founders with whose names they are popularly associated. However, he makes a subtle distinction between ownership and control, and control and management. He wishes to encourage managerial talent and good management. Can efficient management be secured without effective control? Is this not a problem confronting governmental administration and public sector enterprises? Responsibility and control go together, and can be divorced only with grievous consequences. This is true of every situation.

In February 1965, the Twentieth Congress of the International Chamber of Commerce will take place in New Delhi, at the invitation of our Federation and the Indian National Committee. I would like to thank the Government of India for the assistance they have agreed to extend in organizing this Congress. The theme of the Congress will be 'World Progress through Partnership'. Over 1,000 delegates from more than 50 countries are expected to participate. This Congress, I venture to anticipate, will constitute a landmark in the promotion of flow of capital, knowledge and skills from the developed to the developing countries.

I am happy to report that in September last year, the Federation sponsored a delegation to Nepal. We had a round of discussions and consultations with a good cross-section of officials and non-officials. These discussions helped in better understanding of each other's problems and fuller appreciation of the prospects of industrial development of Nepal and the part Indian entrepreneurs may play to assist this development. I am given to understand that since then quite a few Indian business houses have evinced interest in specific projects, and programmes for their fulfilment are underway. This shows that there is scope for collaborative effort in the region as a whole.

Friends, as I lay down my office of Presidentship of the Federation, I would like to briefly share with you some of my thoughts on the outlook for private enterprise in India. The problems that loom across the threshold are many. The outward indications might appear at first sight puzzling and conflicting in the extreme. The central point is that, along with the acceptance of political democracy as a method of governance, there is also emphasis on social justice. These two concepts together constitute the basic urge for national effort. I feel convinced that businessmen will continue to play an important part in furthering social justice through economic development. I am aware that there are many constraints imposed on business; most of them are irksome in the extreme, and worse, they hinder the development process. Further, all those in business continually run the risk of unintentionally contravening some rule or regulation. It is almost impossible for anyone to know why or how a branch of rules has been effected because there are so many rules and not all of them are explicit. This, however, does not prevent either the law or criticism from descending upon us. We have, therefore, to be all the more cautious. Over a number of years now, we have learnt to live with controls, while continually representing to the authorities the need for opening up the operational valves so as to release more fully the productive forces. We must continue to do so, and in so doing we should be able to convince the government, as well as the public, that we fully understand and appreciate the currents that underlie the purposes of development. It is here, I believe, that organizations like our Federation have a two-fold task to perform—one to expose the difficulties that beset business, and the other to explain to the business community the social milieu in which it functions. I have no hesitation in expressing the confidence that, as in the past, the Federation will fulfil its functions. In the end, I would say that we are living in very exciting times, full of problems and challenges. Sometimes we are despondent at our failures, sometimes exuberant at our small successes; but the fact is that we have hard tasks ahead, and if we have to preserve our democracy, we must not fail. In all the various tasks before the country, I have no doubt that the business community will play its proper role.

Presidential Address at the Thirty-seventh Annual Session of FICCI at Vigyan Bhawan, New Delhi, 7 March 1964.

RESOURCES FOR DEVELOPMENT : A GLOBAL VIEW

I am thankful to the organizers of the seminar for the opportunity given to me to speak at this session, on the subject 'Resources for Development'. The problem is undoubtedly vast and complex. It involves not only an assessment of domestic resources but also of foreign resources, keeping in view the need for stability and the prerequisites of international cooperation. Fortunately, I had the privilege of chairing the plan sub-committee of the Federation of Indian Chambers of Commerce and Industry which has recently brought out a document on the subject. I shall, therefore, take the liberty of reviewing some of the broad impressions that I gathered in making this analysis and attempt to fit these findings within the profile of our development programme.

Development itself is a global problem. Today, the distribution of world income is abnormally skewed; what is more, the gap between the developed and developing nations has been widening over the years. More than 50 per cent of the world's income is shared by only 7 per cent of the countries, representing 10 per cent of the world population. Ten countries have a per capita income exceeding US $ 2000; more than 47 countries have a per capita income of less than US $ 200.

Some effort, no doubt, has been made to promote international cooperation for accelerating the development of less developed countries. The UN Resolution on the Second Development Decade proposed that the developing countries should achieve a 6 per cent growth rate and that this should be financed from external savings to the extent of 1 per cent of the GNP of the developed countries. The intentions were undoubtedly lofty; but the results have been rather poor. Since the middle of the last decade foreign aid to developing countries has actually been declining.

I would like to draw your attention to the fact that what has been called aid is often no more than a loan. For the most part, the terms of the loans were harsh; they were tied to particular countries and were given to finance projects which had greater demonstrative value. With all these restrictions and conditions, external aid, the quantum of which was also low, provided only limited relief to developing countries. No spectacular development was achieved. As such, the aid-giving countries were overcome by what has come to be called aid-weariness and the aid-receiving countries, on their part, possibly, by aid-disillusionment. The question was examined in detail by the Pearson Commission. But there has been hardly any improvement in the situation.

This does not mean that aid does not have a role to play in the larger world perspective. It does appear, however, that significant changes have to be made in the quantum, mode and conditions of aid. It has been suggested, for example, that a part of the SDRs allotted to the developed countries should be set aside for giving aid to developing countries. For achieving greater productive use of these resources it would be better if these resources are channelled through international organizations like the World Bank and the IDA which are free from political influences and are governed by economic values. The terms of aid have to be reasonable and repayments spread over a much longer period of time.

As you know, by the end of March 1972 India had received aid to the extent of Rs 12,746 crore. Of this, Rs 3120 crore was under the PL 480/665 Agreement. Grants amounted to only Rs 890 crore. Aid was effectively utilized for financing imports mainly of industrial machinery and partly of components and raw materials. The terms of aid were stringent and, as a result, repayment obligations, including amortisation and interest payments, now amount to nearly a quarter of our export earnings. The uncertainty of aid, the political pressures with which it is often associated and the high burden of debt servicing have all made it necessary for us to reduce dependence on external assistance. However, there are strong balance of payments considerations which make it impossible to reducc aid far below the repayment levels, for quite some time. The provisional aim, therefore, is zero-net-aid by the end of the fifth plan, i.e. 1978–79. Since the major burden in the balance of payments is in respect of repayments it would be in the country's interest to seek rescheduling of debt obligations rather than to look for new sources of aid finance.

The UN Strategy for the Second Development Decade had also expected that the inflow of private foreign investment from developed to developing countries would amount to about 0.3 per cent of the GNP. This target has more or less been fulfilled. The flow of this investment can be considerably enlarged if public limited companies in developing countries are enabled to float shares and debentures in the capital markets of developed countries. This function can be profitably undertaken by the International Finance Corporation which can assume underwriting obligations in this respect. Private foreign investment is also sometimes linked with technical and managerial participation. In this field, the multinational corporations can possibly have a larger role provided they operate within the sphere of national objectives.

On the whole the role of foreign private investment is limited though it can be used as an important catalytic agent. Foreign investment has to conform to certain conditions and enjoys specific tax concessions. I have been pleading, as President of the International Chamber of Commerce, that governments in the investor-countries should give tax protection to the incentives provided by developing countries to foreign investment, technical collaboration or technicians. Otherwise the very purpose of incentives is lost.

The trends in external resources, by and large, are not very encouraging and reflect the crisis of partnership in international development. Even earlier, foreign aid in India hardly exceeded 25 per cent of national investment. But considering the recent trends, it appears absolutely necessary that the Indian economy, in the future, develops almost wholly from domestic resources. Fortunately, this is not impossible.

Before I discuss this problem I would like to refer to certain primary issues which are of great relevance. First, it has often not been appreciated that resources are not the only constraint on growth. There are a number of other limitations which can obstruct economic development and which, therefore, have to be set right before a given amount of resources can be usefully invested. Second, resources themselves are not a fixed pool which can be drawn upon by the public and private sectors. They are governed by economic policies which influence the sensitive attitudes of the people to save and invest. Third, resource generation, considered over a period of time, depends on resource utilization. If resources are used more productively, resource generation also is stepped up. This is essentially a question of economic management to which I attach great importance.

I have made reference to the management issue in its wider sense because, I think, in our economy it has assumed considerable dimensions. I am absolutely sure that if the investment pattern in our first four plans had followed the productivity line consistently, today we might not be faced with a resource problem. A large part of our resources have gone into uses which are incapable of generating further resources. As such, the potential sources of development finance have not expanded. Therefore, in the future, this consideration has to be kept in the forefront. I would, in particular, like to urge that before mobilizing the requisite resources for the implementation of projects it is of utmost importance that the projects themselves are properly selected, clearly defined, thoroughly worked out and made ready for implementation. Mobilization of resources in the absence of these safeguards is bound to be frustrating.

During the past six or seven years, the trends in resource generation have been rather depressing. From 11.1 per cent of the national income in 1965–66, savings declined to 8.5 per cent in 1969–70, and are expected to be about 10 per cent in 1971–72. Foreign savings have also shrunk, relatively as well as absolutely. As such, resources available for investment will, to that extent, be less and the shortfall will have to be made good by corresponding increases in domestic savings.

For the purpose of further discussion we can divide the economy—as is usually done—into three comprehensive sectors, which functionally have different roles to play. These sectors include government, the corporate sector and households. Broadly, we can say that the government and the corporate sector invest more than their own savings. The additional resources are drawn from the households sector. In what proportion the public and the private sectors draw upon household savings is a matter of policy and is more specifically determined by the levels of taxation, the state of the capital market, credit policies affecting banks and term-lending institutions, etc. In 1971–72 (financial year), total domestic savings have been estimated at Rs 4105 crore. The bulk of these savings, viz. Rs 3270 crore or roughly about 80 per cent, originated in the households sector. But the households sector was able to invest in physical assets only to the extent of Rs 1300 crore. The balance, i.e. Rs 1970 crore, was loaned out to the government and the corporate sector directly or through financial intermediaries. It appears that the distribution of the surplus savings of households between the government and the private corporate sector was in the ratio 7:1. However, since the corporate sector investment was small in relation to public sector investment the borrowings financed nearly a half of the corporate sector investment.

The major instrument at the disposal of government for mobilizing savings is taxation. The very first plan indicated that in a country like India, where savings propensity is low, the burden of savings formation would largely fall on the government sector. As a result, it recommended that government should mobilize resources through taxation for the purpose of financing plan programmes. When this recommendation was made the Planning Commission probably did not realize that the government's own savings propensity was not very high. As a result, though the government has raised substantial tax revenues in the past twenty years there has been hardly any improvement in its savings. This point is sufficiently important to need illustration.

When the first plan started in 1950–51, the ratio of tax revenue to national income was hardly 6 per cent; it is about 15 per cent now. If the government's current outlay had increased at the same rate as national income, it should have been possible for government to save an additional 8–9 per cent of the national income. But this did not happen. Almost the whole of the potential savings have been eaten up by current expenditures. Government has been as poor a saver as the people. An essential precondition for stepping up the savings rate in the economy, therefore, is to ensure efficient management of resources and minimize the leakages into non-productive or less productive uses. A little exercise I had made earlier indicated that if these leakages are at a rate equal to the rate of growth of national income, the budgetary surplus would be of the order of Rs 15,900 crore in the fifth plan. On the other hand, if that control is missing, as is the case today, this surplus would fall to only Rs 5200 crore. The difference, you will appreciate, is significant. It measures the importance of efficient budgetary control.

Another crucial source of savings to which even the first plan had drawn attention is the surplus of public sector undertakings. In this field too the performance has not been commendable. The management aspect, even from a narrow, commercial viewpoint, has been violated. This, I believe, can be dangerous because public sector undertakings are now a sizeable part of the industrial sector and are the most viable potential source of investible surplus. Total investment in public sector undertakings is now of the order of Rs 4500 crore. Even a 10 per cent return should have put at the disposal of government gross resources (including depreciation reserves) of the order of Rs 800–900 crore per year. Therefore, considerable effort has to be made to put management on a sound footing, to improve operational efficiency and to rationalize the pricing system so as to enable the undertakings to earn a commercial rate of return.

The government and public sector enterprises thus have a vast and potent capacity for generating resources. Since these sectors are large, they need to receive urgent attention. I do think that if proper action is taken it should not be difficult for the public sector to step up its savings from the current 1 per cent of the national income to about 6–6.5 per cent, in another six to seven years.

Being in the private sector, I am more conscious of the responsibility of industry and business. I am pained to see that the share base of companies has not been widening fast enough. The growth rate of share capital in private sector companies, on the average, has been only about 2 per cent per year. The total number of shareholders, considering the size of the country, is small. With such a small share base it will not be possible for companies to mobilize resources at the rate required by development potentialities. What is also important is that with a small share base it becomes impossible to diversify ownership, strengthen shareholders' democracy and foster the investment habit among the public.

The capital market in India is almost wholly urban in character. At present, there are only eight stock exchanges in major cities like Bombay, Calcutta, Madras, Ahmedabad, Delhi, Hyderabad, Indore and Bangalore. It may be worthwhile to expand this financial infrastructure so that the interest in shareholding may be made more widespread. Of course, this is not the responsibility only of stock exchanges or stock brokers. Companies themselves have to make a concerted effort to popularize industrial scrips, particularly among the rural public who are unfamiliar with this type of investment. I am stressing this point because with the progress of the 'green revolution' considerable amounts of resources have accrued to the rural sector. A substantial part of these can be tapped for productive investment. This responsibility has to be shared by the corporate sector, government and other financial agencies like banks and investment trusts. It is heartening to note that the commercial banks have opened a number of branches in rural areas, particularly in the last three years. However, adequate motivation for people to deposit money with banks, companies, investment trusts, etc., is lacking. A massive savings motivation programme has to be undertaken. This would reduce cash holdings and increase the velocity of circulation of money.

The need for borrowed funds arises because the internal resources of companies are far too inadequate to meet their investment requirements. Nearly a half of the gross investment is financed by depreciation reserves and a further one-fifth by retained earnings. For the balance, the corporate sector has to look for resources from institutions and the general public. The retained earnings of companies have been low because of the nature of taxation which fails to distinguish between dividends and savings. I feel that as a part of the general savings drive, distributed and undistributed profits have to be treated differently for tax purposes, thereby creating an incentive to retain a larger part of profits for ploughing back.

I mentioned earlier that the bulk of savings—nearly 80 per cent—originate in the households sector. These savings have not been elastic because both the capacity as well as the willingness to save have been seriously affected by the pattern of taxation, the rise in prices and the redistribution of income. Let me elaborate this point a little further.

It is found that savings generally fall when prices rise. In India price rise has been brought about mainly by monetary expansion and indirect taxation. Taxation of commodities, particularly of wage goods like cloth, vanaspati, sugar, etc., which have a high weightage in the consumer price index, has pushed up prices, leading to higher wage demands. This process is reinforced by the growth of monetary demand created by budget deficits. On the other hand, rising prices which reduce the value of money have discouraged savings and stimulated current expenditures, thereby leading to higher prices. Unless this vicious circle of taxes, prices and wage demands chasing one another is broken, it will not be possible to promote larger resource generation for higher growth. My specific suggestion is two-fold: first, there should be no increase in taxes on wage goods which have a high weightage in the consumer price index; second, deficit financing should be restricted to meet only legitimate monetary needs in conditions of stable prices.

The redistribution of income, which has taken place in favour of agriculture and the poorer sections of society, is a welcome feature. In fact, development programmes in the future will have to be increasingly directed towards accelerating this process. But its implications for resource generation have to be fully kept in view. A transfer of income to the less privileged sections of society is bound to reduce the overall savings propensity. Studies made about changes in income distribution and growth show that redistributive policies have tended to reduce the general rate of growth by about 1 per cent or so. It is, therefore, necessary to guard against such eventualities by providing powerful savings incentives. A worthwhile measure would be to exempt savings from income tax. At present, contributions to provident fund and life insurance premium are excluded from income assessed for tax up to a certain percentage, subject to an absolute maximum. The inability to save adequately for old age under the present system of taxation has given rise to demands for higher salaries. First, the range of eligible savings has to be enlarged. Second, the percentage of income allowed to be saved free of tax should be increased.

With the sort of savings incentives I have suggested and the type of institutionalization that is necessary it may be possible to raise household savings from 8 to about 12 per cent of the national income in the next six to seven years.

From what I have said it would certainly appear that the necessary increase in the rate of national savings is not easy, though possible. What is important is that resource generation is not purely a matter of arithmetic. It is not as if so much can be diverted from this sector to that. What is called for is evoking a proper response to certain policies and actions. This has become important particularly because the vast bulk of savings originates in the households sector, which is very sensitive to taxes, prices, income distribution, and so on. Therefore, the savings habit has to be deliberately fostered through appropriate policies and an appealing motivation programme. It is equally important that the management of government finances is efficient and the leakages to less productive sectors are minimized. For, as I said earlier, resource generation itself depends on the pattern of resource utilization. The choice of investment must essentially be on the basis of productivity. If this is done it should be possible for us to step up our rate of domestic savings from the current 10 per cent to about 18 per cent or so in the next six or seven years.

This is a task to which the government has to give urgent attention. Saving is really a social choice between providing for immediate improvement in the standard of living on a limited scale and a permanent improvement in consumption in the future on an expanded scale. For a developing country like India, where large masses of people are below the poverty line, this choice becomes difficult. Foreign aid does provide an easy way out. But it is neither possible nor desirable to depend on aid for all time. The less aid we have, the greater the effort we have to make to generate domestic resources. But this would entail a considerable restraint on consumption, particularly of the relatively well-to-do sections of society. One has to accept that for these sections, which include businessmen, traders, the salariat and even industrial workers, who are well above the poverty line, the present standard of consumption will have to be stabilized in order to transfer the benefits of development to less fortunate people and at the same time maintain a high level of investment. The economic acumen of the government will be judged by the success it achieves in this difficult manoeuvre.

Address at the Plenary Session of the International Seminar on Economic Journalists, 6 December 1972.

CHALLENGE OF ECONOMIC DEVELOPMENT

A copy of the Resolution on 'Challenge of Economic Development' is in your hands. In my view, the title of the Resolution is as important as its contents. Although we have been engaged in the task of planning since 1951, and notwithstanding successes here and there, it seems to me that we have not learnt to face squarely the many challenges that economic development throws up. These challenges cannot be met all at once. Neither do they remain static; they take new forms. Developed countries too have to face these challenges from time to time. In their case the problems arise either because of structural changes like balance of payments, or new factors like pollution and oil prices. In a developing country like ours, we are concerned with more basic tasks such as pushing up the rate of savings and investment, building productive assets, providing employment, increasing production, particularly in the field of agriculture, and most important of all, reducing the rigours of harsh poverty.

In my opinion, the factors that determine the growth of production are often outside the field of economics. They belong more naturally to the social sphere and would broadly include education, human energy and enterprise. Our development policies have not put adequate emphasis on these extra-economic developmental factors and, as such, our growth process has not been as high or as rapid as we would have liked it to be.

Meanwhile, here and now, we are passing through a critical period. There is public discontent, frustration, and even anger. These susceptibilities have been taken advantage of by unscrupulous elements and anti-national political parties, resulting in spasmodic violence and unnecessary and unusually high loss of life and property. Violence is no method to resolve any issue, whether economic or political. It is a blemish on organized society, on our rich culture and high tradition. True, public discontent has to be expressed to be heeded. But there are rational and civilized ways of expression.

Public violence may often be politically motivated. But I would like to emphasize that it is also a reflection of the rather aggravating economic malaise, the symptoms of which can be seen in the high rate of inflation and the rapidly growing unemployment. It would be wrong to wholly attribute these to the Indo-Pakistan war, drought, etc. They have much deeper roots. Briefly, the areas of failure are as follows:

— The strategy of planning was not completely attuned to the problems that the country was facing.

— Plan performance fell short of its targets.

— The policies which were expected to create the environment for growth were not always appropriate. Even the good policies lost their efficacy because they were not administered well.

The first plan aimed at a growth rate of only 2 per cent per year and achieved more than 3 per cent. All subsequent plans targeted for an annual growth rate of 5-6 per cent and achieved only 3.5 per cent. The economy was not able to create as many job opportunities as the increase in labour force warranted or as much production as would meet the requirements of the people.

Last year the Federation had published a small but valuable document entitled 'Planning for Results'. What it recommended was a strategy which would create jobs in a manner that would simultaneously lead to production of wage goods. This strategy centres around giving a stimulus to agriculture. A substantial part of the plan resources should be invested in schemes like minor irrigation, soil conservation, development of backward areas, dairying and animal husbandry, forestry, fisheries, rural roads and rural electrification. These schemes will provide employment and, at the same time, increase the productivity of foodgrains and commercial crops which form the base of essential mass consumption goods.

In fact, per capita availability of mass consumption goods has expanded at an even smaller rate than per capita real income, i.e. per capita money income deflated by the price level. More specifically, production expansion in respect of four major commodities, namely foodgrains, edible oils, sugar and cloth, is most urgent. If abundant supply is created of these commodities, which are more meaningful to the less privileged sections of society, their prices will be brought down or at least stabilized.

The four commodities I have mentioned are really agriculture-based. And it is precisely agriculture which has been the weak spot in the production plans. In the last ten years, foodgrains imports, on an average, have been at the rate of 4.8 million tons a year or about 6 per cent of the net production. Food imports have certainly softened the attitude not only of the government but of the nation towards agricultural development. Proper water budgeting for different parts of the country is yet to be done. Fertilizer production has still to catch up with our requirements. I fear that if irrigation and fertilizers are not made abundant enough, the green revolution which has made commendable headway since 1968 will be reversed.

The performance of industry also was seriously thwarted due to a number of factors. As a result, the growth of industrial production in the fourth plan period would be only about a half of the set target. Raw materials like cotton, oil seeds, steel, etc. are in short supply. Last year almost every state, and this year most of the northern states, suffered a severe power crisis. It is my firm belief that if the subject of power development is left to state governments, the type and the level of improvement that is required will hardly take place. My suggestion is that there should be a Ministry for Energy at the centre exclusively concerned with power development. I need hardly say that power development depends to a large extent on other related infrastructure, particularly coal and transport, which have to be simultaneously developed.

The other major impediment to industrial growth was labour. Man-days lost in the first ten months of 1973 were 15 million. A suggestion for an industrial truce has been made by the President and the Prime Minister. I am convinced it is a constructive approach, and I hope that the government will call a joint meeting with trade union leaders and managements of industry to work out the modalities of this arrangement.

The greatest art national management, I believe, lies in keeping different sectors of the economy in step with each other. A shortfall in any one sector has a cumulative effect because of its forward and backward linkages with other sectors. The budget for 1974–75 has rightly made selective increases in outlay on crucial sectors like transport, power, coal, steel and fertilizer, which had proved to be major bottlenecks. It is most necessary that these get translated into actual goods and services.

I referred earlier to the policy dimension of the development process. The nexus between economic policy and performance is indeed close. One has only to look at the tremendous changes in economic policy since 1951 and to correlate them with economic phenomena. Such an exercise, unfortunately, has not been done so far. What I think is very necessary is a factual statistical analysis to weigh the impact of any policy on production, investment, savings, exports, etc.

Consider, for example, price controls. In a situation of rising costs, price controls tend to squeeze the margin of profit and make investment in controlled lines uneconomic. This is what has actually happened. In a number of commodities subject to formal and informal controls, like cement, paper, vanaspati, tyres and tubes, and coarse cloth, shortages have emerged. It appears obvious to me that unless a scheme is devised by which new investment is able to enjoy higher value retention through, say, a dual price mechanism or differential excise duties, additional investment in controlled lines will not take place. I do see, however, that in a very limited number of commodities, which you may call the necessities of life, price controls may have a legitimate place temporarily to ensure adequacy of supply and a proper distribution system supported by buffer stocks.

Let us consider another policy measure, the vague concept of 'large house' in industrial licensing. This concept became a part of policy after the Report of the Dutt Committee in 1969. In the three years before the Dutt Committee reported, the rate of growth of gross fixed assets of the corporate sector was 11 per cent per year, on an average; in the three years after the Dutt Committee Report and the change of industrial licensing policy, the rate of growth of gross fixed assets in the corporate sector dropped to 8 per cent per year. Large projects could only be taken up by large corporations. In fact they also act as catalysts for small and medium-scale industries.

In the past twenty years we have also witnessed nationalization and government takeover of a number of services like insurance and banking, and of industries like cooking and non-cooking coal, copper and textiles. In certain cases, nationalization may be necessary to increase the viability of industries, bring about modernization, achieve full coordination, or expedite growth. These objectives, however, have hardly been achieved. The approach to the problem of state management has to be practical, based on an objective cost benefit analysis. I do not need to quote instances where failures are glaring and the damage to the economy distressingly high.

Let me, finally, briefly touch on another policy measure, taxation on government savings, and its impact. Tax revenue as a percentage of national income in the past twenty-three years rose from 6 to 15, while government savings remained stagnant at 1.5 per cent of national income. Taxation as a savings formation measure, which it was mainly intended to be, has miserably failed.

Every policy creates its own effect which may be good or bad for the country and which may be different from what is anticipated by the policy makers. Policy has to be appraised in terms of its results and modified in a manner that would benefit the country as a whole. I would urge the government to make an assessment of its policies on these lines and to orient its approach in the light of the findings.

In a Resolution which deals with major outstanding economic issues I would be unfair to myself if I do not touch upon one of the most critical problems, viz. the population explosion. This problem has belittled all our development efforts. If population had remained at the 1951 census level, today the standard of living of the people would have been higher by 60 per cent; and if this income had been equitably distributed, there would have been no poverty in the country. The importance of family planning programmes is, no doubt, well appreciated. It is necessary to spread the family planning message to every nook and corner of this country and to provide the clinical facilities that give real meaning to the programme. This is not a responsibility merely of the government. Business can do quite a bit to assist the government in this national task.

It would be a folly to think that development is the responsibility of the government alone. Indeed it calls for partnership and the cooperative effort of all groups. If different national groups work together for the common goal of national well-being, the total progress we are looking for would be within easy reach. No problem is too grim not to be resolved through ingenuity and hard work. Let us do our best to see that the present problems are resolved within the framework of the institutions this country has all along cherished.

Address at the 47th Annual Session of FICCI, while moving a Resolution, 16 April 1974.

PRIVATE ENTERPRISE IN AGRICULTURE

In a rash moment I accepted your kind invitation to be here and to speak to you although I do not have any special expertise that I can share. Indeed, I am abashed at my temerity in addressing experts from diverse disciplines. But I know, I am among friends who will gloss over my shortcomings. Sid Keel invited me to be with you probably because I have the dubious distinction of having served industry for over four decades. Circumstances and the rough-and-tumble of business gave me the privilege of leading my country as the head of many chambers of commerce and also of participating in international debates on economic and business issues. My interest in agriculture is not that new although my involvement is not that full. Apart from purely intellectual curiosity, I have been engaged in horticulture and kitchen gardening. And, of course, my association with fertilizers is pretty old.

In industry, with which I am more familiar, the meddling politician has often tried to compartmentalize business into the public and the private sectors. It is wrong to emphasize formal differences. For developing nations, the question of public and private sectors ceases to have any meaning at all. There is only one sector and that is the national sector. This is true of industry and even more of agriculture.

Agriculture has for long been a much neglected subject. Jean Mayer calls it the 'oldest of sciences—an island empire'. Agriculture provides the basic necessities of life and a vibrant agriculture becomes the *sine qua non* of a progressive society. Yet, this truth seems to be grudgingly realized only now. I was astonished when it was brought to my attention by Nobel Laureate Dr Norman Borlaug, that while medicine, chemistry, physics, management, economics, have all found a place in the deliberations of the Nobel Committee, agriculture and its contribution have not yet been considered worthy of recognition. This is another example of how agriculture has been given a relatively low priority in our socio-economic programmes.

To my mind, man who is a late arrival on this planet compared to other forms of life and who has learnt the art of husbandry of resources only recently, is essentially an individualist. In agriculture, progress has been largely brought about through initiation and enterprise at the individual level. The form of organization is, however, changing because of technological innovations that require operations on an entirely different scale or of a different kind.

But change is not without resistance. The corporation has come to mean for the vast majority of people, size—bigness—big business houses—which in turn bring to their mind fear of exploitation, of concentration of power, of empires and marching armies. These images are exaggerated and the good that the corporation can do is often forgotten. We should recognize that private enterprise has over the years developed skills and expertise which could be used purposefully in solving many of the problems of society. Indeed, science has advanced and the revolution in genetics, the biological sciences, space and other areas has been tremendous; but the pace of such progress has not been matched by developing adequate and responsive intelligence to solve the problems of society which flow from the application of technology. I refer to such problems as the proliferation of slums, artificial scarcity and many of the other ills that beset our society. It is here that private enterprise will be called upon to play a greater role, involving deeper exercise of their capability and responsibility, and in broader areas related to the social good.

The most serious social problem that faces the entire world today is how to use the benefits of science which is 'public knowledge' and technology which has already enabled him to visit the moon—how to tame and direct these powers to solve intelligently and humanely the problems that developed and developing countries have to face in varying measure, the problems of human needs, education, habitat, agriculture, etc.

It would be easy for me to attempt a narration of statistics to describe the role of the private sector in setting up fertilizer plants, pesticides plants, or a viable distribution system. All these have rendered immense service to the farmer in my country as in others. I need not elaborate on this because, to you, it is not unknown. You know even more than I do, of the march of the green revolution in some of the developing countries which accepted the promise of the dwarfs provided by Borlaug and his team, in wheat. Rice has repeated that experience. Here, it must be remembered that production of fertilizers or pesticides by itself is not enough. We need an army of well-trained and well-equipped people to communicate this constant explosion of information and skills to the poor farmers. The productivity of the land which has been used over and over again for centuries has to be replenished and modern science has shown how to do it.

For a moment, let me turn to the scene in my own country. Some of you may remember that many distinguished people had predicted that Indian agriculture was foredoomed. The Paddock Brothers had referred to triage, the life-boat example and included India among those who would not be saved. Yet, India today, with the severest drought in living memory and with other nature-made problems, has shown a remarkable resilience and flexibility in managing its food supplies. How did this happen? It is the fall-out of our agricultural research and innovation, and more importantly, acceptance by the farmers, who are the best representatives of the private sector, of modern methods of cultivation. It is not necessary to dwell on statistics—they can be had from any government publication—to see the new levels of yields reached in foodgrains, wheat, rice and cotton. And it is here that, whether we like it or not—I personally do not like it—the private sector, as it is labelled, has played a fine role.

Some of the largest and most efficiently run fertilizer companies are in the private sector. Some leading companies manufacture, distribute other inputs and educate farmers in the use of them. Despite its comfortable food surplus during the past few years, India has a vast number of poor who have not enough means to buy food. In any successful agriculture, in fact, to move agriculture forward, what is needed is an aggressive campaign to provide employment opportunities for the farmless labour and other rural poor. The majority of India's impoverished millions live in the villages and opportunities for earning incomes to buy the necessities of life acquire great significance. Here again, private organized employment has a role to play and I am glad that in recent years, many companies have taken up work in rural areas—through village adoption programmes, rural road building, strengthening the network of link roads, setting up vocational training centres for men and women, provision of good seed and establishment of 'seed farms', and in other fields of agricultural life.

The experience of the past few years is abundant proof that man has the technological capability to feed the world. Despite our new brahmins, who plead with such passion for organic manure, fertilizers will continue to be our chief source of nutrient supply for impoverished soils; how else, but by using phosphate rock, can you produce the phosphatic complexes required by crops? I am convinced that the physical resources of the earth, when used intelligently with ecological concern, can provide the food required by the world. Having said this, where do we go from here?

We need a new awareness. You are familiar with the 'two cultures' of Lord Snow, the 'dissimilar universes' of Aldous Huxley. The pursuit of professional goals, be it business and industry, science, agriculture, or academic life, calls for a new symbiosis. We can no longer accept that intellectual curiosity is restricted to the theoreticians and thinkers, who know better; and that the poorer calling of the scrivener, the shop-keeper, the tinker and the businessman, is less respectable and, therefore, less relevant. You may recall what John Gardner said with telling force, '. . . a society that scorns excellence in plumbing because plumbing is a bumble profession and exalts mediocrity in philosophy because philosophy is a noble profession . . . such a society is doomed to failure. Neither its pipes, nor its theories will hold water.'

The theme that runs like a refrain in your deliberations, will be quality of life. No one has given—at least I am not aware of it—an acceptable definition of quality of life. I think it was Aristotle who said the State comes into being for life and continues for good life. I daresay, for many, quality of life may mean material comforts—the ease, the pleasure, the refinement that life offers. It pleases the senses; it satisfies the prime needs of man. But, if we seriously consider what we have done with our heritage, squandered the bounty of nature and misused the intelligence given to man by the Creator, we will see the malaise that has taken hold of man. This gives me a sense of unease.

Ladies and gentlemen, permit me your indulgence. I have seen life, enjoyed every moment of it, the thrill and the adventure it offered. I have now reached a stage in my public life when I can share some of my thoughts fearlessly—I mean, without fearing public applause or obloquy. What I say is from the depths of my heart. When I started my business life many years ago, as an industrial apprentice, my father, a distinguished industrial statesmam of his time—far ahead of his own times—gave us one guiding motto: Produce or Perish. That was a necessary condition of life and development then. I have watched the movement of life in my country and in other parts of the world since those innocent years and now think differently. Man's position on this planet is precarious. Our worship of success and growth at the expense of other values has led to an emptiness which reflects the spiritual poverty from which man suffers. Our concern has always been with the material front. In this process, leading to a multiplication of wants, we have lost the sense of beauty and order, a feeling for nature and her wondrous ways. Many years ago, the English novelist, George Orwell, wrote a novel, *1984*, which brought terror and sadness to many sensitive, creative people. Earlier, Aldous Huxley, that gifted and perceptive savant, had written *The Brave New World*. Man today is a sad witness to his own dehumanization, caught in a trap without the hope of release. The worship of the computer and the pill will not open the doors of perception to him. But I wonder if man has achieved the maturity which will make him realize that our future is in the past, for we have squandered away our heritage and are now groping in darkness for meaning and significance. In this ceaseless activity, pursing excellence and efficiency, he has lost the power to appreciate the inwardness of man. It is only by turning himself within that he can come to terms with himself and find peace and harmony in place of tension, terror and tedium. I plead with you, therefore, to bring to your deliberations that sense of humility which is needed to appreciate this wondrous thing called nature and how she operates silently, unseen, beautiful and mysterious—a picture of great order.

One can only hope and pray that with better appreciation of the inherent goodness of man and with the knowledge and power he has acquired, he will be able to work out a scheme of things, innovation, technology, communication of skills, all tempered towards agricultural advance and progress to feed the teeming millions on this planet without degrading man himself and his resources. This requires a new mind which can look at things in their integity and wholeness. A fragmented mind will not be able to grasp the inherent order of nature and accept man as only a very small part of it. To comprehend this, we need a transformation, a mutation; that we may see the whole with man at its centre.

Address read at the 15th Asia Pacific Food Production Conference held in Hongkong, 3–5 December 1974, in Dr Bharat Ram's absence.

CAUSALITY AND CHANCE IN ECONOMIC GROWTH

In February last year, I received intimation that I had been selected by the University of Bombay to deliver the first lecture under the Shri Babubhai M. Chinai Lectureship Endowment. When I received the invitation, I felt both happy and honoured. Little did I imagine then that within a few months we would lose for ever Babubhai, as he was popularly known in all circles, and that the endowment lecture would turn out to be a memorial lecture.

I had the privilege of having in this great liberal a personal friend as well as a philosopher and guide in many matters. His passing away therefore, has been a heavy personal loss to me, and it is one of the reasons why my lecture has been delayed. Babubhai had the distinction of having a long political career both at the state and the national level. While he was brutally frank, he had the rare capacity to make good friends. His attitude towards men and matters endeared him to all who came in contact with him. Businessmen, big or small, not only held him in great esteem but always turned to him for advice on a variety of problems. His early demise has thus deprived the businessmen of India of a great friend, and the country of a great son.

I am not an academic man and as one in business I am concerned with the practical problems of management and the efficient running of enterprises. While the endowment lecture is intended to cover a subject related to the theory and practice of business management, I have chosen a wider topic which relates to management not at the firm or micro level but at the national or macro level affecting the whole economy. The subject of economic development is not only important but is as old as the father of modern economics, Adam Smith. I have had the privilege of learning its applications largely through practical experience in the workshop and the boardroom, and at discussions with practical men of industry and commerce at home as well as in international forums. I shall try to do justice to the honour accorded to me by piecing together the elements of causality and chance in the economic growth of nations.

Economic ideas have travelled a long way since Adam Smith wrote his famous 'Inquiry into the Nature and Causes of the Wealth of Nations'. There has been so much sophistication through the use of so much mathematics that it is baffling to many. However, many of the basic questions remain unsettled even today. In fact, the fundamental questions raised by Adam Smith, namely, what factors are responsible for economic progress, and what policy measures could be taken to induce rapid growth through the creation of a suitable environment, are still not fully settled. It is also necessary to inquire whether there are determinate causes for economic progress or whether there are more elements of chance in the causation process over which comparatively less control is possible.

The question became more pertinent when after the termination of World War II, many countries which were economically underdeveloped, usually thought to be due to political subjugation, became politically independent and started to inquire how to stimulate economic development. India was at the forefront of such nations to whose fold some were being added from some continent or the other almost every year. The subject of economic growth became not only fashionable and modern in the economic world but also of vital and primary importance to those nations. The advanced nations also got interested because many of them were eager to assist economic progress in the less developed countries and wanted to know the way to do it. Analysis of the causes of underdevelopment, the dynamics of economic progress, and practical measures to help economic growth were essential topics in all discussions.

What is Economic Growth?

It is not easy to give a simple meaning to the concept of economic development or economic growth because economists are not in complete agreement in accepting any given definition. This is due to the reason that there are vast disparities in natural endowments, in cultural heritage, in social and political institutions and in economic structure between one country and another so that a single criterion to distinguish developed countries from undeveloped countries is likely to be confusing. Definitions combining a number of indications of underdevelopment have also proved to be unsatisfactory because they include so many variables as to become descriptive rather than analytical. Economic development can be described as a process by which an economy is transformed, from one whose rate of growth of per capita income is small or negative to one in which a significant self-sustained rate of increase of per capita income is a permanent, long-run feature.

Factors for Economic Growth

It is now generally recognized that a number of factors may be jointly responsible for the economic growth of a country. Growth of output is thus said to be dependent on:

(i) natural resources and their rate of growth;
(ii) the labour force and its composition and quality;
(iii) capital stock;
(iv) the country's fund of applied knowledge of science, technology and organization; and
(v) the social, economic, cultural complex of economic institutions, political system, cultural values, etc. which go to make one nation more vigorous and enterprising than another, providing the urge to work and go forward from one success to another.

It is to be noted that the variables are not unrelated to each other. In fact, the rate of change of each one of these variables is related to one or the other variables in the system. There may be exogenous forces also which affect these variables. Thus, international flow of capital and labour may change the quantity and quality both of capital and labour stocks. Such flows may also affect the socio-cultural complex. Perhaps, it is more correct to say that all these factors taken together with their interactions with each other are jointly responsible for economic growth.

Amongst these factors, the first one, viz. the existence of reproducible and non-reproduceable natural resources, is largely a matter of chance. Thus, the presence of oil and natural gas in Western Asia, Northern Africa or the Northern American region, the presence of coal and other minerals in Europe and America, or the presence of thorium in Kerala in our own country are due to certain geo-physical factors which for all purposes must be taken to arise out of chance and cannot be made to happen on order as and when any country wants this through some deterministic action.

But the existence of natural resources by itself is not sufficient to cause economic development. The people of the country must have the urge and the will to exploit such resources through conscious human effort. Even if the urge is present, in the case of many countries, in Europe and Asia, for instance, after the attainment of political independence, lack of technical knowledge and capital stock may hamper growth of output. International flow of capital and technical knowhow may compensate to a certain extent. Surprising as it may seem, in most cases, economic growth depends mainly on non-economic factors such as social values and cultural milieu. The valuation of material goods is often determined by religious attitudes and ascetic ideas.

Greater than religious belief is the attraction of wealth which serves as a means to power or a mark of superior social status. Wealth is desired by men as a means to power whether it is economic power over employees or competitors, or political power. In modern capitalist societies anyone who becomes rich can move into the highest social circle. In many other communities this is not so. 'Thus in Hindu society it is the priestly class; in China it is the learned men; elsewhere it is the soldier; in any country the young men would try to distinguish themselves in the way which wins highest distinction. If the way lies in war; in hunting; in religion; in bureaucracy—wherever it may lie, thither they will go.' They will turn their thoughts towards economic activity, if successful organizers of economic activity can achieve the highest honours. Thus, in the early days of Soviet Russia, there was power and glory for the party men or the trade unionists but not for the managers of factories or organizers of economic activity. However, the factory manager is now highly privileged and rewarded with special privileges and moves in the highest social circles.

Although wealth means respect and prestige in every country, the profession of making money has to compete with other ways of acquiring social status. The relative status of such activity depends on the proportion of intelligent and enterprising young men attracted to this way of life. It is sometimes believed that the relative status of money makers is higher in the USA than in the UK and higher in England than in India. These differences are sometimes said to account for the differences in the rate of economic growth in these countries. In a similar manner, the lower status of traders and merchants in Spain than in Elizabethan England is considered to be relevant in explaining why Spain failed to exploit economic opportunities in the sixteenth and seventeenth centuries and lost to England its hegemony as a sea power.

The spirit of adventure has been responsible for economic growth in many countries in the past. It was this spirit which opened up the new world in the western hemisphere. The existence of such a spirit of adventure amongst the people of the land is, no doubt, a chance factor. But other circumstances sometimes help in fostering such a spirit. For example, the law of primogeniture prevalent in England is considered to be responsible for the enterprise and mobility of all the sons except the heir, which provided the driving force among early colonialists of British stock in developing the USA, Canada, Australia and New Zealand. The spirit of adventure involves some risk-taking which is partly a matter of temperament and partly a matter of tradition. Temperament is largely determined by a variety of factors which are due to the chance element. But the law relating to property going mainly to the first son built up the tradition of other sons in that country having to move out of the country to seek fortunes far and wide, across the seas, in distant lands.

The factors that inhibit the spirit of adventure are taboos and prejudices. A well-known example is the Indian attitude to the sacred cow, according to which even cattle of inferior quality cannot be killed or restrained from breeding. The result is an excessive number of such cattle which act as a burden on the farmer's meagre resources. Such prejudices are also in existence in western societies, as in the prevention of using human excreta as manure in fields thereby wasting valuable minerals into the sea. There may be taboos in relation to family life particularly in respect of the sort of work to be done by women or those in respect of birth control. 'Prejudices in relation to livestock and also in relation to family are currently religion's most deadly contribution to the maintenance of poverty in many parts of the world.' Fortunately, such prejudices can be gradually overcome by the process of development itself and need not be left to be rectified to matters of chance.

The spirit of adventure is so inherent in economic development that when the French economist J.B. Say first used the expression 'entrepreneur' to describe a businessman, English translators were confronted with the problem of finding a synonym in English and were forced to fall back upon the word 'adventurer', a word commonly applied to sedentary merchants of London at the time of Elizabeth and James I. Say described the entrepreneur as an economic agent who

> unites all means of production—the labour of the one, the capital or the land of the other—and who finds in the value of the products which results from their employment the reconstitution of the entire capital that he utilizes, and the value of wages, the interest and the rent which he pays, as well as the profits belonging to himself.

Say also outlines the special personal qualities of the entrepreneur as follows:

> judgement, perseverance, and a knowledge of the world as well as of business. He is called upon to estimate, with tolerable accuracy, the importance of the specific product, the probable amount of the demand, and the means of its production; at one time, he must employ a great number of hands; at another, buy or order the raw material, collect labourers, find consumers, and give at all times a rigid attention to order and economy; in a word, he must possess the art of superintendence and administration. . . . In the course of such

complex operations, there are abundance of obstacles to be surmounted, of anxieties to be repressed, of misfortunes to be repaired, and of expedients to be devised.

In the promotional and survival purposes which entrepreneurs serve, there are three important processes, viz. innovation, management and adjustment to external circumstances. It is interesting to note that Schumpeter, the great theoretician who extolled the role of the entrepreneur, finds innovation to be the greatest characteristic of the entrepreneur. He describes his role as follows:

> The sole distinguishing characteristic of the entrepreneur is that he is an innovator. By forcing the means of production into new channels he provides the economic leadership that spearheads a dynamic change. The entrepreneur is not necessarily the head of a business and may not even be permanently associated with a particular firm. Although he may assume managerial functions, these do not necessarily define his work as entrepreneurial in character, i.e. the entrepreneur must not be confused with a manager of an enterprise. Similarly while the entrepreneur may be either an inventor or a capitalist or both, he will perform his functions merely by coincidence. By nature he is an innovator, no more and no less.

Given the rate of population growth, the dynamic evolution of an economy is determined by the rate of innovation which, according to Schumpeter, is a function of entrepreneurial activity. It depends, in turn, upon the distribution of entrepreneurial talents and upon the existence of economic institutions providing credit to finance risky undertakings. Such institutions, motivations and rationality constitute the socio-cultural framework conducive to the manifestation of the talents of the entrepreneur. Since innovations appear discontinuously, economic development is inherently cyclical in character. However, from a secular point of view, continued technical progress is likely to result in an unbounded increase in total per capita output since historically there is no diminishing return in technological progress.

No doubt, the existence of innovative people in a community is largely a matter of chance. Men introducing new commodities, like Ford, or new systems of economic organization, like Woolworth, are few in number. They are a rare phenomenon providing economic impetus to the society. But once the atmosphere is set for encouragement of the entrepreneurial spirit, many more appear on the scene. Only a few people have those qualities of leadership and only a few can succeed. However, if one or a few have advanced with success, many of the difficulties disappear. Others can follow the pioneers; their success again makes it easier for more people to follow suit until finally the innovation of the entrepreneur becomes familiar and its acceptance a matter of choice. Evidently, this is because the socio-economic complex after the introduction of new products or new methods by pioneers has undergone fundamental changes so as to foster the development of many such people in order to provide an adequate supply of such men for continuous buoyancy of the economy. We can perhaps say the same thing about India also. The number of entrepreneurs fifty years ago was only a few. But today, there are many more, even though the numbers are not as large as in more advanced countries like the UK or the USA.

Very similar is the case with technical and scientific innovation. The advent of the capitalist form of production in England was possible, according to Arnold Toynbee, due to four great innovations which revolutionized the cotton textile industry—'the spinning-jenny patented by Hargreaves in 1770; the waterframe invented by Arkwright the year before; Crompton's mule introduced in 1779; and the self-acting mule invented by Kelly in 1792.' However, none of these could possibly have revolutionized the textile industry had it not been for James Watt's patenting of the steam engine in 1769 and its application to cotton manufacture fifteen years later. Once the crucial set of inventions conquered the main fields of industry, the pace was set for similar changes in other fields, and other inventions and technical changes followed. Thus, the invention of coal smelting in the early eighteenth century and the application of the steam engine in 1788 to blast furnaces changed the character of the steel industry. Similar was the case with innovation and technical change by entrepreneurs in other countries of the West like Germany, France and the USA.

One conspicuous fact about the earliest inventions and discoveries, whether in England, Germany or the USA, is that all of these—steam engines, inventions in weaving and spinning, new ways of smelting ores, machine tools—came from practical men not necessarily endowed with much of a scientific background. Although there is still scope for such discoveries at the practical level, scientific discoveries since the beginning of the twentieth century have now become the major source for technological progress. The primary impact of scientific knowledge has been to bring about some fundamental changes in the processes of invention and technological research. Not only is it now necessary to have some scientific background to become an inventor but a large part of these activities has now passed beyond the capability of individuals working on their own and is feasible only in well-equipped laboratories staffed by a team of scientists. In advanced industrial countries such laboratory facilities are available in universities and other research institutions, or in research organizations set up by the private sector, or even in the laboratories of giant corporations. In fact, many of the great practical inventions of recent years have come from private laboratories. To give an example, the invention of nylon was made by Carruthers only after he went over from a university to the laboratory of the private sector firm Du Ponts. Terelene was invented by Imperial Chemical Industries in England. However, the private sector in underdeveloped countries generally lacks the resources to set up such laboratories and to finance research activities, although there could be exceptions. Another impact of the new development has been to make invention and research comparatively much more expensive.

There is no doubt that one of the deficiencies of underdeveloped countries is their failure to spend sufficient funds on research and development of new processes and materials suited to their circumstances. Institutional difficulties are partly responsible for this state of affairs. In industrial countries private entrepreneurs can afford to spend, and are generally prepared to spend, considerable sums on industrial research because of the hope of getting back sufficiently in return out of the results. Underdeveloped countries are, however, largely agricultural and there are hardly any private interests financing research except a few large commercial companies in specific fields such as rubber, sugar, etc. The result is that in underdeveloped countries industrial research primarily devolves on the government, whereas in industrial countries these are matters related to private interests.

Before I close this section on innovation and research I intend to touch upon another topic, viz. the need for adequate training facilities in the right directions. Economic development requires adequate facilities and training at all levels. It should not be left to chance but should be guided by the authorities by setting the priorities for different types of training and providing for the growing needs of skilled and trained personnel in various fields with the continuous growth of industry. One important sphere of education and training which is often forgotten is administration. Economic growth creates a very great demand for administrators in public services as well as in business. Underdeveloped countries have a multitude of businessmen in small trade. Large-scale industry and organized manufacturing require an equally large number of people capable of managing such large undertakings efficiently. Management of a large number of employees at different levels of education and training, and administration of huge volumes of resources of a wide variety are involved in large-scale organized manufacture. This requires special skill and acumen on the part of the men entrusted with such work at different levels.

Great entrepreneurs are born, not made. Some knowledge of business can be gained in business schools. But an important part can be learnt only through experience at the job, and the rest depends on personal qualities, on the temperament and character of persons entrusted with the management of the enterprise. Business schools can teach how to keep records of stocks and orders, or how to handle physical resources or finance, how to manage by proper selection of staff and delegation of duties, methods of training, etc. But they cannot teach a businessman how to get on with his staff so that both loyalty and efficiency are inspired.

A commercial sense, cutting out wastages, adjusting the use of resources to the flow of output, intuitive decisions as to what price to pay or to charge, these are qualities which are peculiar to certain men who become leaders of industry. No doubt, some competence can be attained through experience in administration, or by working in more efficient firms in advanced countries or at home. Countries in the initial stage of development might also find it profitable to send some of their young people abroad to get training in business management in more efficient firms. Competition is also vital to business. Businessmen are likely to make use of the facilities for training and advice and seek out all the ways of improving their own efficiency in business management if there are incentives to do so. The most powerful of such positive incentives is the fear of loss of business and bankruptcy, both of which depend upon the existence of competition.

Re-awakened interest in economic growth has naturally turned attention to the role of capital which is considered to be the most important factor in economic development. The basic problem of capital formation can be stated as follows. The actual state of capital in existence in different countries is determined by the action and reaction in the past of a number of economic and non-economic forces, some of which are exogenous and others endogenous factors which arise within the system. These factors together constitute the demand and supply forces of capital formation. The demand for capital is governed by the inducement to invest. This has been usually low in developing countries with low income. The result is low buying power of the people in the country. The lower income is ascribed to low productivity because the amount of existing capital is small which in its turn is due to the fact that the inducement to invest is low. Similarly, on the supply side capital formation is governed by the capacity to save. This is found to be low in developing countries with low income which leads to a shortage of capital which in turn results in low productivity. The latter results in low real income which leads to a small propensity to save. Thus goes the vicious circle of poverty both from the demand and the supply side, the action and reaction of both the supply and the demand forces tending to keep a low income country perpetually at a low level.

The supply of capital for economic growth presents a more serious problem and has to face some fundamental difficulties. Economic growth requires a continuous stream of investment in a wide field of activities. The immediate question is, where to get resources for such investment. The basic difficulty lies in the fact that the process of investment does not automatically generate any savings. In fact, the savings and investment decisions are in general taken by different sets of people in the country. Whether there is a balance is a matter of chance. If savings are more than investment, there will be depression because producers of consumer goods will be making losses. This is unlikely in a low income country where there is an inherently low propensity to save, leaving little margin for investment to increase productivity. More generally, savings are likely to fall far behind the investment required for all-round economic growth. In such a case, expansion of output is possible only if there are idle resources of land, labour and capital. If there is none of these, any investment above the current level of savings will result only in inflation.

All developed countries have borrowed in the past. England borrowed from the Dutch in the seventeenth and eighteenth centuries and was the chief lender to almost every other country in the world in the nineteenth and twentieth centuries. The USA, now the richest country, borrowed heavily in the nineteenth century and was a debtor country till the beginning of World War I, but is a major lender today. The main source of foreign finance is by way of direct investment or by grants of loans from foreign countries. There has been a decline in direct business investment. Britain, the chief lender in the past, had invested between 1875 and 1914 about two-thirds of all additions to the stock of capital whereas the chief lender of today, the USA, is far from that level; to reach a comparable level of investment, the USA will have to invest the Marshal Plan thrice a year. This is very low as compared with either the 1920s or the years before World War I, even after allowance is made for increase in world production and prices. The reason for this decline is that there has been deficiency both on the supply and demand side. Most of the savings in Europe and America are now largely diverted towards home investment. There has been a relative decline in personal savings.

There are, in addition, inhibitory factors restricting direct business investment such as fear of arbitrary action by foreign governments which may refuse transfer of profits or repatriation of capital or may even go to the extent of nationalization. The demand for direct foreign investment has also declined in the sense that such resources are no longer required in several spheres of industry in some countries.

Direct business investment for economic growth in low income countries has, no doubt, the advantage of going directly to capital formation. Normally and almost inevitably foreign investment by entrepreneurs creates a real advantage for the productive capacity of a primary producing country. Moreover, such investment carries with it modern technology and know how.

The subject of technological change falls partly under economics and partly under the social sciences. Technological change depends on growth of knowledge itself, both technical and organizational. Much seems to be determined by circumstances outside the system, that is, by chance factors. It should, however, be pointed out that the existing technical knowledge does not automatically increase productive efficiency. Its application to the production process depends on certain features of the economy itself. There is always an excess supply of untapped investments that can be exploited under private economic conditions as is actually seen from the past economic history of England and the USA. Industrial innovations are more likely to come through application of existing techniques than through new research. It follows that the rate of innovation of technical change in most economies is not limited by a lack of technical knowledge but by some features of the economy.

The classical view is that technical change is determined by the rate of capital formation and continuously increases with progress in capital accumulation. This happens due to the rationality of entrepreneurs, according to Adam Smith; but according to Marx it is due to cut-throat competition to exploit the best possible of techniques in production. Another view is that technical progress is not automatic with capital formation but it is really indicative of the strength and effectiveness of entrepreneurial activities.

The extent to which credit institutions are prepared to supply the potential innovator with financial resources would be another determinant of the rate at which new techniques can be adopted. The policy recommendations from this analysis are clear. Appropriate financial institutions must be set up or those existing strengthened in order to mobilize savings, channelize them into venture capital. Socio-cultural changes that encourage quick acceptance of technical changes should also be fostered.

The socio-cultural environment is less of a measurable economic quantity. According to classical economists and the moderns, the evolution of the cultural and institutional structure in any community depends on a number of extraneous factors. In that case, it may be directed into desired channels, to some extent, through certain policy manipulations operating on those factors. It is perhaps more likely that the components of the socio-cultural environment and those of technology are inter-related.

While we need not go to the extent of considering production relations, i.e. technology, as determining the character of society, as done by Marx, I feel we can say that there exists some implicit relationship between technology and the socio-cultural complex without any certainty about the direction of causation. Just as many examples can be quoted to prove Marx's point, illustrations can prove the reverse relationship as well. Therefore, in my view, the probability is that any policy decision in respect of the variables in the economic system does affect the socio-cultural complex also.

The Babubhai M. Chinai Endowment Lecture delivered at University of Bombay, 9 September 1976.

CAUSALITY AND CHANCE IN ECONOMIC GROWTH : THE INDIAN SITUATION

In the last lecture, I dealt with some factors affecting economic growth. I pointed out that there is no simple explanation for economic development or for the question as to why one country is poor and another rich. Various factors taken together, their relations with each other and their interaction determine the course of economic evolution of any country. In today's lecture, I shall concentrate largely on an application of these theses to the Indian situation.

Land and People

There have been many speculative and emotional views regarding the natural resources of India. It has been usual—almost as an aspect of our nationalistic spirit—to believe that our country is very rich in resources. Actually, we find that while there are some minerals like coal which are plentiful, there are others which are not sufficient for our requirements. Since Independence, India has tried to assess her wealth of natural resources of every type more vigorously and in a more scientific manner. Organizations like the Geological Survey of India, Indian Bureau of Mines, Oil and Natural Gas Commission, etc. have become very active in the exploration of unknown wealth under the earth and sea. As a result, many discoveries have been made. To give an instance, India was producing not even half a million tons of crude oil in 1947, whereas today about one-third of our crude oil requirements, amounting to about 8 million tons, is being met from indigenous wells. Initial explorations for offshore oil at Bombay High have been so promising that it is no longer an idle dream to achieve self-sufficiency in this basic sphere when other areas in Kutch and the Bay of Bengal basin are fully examined. For, as the experts say, there is hardly any bay or deltaic region in the world which does not have any oil or natural gas. Coal production which was hardly 30 million tons then has gone up to nearly 100 million tons. Geological explorations continually bring to the fore more and more resources which are available within the country. The mineral wealth of the country has considerably increased as a result of these explorations, and we can rightly hope for more and bigger findings in the future.

As regards her people, India has never lacked initiative and entrepreneurship. In the past Indian merchandise found its way to distant markets in the Middle Eastern, African and European countries. In modern times, even during the British rule there have been a number of industrial pioneers who worked under the most unfavourable circumstances under a foreign government which was naturally more eager to protect and develop its own home industries. The story of the installation of the first Indian steel plant is an eloquent testimony of India's entrepreneurial talents.

With the appearance of more favourable circumstances after Independence, Indian entrepreneurs took up the challenge of industrializing the country even though their field of activity was limited by the Industrial Policy Resolution announced immediately afterwards. During twenty-five years of growth, a wide range of industries have been established covering many consumer goods not previously produced in the country. Many producer goods were taken up for the first time and a foundation was laid for the capital base for industrialization. Machine-building capacity of various types essential for the building of industrial India was set up by Indian enterprise, both in the public and private sectors. Hundreds of items of manufacture are produced every year by Indian entrepreneurs in the engineering and chemical industries. As the UN Team for Export Production that visited India in 1966 commented, 'India should better be called an already developed country rather than a developing country.'

In fact, Indian industry is now venturing to set up units in many countries abroad, even in advanced countries like the USA, Germany and UK. As many as 67 joint ventures of Indian enterprise are in production as on 1 January 1976. Sixty-eight projects are under implementation covering industries like food, textiles, paper and paper products, leather and leather products, rubber products, plastics, chemicals, steel, metal products, machinery, automobile ancillaries and electrical machinery.

In fact, the ingenuity and enterprise shown by the Indian people in different spheres of business activity have been astonishingly varied and widespread. I should not be taken to be boasting if I say that some of our industrialists can be favourably compared with their counterparts even in the most advanced countries and are in no way inferior to them in business acumen, managerial ability and industrial dynamism.

The broadening of the entrepreneurial base in India is particularly evident in the phenomenal growth of the small-scale industry. Today small-scale entrepreneurs are producing 38 per cent of the industrial output of India with Rs 1450 crore of capital and employing 2.2 million persons. These figures are exclusive of the business activity on a household basis. Their contribution to exports is rising day after day. Out of 2400 items of products covered by the recent census, over 31 per cent were exported, the value of exports amounting to Rs 150 crore in 1972. Advanced countries like the USA, the UK, USSR, and Japan are the most important consumers of products of our small-scale entrepreneurs.

Technological Change

Technological change requires considerable expenditure on research and development. In India, the government has been at the forefront of such activities. It has set up a chain of national scientific laboratories for conducting research and development work under the general guidance of the Council of Scientific and Industrial Research.

Besides being expensive, research is a long-drawn process. Wide and fundamental changes have taken place in various fields of science and technology, and industry has benefited substantially through many significant changes in technical processes increasing productivity and expanding the availability of multifarious consumer and producer goods to Indian citizens. Much of this has happened elsewhere in the world and has travelled to India through collaborations between Indian industry and their foreign counterparts in projects which have been set up in India. No doubt some work is being done in the scientific institutions of the government as well as by industry. However, much of this is centred around borrowed or imported technology. In many instances it has been found that the results of research have been used rather hastily in projects, as a result of which the projects fail and people lose confidence. It is therefore no surprise that research in India is still at the periphery and has not been able to create the basic infrastructure for scientific and technological changes. Evidently, very much more will have to be done both by government and industry before we reach the threshold of such a watershed.

It would be useful to compartmentalize research work into designing and processing so that it gets directed more towards certain specific industries like cement and sugar. I would suggest that concentration in specific sectors like the automobile industry covering different types of vehicles from mopeds to heavy commercial trucks, their numerous components and accessories, would be specially fruitful. In this matter there is urgent need for greater coordination between the research work done in government institutes and that done by the industry. Research wok in Indian universities should also be encouraged.

Capital Investment and Savings

I have a few comments to make on various aspects of capital formation which is a very important factor determining economic growth. Capital investment in India has not proceeded at the rate contemplated at the beginning of the plan. When the second plan was formulated, elaborate calculations were made to show that capital investment would rise from 7.3 per cent in the first plan to 10.7 per cent in the second and to 17 per cent by the fifth plan. The rate of growth of domestic capital formulation, however, in fact, was much slower. Although domestic capital formation at current prices came up to about 12.6 per cent by 1960–61, it remained almost at that level throughout the third plan and thereafter; even in 1974–75, the rate of capital formation was only 12.8 per cent. In contrast, advanced countries like the USA invest nearly 20 per cent of the gross national product.

Savings

Capital formation needs to be matched with proper growth in savings. In India savings have always lagged behind investment and have been slow to rise. Domestic savings stood at 9.3 per cent by the second plan, and rose to 11.2 per cent by the end of the third plan. But it became stagnant thereafter and is still at 11.8 per cent in 1974–75. Domestic savings come largely from three different sources. The major contribution comes from the household sector. Then there is the savings of the corporate sector which industry ploughs back for reinvestment. Lastly, there are government savings which in a sense are of the community as a whole.

Household Sector

In the savings potential envisaged for the fifth plan, private savings constitute about two-thirds, of which the major contribution of 57 per cent is made by the household sector. This sector is a heterogenous group consisting of individuals, unincorporated enterprises, non-profit-making organizations, trusts, charitable and religious institutions, etc. It includes wage and salary earners as well as households in rural areas. That the greatest contribution in savings comes from this sector does not necessarily mean that the propensity to save of individuals within this sector is high. In fact, the savings of this group of income-earners are proverbially low. While a major part of income in India comes from agriculture, much of the savings in the rural areas is frittered away in unproductive expenditure, on social and religious functions like weddings, celebration of festivals, etc. There is very little margin left for income-earners in the villages or wage and salary earners in general for savings to be channelized in large quantities for productive investment.

It is necessary that suitable measures are taken to change the social and economic background of our rural society. This is, no doubt, a long process but a beginning has to be made, if the propensity to save in the rural areas has to be improved in a substantial manner. Saving is a habit, and creation of savings by propaganda and financial incentives is necessary to stimulate the habit among all classes of people. Savings institutions like the Unit Trust have been set up, and many commercial banks have joined in the savings campaign. But I am of the opinion that there is still considerable scope for intensive activity in propagating the benefits of savings, particularly in rural areas. I do not think stock-exchanges and associations have made sufficient efforts to tap these very important sources of rural savings. Research also indicates that there is significant transfer of income from the industrial sector to the rural sector. Thus there is urgent need for tapping rural savings to the maximum possible extent through various campaigns and incentives for investment in productive enterprises.

Government Savings

Government savings are substantial, constituting one-third of the total. The importance of government savings is underscored by the fact that there is a large part of gross fixed investment which is required for public works and public utilities. In industrial economies, these come to nearly 7 per cent of gross national income. But in India, a policy of progressive socialization of industries has been made inherent in the Industrial Policy Resolution announced immediately after Independence. The contribution of public sector undertakings with a total capital investment of more than Rs 7000 crore towards government savings is about 41 per cent which comes to 13.5 per cent of the total national savings. Vigilance is required not only for getting maximum savings from these units by increasing the efficiency of their operations and improving their savings capacity but also to see how government surpluses are spent.

Corporate Savings

Private corporate savings through ploughback of retained profits are an important source of savings. Today, one of the major factors inhibiting the growth of corporate savings is the high rate of corporate taxation. These taxes together with the surcharge amount to about 67 per cent which leaves little margin for building up reserves. The result is that the normal requirements of depreciation of industry cannot be made, and with increasing costs, industry finds it difficult to modernize—leave alone invest in new capacity. It is unfortunate that the development rebate which helped industry to expand and diversify has been withdrawn. The investment allowance which was introduced in this year's budget is only on a selective basis. In the absence of modernization of machinery and equipment, the productivity of industry is also kept at a low level. Another aspect of the high corporate taxation is that the competitive position of Indian export goods is adversely affected in comparison with competitors from industrialzed countries like the USA, UK, France, West Germany and Japan where corporate taxation is at a very much lower rate, between 22–52 per cent at the most.

Pattern of Investment

The pattern of capital investment in India is also somewhat different from that of advanced countries where the largest investments are in housing at 25 per cent, public works and utilities at 35 per cent, and manufacturing and agriculture at 30 per cent. In India, agriculture including irrigation absorbs about 20 per cent and manufacturing about 28 per cent. Investment in housing in India was not shown separately; but in the fifth plan, about 8 per cent of the investment has been mentioned as being on housing and sites. It is presumed that a considerable part of the manufacturing investment is inclusive of housing. Investment in stocks in advanced countries is between one-third and one-half of national income. Thus, with income rising at 3 per cent, the addition to stocks should be about 1–1.5 per cent which in advanced countries may come up to 12 per cent of the total. The exact corresponding figure for this item is not separately shown in Indian plans. However, it is essential to make separate provision for stocks because otherwise with the growth of economy, various types of shortage of raw materials and consumer goods might develop holding up expansion. My suggestion is that the planning authorities in India should specially make provisions for housing, including those required for industry, as well as for stocks. A clear picture would enable the country to avoid unforeseen shortages and bottlenecks out of ignorance about the correct situation in this respect.

Efficiency of Investment

Efficiency of investment is another important aspect of capital formation. In India, the overall marginal capital output ratio was less than 2:1 in the first plan; but it was envisaged then that it would be well over 2 in subsequent plans, rising to about 3.7 by the fifth plan. In actual fact, however, the marginal capital output ratio was less than 2 in the second plan and for the fifth plan, it is envisaged at 2.7. A large part of the investment in India is in agriculture which tends to bring the overall marginal ratio down. Investment is not high in industry either. In a majority of instances as well as for industry as a whole it is about 2 or even less, although for small-scale units it has worked out to nearly 3 in many cases. Various socio-economic factors, labour legislation and trade union activities have contributed to keep the productivity at a low level. Often, it is not realized that there is a close co-relation between size and efficiency which in the economist's jargon is called 'economies of scale'. I am not making a case for the so-called big houses, but I am certainly in favour of ensuring that only enterprises of optimum size are established. Against the fear of concentration of economic power must be weighed the interests of the consumers as much as the rational use of our limited financial resources. The important matter of dispersal of industries must not be confused with the size of individual units. The logic of survival, let alone growth, demands that every unit and corporation, whatever be the size, in whatever industry, expands steadily and surely. If this does not happen, the unit/corporation is bound to become sick. At the micro as well as macro level, there has to be continuous forward movement and the closest parallel is an aeroplane in the air. Whatever the reason, the low capital output ratio is an indication that efficiency of investment in India is comparatively low, as low as one-third in comparison to China in the first decade of planning, as observed by Malenbaum and others. Evidently there is considerable scope for increasing the productivity of our investments both in industry and agriculture after diagnosing the reasons for low efficiency and taking suitable measures.

Foreign Capital

While foreign capital, no doubt, has been responsible for initiating the process of industrialization in the country, its role during our planning era has been comparatively small. For instance, out of a total investment of about Rs 47,560 crore envisaged in the fifth plan, the net inflow of funds from outside the country has been put only at Rs 2430 crore. Thus, about 95 per cent of the total investment is proposed to be financed from domestic resources as against 84 per cent envisaged in the fourth plan.

The significance of foreign capital investment in the past lay in its impact on critical sectors constituting the infrastructure such as transport, railways, etc. That was due to the free play of market forces which led capital wherever it was most profitable. Today, foreign capital investment is controlled and guided in the desired directions by the government. The procedure involved in its administration had till recently deterred many a foreign investor intending to set up industrial capacity in India. Such delays have no doubt been reduced due to the new outlook of the government, but have not been completely eliminated.

In the present situation in India, the role of foreign capital needs to be looked at from a wider perspective with a view to reorienting it towards dynamic growth of industry. In more than two decades there have been some significant changes in the basic industrial structure with capacities installed in a wide variety of industries covering basic items and filling in many gaps in our industrial structure. It is well known that huge capacities have been installed in various types of machine building, both in the public and private sectors. These undertakings, particularly the public sector units, despite their recent improvement in capacity utilization, still have a considerable margin left for supplying machinery and equipment to new industries. Industrial capacity for building machines and equipment installed at considerable foreign exchange require to be fully utilized.

Hitherto, foreign capital resources whether for technical collaboration or for equity participation were often found to be directed towards a miscellany of industries rather than critical projects essential for creating an industrial base. In my opinion, foreign capital can play a substantial and crucial role in augmenting our resources if it is canalized to industry, whether in the public or the private sector, in large critical projects. Thus, personally, I would welcome, for example, a time-bound project, say, a steel plant of 10 million ton capacity, on the basis of an agreement on product sharing, with foreign capital.

Growth and Price Stability

Savings having continually fallen short of investment year after year, India has had to take recourse to deficit financing. The net deficit in twenty-six years between 1950–51 and 1975–76 comes to a total of more than Rs 6000 crore. Deficit financing and creation of money are not necessarily bad as such, and are, in fact, recommended by many for stimulating investment so that it will ultimately increase productivity and living standards. Inflation for creating useful capital has an inherent tendency to destroy itself because sooner or later, there would be an increased supply of goods. But there is no way of ascertaining whether and how much of this huge amount of created money has been utilized in the creation of productive capital, and how much has resulted in an increase in the general level of prices. Leaving out of account the price increase since the beginning of planning, there has recently been a steep rise of about 50 per cent in two years' time, just before its arrest last year through some policy measures. Without going into statistical calculations, one can easily conclude that such a violent fluctuation in price would have more than counterbalanced any gain obtained through the creation of new capital by deficit financing.

In general, I have a feeling that in India, comparative price stability is an essential condition for growth, the creation of money and small price increases being conducive to economic growth only to a limited extent and that too only if used in quick maturing projects, intermittently and in small doses. In a predominantly agricultural country like ours, the movement of prices depends largely on the success or failure of agricultural crops, as has been noticed from a study of inflation and agricultural production trends in recent years as well as in the past. Agricultural production in India, despite the improvement in irrigation facilities, is still largely dependent on the vagaries of the monsoon. A more than 50 per cent increase in the general price level recently is a grim reminder of the need for price stability in the economy. Any gains achieved through economic growth get nullified by such violent fluctuations in prices which result in complete distortions in various sectors of the economy.

One way of reducing the amplitude of price fluctuations is to build up reserves of various agricultural crops like wheat, rice, edible oils, cotton and jute. We have already accepted the policy of bufferstocks in foodgrains. Such a policy should be extended to cover other agricultural produce, and bufferstocks should be created not only from our surplus, whenever available, but also from imports from other countries through forward contract. I would suggest that a priority programme of building up bufferstocks of other agricultural produce should form an essential feature of any plan for economic growth and price stability in our country.

Conclusion

In conclusion, I may summarize as follows. There is no single explanation for economic development or for the question as to why one country is poor and another rich. Poverty in a country like India cannot be solely ascribed to deficiency of capital or to a lack of entrepreneurial talent or to an adverse ratio between population and resources or even to an unfavourable socio-cultural and institutional complex, just as the wealth of a country like the USA cannot be explained solely by the chance abundance of any one of these factors. Similarly, a complete explanation for development or underdevelopment cannot be provided by focussing attention on any single relationship like savings-investment or innovation-entrepreneurship. There cannot, therefore, be a readymade prescription as to how to achieve economic growth quickly. Economic progress depends ultimately on the simultaneous influence of a number of factors like land, labour, capital, technology and socio-cultural environment which are inter-related. These relationships and the interactions between these factors determine the course of economic evolution in any country.

The greatest chance factors are the existence of natural resources, both land and people; but can we consider these as completely dependent on chance or can these be considered to be deterministic in a way? The existence of coal and steel side by side in Britain, or oil in the West Asian countries, is no doubt, a matter of chance. But these also required men—entrepreneurs and innovators—who acquired knowledge about their existence and use and had the urge to exploit them. The socio-cultural environment can influence the incentive to cultivate such knowledge. Russia has now discovered many natural resources in Siberia which was at one time supposed to contain no economic resources. India is not accepting its destiny, but is trying to find oil within its borders and out in the seas. Further exploration may completely change the picture, as it did in China and Russia. Japan, without an ounce of iron ore, is producing more than 100 million tons of steel. Certainly there have been great names amongst entrepreneurs in Europe and America in the past as well as in India today. But favourable changes in the socio-economic environment has probably made the scope for entrepreneurial activity much more extensive in India than elsewhere, resulting in the appearance of many more entrepreneurs and innovators today than in the past. My conclusion, therefore, is that economic growth depends ultimately on the entire complex of relationships that characterize the economic and social life of the community. Even the character of a few chance elements can be made to undergo fundamental change through the impact of technological change and changes in the socio-cultural complex of society.

The inter-related character of the various determinants of economic growth leads to the conclusion that long-run changes in growth patterns cannot be induced until and unless changes are brought about in at least one structural parameter or constraint of the economic system, such as the propensity to save. A significant change in behaviour is possible only through large shocks or impulses introduced into the economic system through deliberate policy measures. Such shocks and impulses represent the 'critical minimum effort' which serve as a threshold for practical economic stimulants to develop. A gradualistic approach in economic development is not likely to be successful.

The 'critical minimum effort' has to be directed towards changing the structural characteristics of the economy which retard economic growth. Thus, one necessary condition for economic development is that the production function, after taking into consideration the effects of technological progress, must be subject to increasing returns to scale so that productivity continues to increase, otherwise sustained growth of per capita income would not be possible. Some appropriate combination of technical and institutional changes would seem to be necessary for creating the conditions in which the potential of economies of scale can become effective. Technical progress has to be continuous and systematic both in agriculture and industry.

In any case investment has to be accelerated for economic growth. New investment will always be required to initiate technical change because all innovations require some fresh capital for implementation. The identification of development with the creation of systematic conditions for increasing returns to scale suggests that there should be greater provision for overhead capital and external economies. The important sources of external economies are provision of an efficient transport system and public utilities as well as education and health. Investing in social capital thus forms an essential part of an overall plan for growth. This however, is generally outside the scope of private investors and comes within the capability of only government agencies. There are other reasons why government role in planning and initiating economic growth becomes more crucial. Purposive socio-cultural and technical changes can be introduced only through the medium of government agencies. Further, it has in its fiscal system the machinery for diversion of resources into those sectors which are most capable of systematic exploitation of technological innovations and increasing productivity.

Thus we find that both from the point of view of theoretical considerations as also their application to India, broadly speaking, it would be correct to take a pluralistic view regarding the causes of economic growth. India's economic condition today is neither due to only a lack of entrepreneurial talent nor solely due to lack of capital nor due to an unfavourable relationship between saving and investment. Technological changes and changes in the socio-cultural complex of society can be brought about by making certain efforts and taking deliberate policy measures. I have tried to indicate the ways and means to expedite economic growth in certain fields.

Although chance factors may to some extent determine the course of economic development, we cannot take a fatalistic view. On the other hand, planning is based on the premise that economic growth can be directed in desired directions. Maybe, our planning efforts have not been entirely successful because we have not considered how we can fashion it in a better way. The fortunes of a nation as in the case of an individual depend primarily on the will to think boldly and to act courageously. Not all actions will be rewarded, but satisfaction lies in the thought that there has been no lack of effort.

The Babubhai M. Chinai Endowment Lecture delivered at University of Bombay, 10 September 1976.

DEVELOPMENT IN THE NEXT QUARTER CENTURY

I am privileged to have been invited to address the Annual Convention of the Bombay Management Association. The theme of this Convention as I see from the subjects listed in different Sessions, which will be held today and tomorrow, relate to the different aspects of development in the next quarter century. The theme in itself is thrilling and naturally allows observers to go into high flights of fancy. But I would rather desist from this temptation and look at the problems as they exist, as they are likely to emerge and the type of action and policies that have to be initiated to achieve national goals.

As you are certainly aware, many exercises have been undertaken by various institutions to project the possible and desirable trends in the Indian economy by AD 2000. These exercises, no doubt, satisfy our curiosity and give us a glimpse of what India would be like at the end of this century. Some of them indicate the type and level of effort that has to be made to reach that position. In many exercises sophisticated mathematical models have been used to appeal to our intellectual instinct and these appear to impart a degree of scientific precision to the predictions.

I have a feeling, however, that these exercises do not even amount to good speculation. We live in a changing world where sociological changes, international pressures, technological advancement, change in tastes and preferences, continuously interact and influence economic trends. Take, for example, technology. It is difficult to predict what direction technological change will take in the next twenty-five years. If we look back a little we shall find that technology has drastically altered bringing about new relationships between different industries. It was Schumpeter, I believe, who identified technology as the single dynamic agent of economic development and change. There is enough historical evidence to show that technological change has contributed far more to economic progress than capital accumulation or larger employment. This point only indicates that in all predictions about the future we are on slippery ground and any projections about production requirements can at best be broad indices.

Take, again, the international situation. Few had predicted the oil crisis, the currency crisis or the recession through which the world economy passed in recent years. These international disturbances find their echo in all national economies. New international arrangements in the field of commodity trade, transfer of resources and technology, debt relief, etc., are being thought of and it is difficult to judge at this time what shape these arrangements will finally assume. I am referring to these international dimensions of national development only to indicate that the external environment is important and can very much influence our own domestic developmental effort.

What I am saying is that futurology is replete with limitations, exposed to considerable uncertainties and as such has to be viewed with abundant caution. I am not suggesting that these exercises are mere idle pastime. In my view, the importance of such analysis lies in indicating the broad path we have to follow in regard to economic, financial and management policies. I would consider it an achievement if in the next two days we are able to at least identify the imperatives which have been dictated by socio-economic conditions and the approaches that the country needs to adopt in order to secure the goals that are nationally accepted.

Look at the objectives first. There can be no two opinions that we have to achieve the highest possible standard of living in the shortest possible time. There have been some hints that it should be possible for India to reach the standard of living currrently prevalent in Europe by AD 2000. It is difficult to fix a precise target. But that is not important. All that we have to aim at is fixing the right direction, making the right effort and ensuring that the benefits of devleopment reach the wider sections of the people.

Again, it will be generally accepted that the economy should aim at a level and type of development which would provide full employment to all available labour. Without full employment it will not possible to have an egalitarian society based on the dignity of the individual and the welfare of all citizens. Today, about 40 per cent of the population is below the poverty line in the rural sector and possibly about 50 per cent in the urban sector. Most of the urban poor are the unemployed wage earners, mainly those who have migrated from rural areas in search of jobs. In the rural sector the bulk of the poor are agricultural labourers, who are only seasonally employed, and small and marginal farmers.

Although there has been some influx of labour from rural to urban areas, it can be reasonably assumed that the vast bulk of the rural unemployed are not mobile, and consequently development measures will have to be taken to backward districts rather than the unemployed to centres of development.

The third objective which I believe is sufficiently important to be mentioned is self-reliance. As a country, we cannot depend on aid for ever. When the draft five year plan was framed, it was believed that by 1978–79 we would reach net zero aid position. This objective had to be given up when the plan was finalized last September, in spite of the phenomenal increase in our foreign exchange reserves. Let us not, however, mistake self-reliance for self-sufficiency. It is not as if we have, or can, produce everything that we need. If we have a closed economy isolated from the mainstream of world development, we shall find ourselves burdened with extremely uneconomic production. The more open the economy, the higher is the benefit resulting from international specialization and division of labour. In my view, all that self-reliance implies is balancing the external payments position in such a way that there are neither chronic deficits nor chronic surpluses. We should be able to export enough to be able to earn foreign exchange for our imports. This is what I would call self-reliance.

In short, the three major objectives which development should promote are: self-reliance, full employment and a higher standard of living. How we can achieve these in the shortest time depends on our own ingenuity in deploying national resources, whether in the public or in the private sector, for securing high and healthy development. We have experimented with a system of mixed economy and my assessment is that the results have been qualitatively as well as quantitatively satisfying. The mixed economy model shaped by Pandit Jawaharlal Nehru has been the most effective device to channel the energies of the nation into a productive endeavour shared by all sections of the community. The government has set up large enterprises. This is true not only of projects like irrigation, power and transport but also heavy industries which have involved huge investments in a short span of time. The private sector has shown the vitality that is called for and ventured into new lines of manufacture.

In the past twenty-five years, we have achieved substantial progress in agriculture, industry and infrastructure. Our agricultural output, for example, has more than doubled and that of industries more than trebled. Industry today employs more than five million workers, produces one-fifth of the national income and undertakes about a half of the nation's exports. It has sponsored research as a step towards self-sustaining progress; it mobilizes resources from the public and generates its own savings; it provides the vast bulk of tax revenues to government. India today can claim to be among the first ten most industrialized countries of the world.

Where do we go from here? Of course, I need hardly emphasize that our development potential is immense. There are rich minerals within our earth, abundant wood in our forests and we have great rivers to provide energy. Our enterpreneurial and management base is sound. We have skilled workers and technicians. We have all the wherewithal of growth and it should be possible for us to be a major economic power if we utilize our resources, talent and skills for the uplift of the nation.

It is also obvious that any growth of the gross national product would be diluted and the benefits to the people reduced, if the size of the population which shares this income is allowed to increase without limit. Our population has been expanding at a rate of more than 2 per cent per year. If this rate continues, even a doubling of the GNP in the next twenty-five years will make no difference at all to our standard of living. This aspect has engaged the attention of the government and serious efforts are being made to reduce population growth through family planning measures. The problem, of course, is immense, particularly because of the large number of villages to be covered and the high extent of illiteracy that prevails. But I am sure, the government has been able to assess problem and it may be expected that worthwhile results will soon follow. Our endeavour should be to stabilize the population growth by the middle of the next decade.

When we consider the problem of development itself, three major areas involving policy choice come to mind. First, it is relevant to question what type of goods to produce; second, what methods of production to adopt; and third, how to mobilize resources to finance the large investments involved. I will take the liberty of giving my views on these major issues, keeping at the back of my mind, the three national objectives to which I made reference earlier.

Look at the logic of development. If we divide the national income broadly into three conventional categories, i.e. agriculture, industry and services, one does find a gradual shift, as development proceeds, from agriculture to industry and services. Nearly half of our national income consists of agricultural goods, another fifth of manufactures and the balance of services. The elasticity of demand for agricultural goods, particularly foodgrains, which constitute about two-thirds of agricultural production, is comparatively small. Therefore, as development proceeds, the demand for agricultural goods will rise much less than the demand for industrial goods. This shift in production will also involve a corresponding shift in employment. But we cannot think of reaching a similar stage of development in this country as, for example, in the USA, where agriculture contributes only about 3 per cent to national income. Our agricultural sector is bound to remain important though its relative size may shrink over the years.

In the agricultural sector itself a shift will have to be engineered between foodgrains and cash crops, and among foodgrains, from cereals to pulses. The production of cash crops has not been commensurate with the demand and this imbalance is reflected in the change in the structure of prices. Similarly, the production of pulses, which are a major source of proteins to most Indians, has not adequately expanded. This deficit needs to be made up. A restructuring of agriculture is thus called for.

The development of agriculture, because of the economic linkages between sectors, will require development of agro-based industries like fertilizer, tractors, etc., and of industries which utilize agricultural products like textile, sugar and oils. This follows from the logic of inter-balance between the different sectors of the economy. But there is a basic factor which has to be built into the production frame that is devised. And that factor is employment. We want more goods with greater use of labour rather than of capital. This involves policy choices which have to be carefully made.

I am mentioning this specially because employment has been one of the weak factors in our five year plans. In spite of the massive investment that has been made in industry and other sectors, unemployment has not been reduced; on the contrary, it has increased with the implementation of successive plans. This has been so because the industries which came to be developed particularly in the public sector were such that they entailed a high amount of capital per man employed. That is to say, the employment potential of investment was rather small. The consideration for the choice of industry was that we have to make growth self-sustaining and for this purpose we have to manufacture the different types of capital goods and equipment that are required. This is true, but only partly. For, we have an open economy and we can import all types of goods that we like in exchange for the type of goods that we produce more efficiently and more cheaply.

Since our major endowment is labour and not capital, we should, I believe, specialize in the production of labour-intensive goods, market these to the developed countries where labour is scarce and import goods which are capital-intensive. This type of production specialization and exchange would promote better utilization of our resources, provide fuller employment and ensure a higher rate of growth. I would particularly mention that greater investment should go into construction activity which not only leads to greater employment but also fulfils an important need, next only to food and clothing.

It needs to be recognized that production does not take place in a vacuum. It calls for a proper climate which is created by the policy framework that is addressed to the nation. What is more, policies are not sacrosanct; they are not permanent. They have to change according to circumstances and remain dynamic all the time in response to economic requirements and needs.

I feel that a review of our economic policies has become absolutely necessary at this juncture. I say this because our scale of production by international standards is small, our costs are high and we are unable to compete effectively in world markets in spite of the advantage of lower wages. If natural economic forces are allowed greater play, we should be able to organize production on better lines, and take full advantage of scientific management and technological advancement.

The policy structure that was devised some years back has served its purpose and we have been able to build a fairly large industrial base. We have completed the first stage of industrialization and we now have to go on to the second stage which requires far greater entrepreneurial and management abilities on the part of business. For this reason I would plead that government should re-examine the whole gamut of economic policies and create conditions for more efficient and effective utilization of resources. More specifically, I would suggest that an analysis be made of the impact of current policies on development and that the framework be refashioned so as to correct imbalances and expand oppurtunities for development. The policies relevant in this connection are the whole range of land reforms, industrial licencing, company law, MRTP, import control and price controls.

The same argument could be extended to the third area I mentioned, viz. resources. It is obvious that a high level of development will call for generation of adequate investible resources. I have a feeling that our fiscal and monetary policies have not given sufficient importance to savings formation either in the households or the corporate sector. The whole emphasis in the past four five year plans has been on transfer of resources.from the people and companies to the government. It was expected that the government would use these resources for development; but this did not turn out exactly as was forecast by the planners. The ratio of government savings to national income has remained more or less static, although the ratio of tax revenue to national income rose from 5 per cent to 15 per cent. A natural conclusion is that these resources were not entirely used for development purposes.

The tax system has to be such as would generate more than proportionately larger revenues with the increase in national income. That is to say, the income elasticity of tax revenue should be more than unity. The Jha Committee which is examining the structure of indirect taxation will, I hope, be able to find an answer to this problem. What I am concerned about is that our system does not provide sufficient incentives for savings formation to households and the corporate sector. These are the prime savers in the economy and it is imperative, if the rate of development has to be high, that these sectors have adequate incentives to save a larger part of their income. A review of the tax system from this angle is, therefore, equally essential.

I have touched on some of the parameters which govern the rate and pattern of development. After all, development is a joint effort and its fruits are also shared jointly by all sections of the community. It is for us to contribute to the national effort, to see that as entrepreneurs or managers, as workers or farmers, as technicians or teachers, we fulfil our obligations to the best of our ability.

Inaugural address at the Ninth Annual Convention of the Bombay Management Association, Bombay, 10 December 1976.

POVERTY AND PROGRESS

I feel honoured to give this G.D. Somani Memorial Lecture. Shri Somani was not only a business leader but a good friend. He was a constructive parliamentarian, a dedicated nationalist, a philanthropist, a social and economic reformer. In him was combined old-world courtesy and the modern urge to get things done. His main objective was to develop the economy. I have, therefore, chosen 'Poverty and Progress' as the topic of my lecture.

The facts of poverty are now generally known. There are differences as to the causes. It used to be fashionable and emotionally appealing to ascribe poverty to a foreign controlled government. Foreign rule was considered the main obstacle to improving the living standards of the people. After the country achieved freedom, analogous reasons ascribing poverty to governance by a particular party are advanced for the stunted growth of the economy.

Poverty is not a modern phenomenon. Poverty has been in existence in ancient times even as today. Just as some nations have been more prosperous than others, so some sections within a nation have been poorer. In modern times the problem of poverty has assumed a central position because of the development of greater consciousness with regard to the comparative wealth of nations and of various strata of society within a nation. Politicians, whether in power or in opposition, take vows for the removal of poverty.

Poverty in India at the time of King Ashoka cannot be compared to that in modern times. Some economists raise the important point as to why economic growth has been so unsatisfactory even in developed countries. Is it because problems of distributive equity loom larger today?

Before we come to a solution of the problem of poverty it is necessary to focus attention on the issues involved. Some observers have noted a strong urban bias in the Indian economy which has curbed the development of the rural sector. The primacy of industrialization followed by urbanization and investment of rural surpluses has been questioned because the poor have remained poor. About 60–80 per cent of the people in developing countries.generally depend on agriculture.

The new party in power has rightly stressed that in a predominantly agrarian economy like India, the massive problem of poverty with its concomitant evils of underemployment and unemployment can be solved only by developing agriculture. Resources have been raised for agricultural and rural development. This is supposed to include power for agriculture, and additional outlays envisaged for the development of roads, transport and education in the villages. Agricultural production can be realistically raised much higher in our country. The achievements of the past thirty years, though limited, are not inconsiderable. However, the yield per acre of our major food crops, rice and wheat, are still very low. The techniques or mysteries of higher production are not unknown today. It is essential that the institutional framework of the land system is radically changed through suitable measures.

Development of agriculture does not preclude development of industry. In fact, the two sectors go together. Many industries are based on raw materials required by agriculture. Fertilizers, pesticides, tractors, pumps, etc. are essential inputs in agriculture.While industrial policy must necessarily aim at achieving a high rate of growth of production and increasing the employment potential, removal of poverty requires that production should be maximum.

The efficiency of capital investment in India during the first decade after Independence has been only one-third that of China. First, I must point out the allergy towards the large-scale sector. Large-scale production, it should be realized, has a positive role to play in our industrial development.Another question I would like to raise is about the definition of small-scale industry. It is well known that the cost of projects has gone up several-fold during the last few years and the return on investment has become even negative in some cases. It is doubtful whether the current definition of small-scale industry is realistic. Similarly, the concept of cottage and village industries is not clearly defined. Inputs whether in the cottage and village industries, or in any industry in the small-scale sector, may be a product of the organized sector of the industry. A flexible view would be more practical.

Apart from efficiency, it is necessary to ensure quality standards. First, it is necessary to locate the development potential of different types of village and cottage industries by area surveys and formulate realistic proposals on the basis of knowledge of local talent and resources. It is necessary to develop entrepreneurship. This can be done through management institutions and term lending institutions.

The advanced industrialized nations are evolving new and more efficient techniques. In sugar production, crushing capacity of 2000 tons per day used to be considered most efficient. But today sugar machinery with double the capacity is being used for greater efficiency. Similar instances could be provided from textiles, manmade fibres, chemicals, etc. Research studies have indicated that traditional techniques are inferior.

The sub-division of industry into four sectors and the industrial caste system is influenced by political overtones rather than based on techno-economic considerations. The products coming under each category have to be decided subjectively. By putting barriers to operational manoeuverability, inefficient producers are likely to be protected from efficient producers. Control by bureaucracy is then likely to spread in accordance with Parkinson's Law besides creating a breeding ground for anti-social practices.

There remains a lot of confusion on the basic tenets of industrial policy. Important members of the present government are reported to have stated that the provision for large units to rely on their own resources for expansion was to prove it's oft-reported claims that it alone was in a position to undertake expansion and new projects because of the resources and technological skills it commanded. If this was the objective, the government should clearly declare that large-scale units could be free from any other restrictions. Distrust of any particular sector is inimical to the growth of the economy and would push the goal of removal of poverty further away. The most important area for economic progress is infrastructure, comprising power,water resources, transport and various essential services.Industry is suffering from shortage of power. The shortfall was 7 per cent of the requirement in 1976, but as of December 1977 the shortfall has gone up to the nearly 14 per cent. The targets for setting up generating capacity have never been attained since the beginning of the plans.

Power supply in our country is characterized by high transmission and distribution losses as high as 30 per cent, compared with the average of 6-8 per cent observed in other countries. Besides the load factor has been 50 per cent of the installed capacity. To some extent, power shortage can be reduced by inducing industries to operate more during off-peak hours by offering them incentives in terms of lower tariffs.Industry should also be allowed to set up captive power plants.Transmission losses can be reduced thus. It is necessary to improve upon the existing capacity of power generation besides expediting the completion of projects in hand.

India has several mountain ranges and large river systems which imply vast potential resources for hydel power. As assessed by the Power Economy Committee in 1971, the total potential of water resources is more than six times the capacity installed for generation of hydro-electricity. The more recent Fuel Policy Committee recommended that a systematic delineation of the water power potential should be made as soon as possible.If the concept of a National Power Grid is implemented, electric power from our water resources can be developed wherever it is possible to do so economically and then it can be fed into the National Grid for transmission and distribution.

The need for balanced development of our economy is now generally accepted. One way of persuading entrepreneurs to go to underdeveloped areas in our country would be to enforce a rational wage policy which will not only take productivity factors into account but will also allow wages in underdeveloped areas to go up only gradually.

Population control, it should be realized, is an essential precondition for improving the standard of living of the people.

Economic progress cannot be measured only in terms of agricultural and industrial goods. It is necessary that a majority of the people are provided with basic social amenities like education, health, housing and transport. Investment in housing which is a capital intensive activity has become unattractive due to poor returns and in recent years there has been a further slowing down due to the ceiling on land holdings in urban areas.

The transport sector is generally known to be one of the most powerful generators of employment.There is immense scope for extending the transport network, particularly the road transport. There is very large potential for direct employment in linkage industries such as electrical equipment, paints, furnishing. Repair and maintenance provide employment. The construction of roads and their maintenance also require a large number of skilled and unskilled workers.

In a poor country like India it is only a few who can save money, and these relatively affluent people are not large consumers of the necessities of life. The so-called 'conspicuous consumption' by this section is not without the benefit of creating employment.I now come to a related point. As I said earlier, only a few in our country are in a position to save. If development is to depend upon such meagre savings, then we can forget about fast development. Monetary savings do not automatically create demand and these savings are used by others who create demand for different types of goods. It will be futile to depend upon the savings of the community alone. In this context, deficit financing has a special role to play.There has to be a trade-off between stagnation and unemployment on the one hand, and growth and greater employment on the other.

We have a growing population which if stabilized by popular

education and suitable control measures would provide the labour base for any gigantic task in agriculture or industry. Further, India is not lacking in natural resources. Our proved coal reserves are considerable but explorations have gone only up to a depth of only about 2000 feet as against 3000 feet or even 6000 feet in some places. We have only started exploring our oil resources.

If the past be any guide and the present a portent for the future, we have to reluctantly resign ourselves to slow growth, wastage, indecision, and some kind of 'working chaos'. It will be a shame if malnutrition, disease and unemployment continue to pervade a large segment of our population which is also growing. The stakes are too high.The development process itself is extraordinarily complex. It must be ensured that past mistakes are not repeated.

—Too much time is lost in policy formulation, and the final product often has the characteristic of a politician's set of promises before an election—there is something in it for everyone.

—Time is money, and delay is extremely expensive in an inflationary era.

— We either too easily permit or too readily prohibit the different vocal sections expressing their disappointment. In so far as development is about and for the people, every section has the right to disapprove or seek change.

— The tendency to change horses in midstream has cost the nation dearly. We abandoned the community development scheme, and are now trying to re-introduce it in some form or the other. Family planning has almost become a dirty term.

— There are far too many myths and prejudices about what should be the size of the operating agency, whether some establishments should be allowed to grow at all and the like.

Many similar points can be made, but I hope I have made myself sufficiently clear to chart out the kind of fundamental shifts in policy and attitude that are necessary if growth is to succeed in any acceptable time-frame.

Maybe, structural flaws in some form will always remain; exploitative and irrational relationships will not altogether disappear. It is often difficult to be optimistic, but it is certainly a coward's attitude to despair of events.

Address at the Fifth G.D. Somani Memorial Lecture, Bombay, 27 January 1978.

FRESH OUTLOOK FOR FASTER DEVELOPMENT

It is a great pleasure for me to be here and share with you, if not the answers, at least some of the questions which have been bothering me. Today I find that while the economy is in a healthy state, there are clear indications that growth may not be a sustained process which, at this time is, in fact, most imperative. I have wondered why is it that we as a country have not been able to do as well as some others which entered the development race at about the same time as we did. The answer to this single question is so puzzling that I thought I may take this opportunity to at least make a beginning towards an introspective analysis of ourselves as a country, as a government, as a people.

The Janata Party has been in power for nearly two years now, and quite understandably, it is faced with an identity crisis. The party did not exist before the last elections and it did not possess a ready economic philosophy which could be put into operation. Even after two years it is not in a position to chalk out the right course of action possibly because of the different pulls and pressures from people who are committed to very diverse ideologies.

In recent months particularly there has been an intense debate which has brought back to the surface some very basic issues. We again find ourselves asking whether it is the public or the private sector that should be promoted, whether it is small or large industry that should be developed, whether it is industry or agriculture that should get prominence in plan programmes. What is surprising is that these issues are discussed as if there is a clear choice between public and private, small and large, agriculture and industry. We have had a long history of development and the economy after five five-year plans, has achieved a certain status, is governed by a certain policy mix and is on a certain course of development. To raise basic issues at this point in history is futile because the economy has to be taken forward from where it is. We cannot now, even if the government so desires, change the total complexion of policy without creating very adverse effects which both in the short and the long term may be too harsh upon the people who are looking for quick improvement in the quality of life.

I am particularly distressed by the debate which has been started about the nationalization of a number of premier private sector industries, particularly steel, automobiles, aluminium and paper. It is not only the development of these industries which is likely to be affected; the uncertainty and the credibility gap will dampen the development of other industries as well. It does not need great foresight or an analytic mind to accept that such proposals have been mooted much less for their economic worth than for the political leverage that they provide. There is somehow a feeling, which I have always discounted, that people are carried away by measures which bring greater economic activity under state control.

People are aware of and resent the abnormal price increases in most of the nationalized industries like coal, copper and several others. There is no nationalized industry which has been able to maintain prices or which is not making very substantial losses. It must not be forgotten that all this is at the cost of the consumer. The time has come, therefore, to think of denationalizing some of these industries and bringing them into the competitive system. This would be a useful experiment.

One of the arguments for nationalization has been sickness in the industrial sector. It is not realized however that this is often due to the government's own policy. This was so, for instance, in the case of cotton textiles. After the controlled cloth obligation was removed the industry became healthy once again. I am not underestimating mismanagement on the part of some managers in the private sector. Besides, there is also a natural process by which a firm or an industry withers away because of economic factors either linked to demand or to supply. These units and industries may have to be scrapped rather than artificially supported through measures like nationalization.

Under these circumstances, to suggest that more industries should be brought under state management appears, to me at least, callous. There is little consideration for the welfare of the people which, it cannot be denied, should be the ultimate test for judging the reasonableness of any economic policy.

As I said, we are not starting out afresh on development. We have to go forward from where we are. Fortunately, the conditions today are fairly good. Agricultural production is satisfactory; industrial production has been growing at a rate of 7 per cent since April last year; prices have been stable; and there is a sizable foreign exchange reserve to back the rupee. There are also certain constraints. Investment, particularly in the private sector industries, is low; there is shortage of power, steel, coal, aluminium, caustic soda, cement and some other crucial commodities; there is considerable labour unrest; and exports have been declining.

Many of the shortages that we see today are due to wrong policies adopted earlier. The government has to learn from past mistakes. With the natural resources and skills that we have, if correct policies had been followed, there should have been no shortages today. It is necessary for any rational economic policy to build on the plus points and to correct the negative aspects so that the economy is put on a steady growth path.

The fundamental requirement, I would say, is to transform the available labour, skills and finance into a high rate of development. Who invests is pertinent, so too whether the investment is appropriate, whether management is efficient and whether the use of resources is such as to give the highest benefit to the people. Unfortunately, such an attitude has not been seen on the part of government. I hope the next budget which is only a week ahead will seek to maximize effort, savings, investment and production.

My assessment is that the economy today requires psychological and economic stimuli. If development remains the privilege of the government it would hardly ever be achieved. If it is brought down to the people enabling them to use their capacities to the full extent it will reach its peak. It is in this context that the budget and the scheme of taxation have to be formulated. I would like to suggest some urgent modifications which are necessary.

First, it needs to be accepted that new investment is imperative because shortages of a number of commodities have surfaced and without expansion of capacity additional production will become well nigh impossible. However, investment is not rising as fast as it should because new projects, due to high investment costs, have become non-viable. The problem is two-fold. A new company should be able to compete with established companies in spite of the higher depreciation and interest charges. This can be achieved by extending the excise duty rebate scheme and relating it to the capital intensity of the project. Further, the companies must be in a position to mobilize sufficient capital from the public without depending on the financial institutions. The Finance Minister had mentioned last year that the corporate sector should generate its own resources. This is indeed a laudable approach, provided the government enables the corporate sector to generate resources by reducing corporate taxation.

Second, there should be a strong incentive for savings formation. This could be achieved if the basis of taxation is shifted from income to consumption. For instance, an individual could be taxed on his income minus the savings which are invested in specified form like bank deposits, company shares, government securities, fixed assets like plant and machinery, buildings, etc. This would immediately give considerable fillip to savings formation and, with the larger investment which people and companies would desire, the economy would be put into a faster development orbit.

It is very important that the rate of development is stepped up to achieve the maximum potential. I am convinced that it is only growth that can be an effective instrument for promoting employment. While the pattern of growth is important the rate of growth is, in my view, even more crucial. It is possible to achieve high growth and, at the same time, design a pattern of development which would create larger employment opportunities.

Development is an integrated process. If any sector develops too fast or too slow, the whole process is held up due to structural imbalances. To promote a higher standard of living it is certainly necessary to have an expanding agricultural base. But this should not be looked upon as an alternative to faster growth of industry. In the fifties and sixties, for instance, we witnessed that a 1 per cent growth in agriculture generally requires a 2 per cent growth in industry. This pattern may not hold good for all time. But there is a structural relationship which necessitates that the growth of industry has to be at a certain rate in the context of the overall target that is sought to be achieved.

In recent months the development of industry has been thought of at two levels, viz. small and cottage, on the hand, and large, on the other. This controversy, again, is overdone. There need not be any conflict between large and small or small and cottage. The products which are manufactured by the cottage sector are entirely different from those manufactured by the large sector, excepting a few where a problem of choice does arise. To exaggerate this limited problem and to blow it up beyond all proportions would be to underestimate the role of the large sector which itself stimulates the development of small and medium industries.

The point I am driving at is that economic development by and large, should be entrusted to enterprises which can deliver the goods at the least cost. This helps resource generation, steps up the rate of growth per unit of investment, enhances our capacity to compete in international markets and raises the employment potential of the economy. The system under which the public sector operates is not quite conducive to efficiency, and a greater element of competition among public sector enterprises and between enterprises in the public and private sectors would be helpful. One suggestion I would certainly like to make is that the public sector enterprises should allow and, indeed, encourage holding of shares by the general public. This would reduce the burden on the budget and consequently the need for additional taxation. It would also introduce a greater element of discipline in the management of public sector undertakings. The exposure of these companies to the scrutiny and vigilance of shareholders would itself promote greater efficiency.

The public sector is vital in a number of activities like power generation, road construction, transport, provision of drinking water and similar economic and social infrastructure facilities. Unfortunately, these activities have been somewhat neglected and the less pertinent, though probably more demonstrative, areas like industry have come to acquire greater interest.

Development ultimately depends on each one doing his job efficiently; and the job can be efficiently done only when it is entrusted to people and organizations who have the capacity to execute. Ideologies are nice, elegant, intellectual exercises. In the modern world it is neither socialism nor capitalism, neither the left nor the right, that can give results. Most free enterprise economies have a substantial contribution by government in the national income; and most socialist countries have now allowed private industry to supplement the state's efforts. Mixed economy is the new concept, the kind of mixture varying from one country to the other. We started our development under this system and it has certainly given results. I only hope that the government will not create serious distortions which would adversely affect future development.

What we need most urgently is to inculcate, to quote Dr Arthur Lewis, a 'national ethos', so strongly visible in countries like Japan, Germany and Korea, and which is missing in our own. However, as long as we remain a divided house we are unlikely to grow. To develop a sense of priority, to be able to put national needs before individual gain or political expediency and to have pride in everything we do is a matter of national character. As long as this is not built up, we may not be able to achieve very significant results. These are values to which not only the people, business and trade must address themselves, but values that the policy-makers must imbibe.

Address at a conference in Calcutta, 21 February 1979.

MANAGEMENT OF THE ECONOMY AND INDUSTRIAL GROWTH

We are on the threshold of a new decade. And if we cannot look back with enough satisfaction, at least we can look ahead with great hope.

In the seventies, industrial development was extremely low key. On an average, the growth rate was about 4 per cent per year. More recently, development was arrested because of the severe constraints imposed by shortage of power, coal and transport. Earlier, development was exposed to other limitations which made it impossible for industry to maintain its performance in the fifties and the sixties or match the potential it possessed.

Industrial development in the seventies did not quite pick up because of the halting agricultural growth which acted as a drag. The drought of 1965–67 had brought home quite clearly that unless agriculture develops, industrial progress will not be feasible. It was natural therefore, that the government concentrated its energies on promoting agricultural progress which, at least in the case of foodgrains, has given handsome results. In the matter of about a decade, production of foodgrains almost doubled. With this correction in the pattern of production it should be possible for industry to push ahead great at speed in the future.

Looking at our potential and the performance of other countries I have come to believe that in the eighties industry will be in a position to develop at the rate of at least 10 per cent per year. The Planning Commission, I believe, has planned for a growth of only about 7 per cent in 1978–83. I am visualizing a higher rate because I can see the opportunities that present themselves and the changes in the political environment which can bring them to fruition.

A 10 per cent annual increase in industrial production will necessitate a vast investment effort and call for corresponding development in other related areas. For instance, expansion of industry is not feasible without corresponding development of power, railways and other infrastructure which supply the necessary inputs. Hence, development of industry is not an isolated issue; it is connected with the rapid progress of the whole economy. Looking at the interrelationship of sectors it seems to me that a 10 per cent growth of industry is feasible only when the economy is itself in a position to grow at least at 7 per cent per year.

The present problems which have arisen because of shortage of power, coal and transport emerge from the fact that those sectors have become the monopoly of the government. It is not my suggestion that coal should be denationalized or that electricity undertakings should be handed over to private enterprise. But I do believe that it is important that in a mixed economy the different agencies of development compete with each other to maximize growth. I would, therefore, say that in coal, electricity generation or any other sector government and private enterprise should participate without any reservation so that the best in each is brought out and through competition the efficiency of each is maintained and enhanced. If an integrated programme of industry and infrastructure is evolved on a development sharing basis, there is no reason why we cannot achieve a 10 per cent growth in the economy as a whole. All that this will mean is doubling of our per capita income which today stands at only Rs 1200, less than half that of China, Thailand or Indonesia. Even if the proposed growth is achieved, at the end of this decade we shall be enjoying only the same standard of living as these developing countries have today.

To promote high development, great management skill is called for at the national level. I can say without hesitation that speedy development of industry cannot take place in the present economic environment. This is so for the simple reason that progress is constrained by policies which are not conducive to rapid development. I would like to offer certain suggestions in this regard because I am firmly of the opinion that unless growth is maximized it will not be possible to secure any other economic objective to which the policies have addressed themselves. Whether it is provision of employment, improvement in the standard of living of the common people, reduction in inequalities of income, balancing the external resources position or achieving a high degree of self-reliance, it is maximization of production which alone can do the trick. If this objective is diluted or made subservient to any other policy parameter, we shall not be able to secure any worthwhile result.

This is no mere rhetoric. It is what we have seen happening over the past decade. Policies which were devised to prevent the so-called concentration of economic power have only diluted growth; policies which were devised to take away through taxation a large part of the income of the relatively well-to-do classes have checked savings and investment; policies which were devised to create savings in government through high excise duties have only led to inflation. It is my firm belief that unless production is made the central theme of our economic effort, and therefore of policies, we shall not reach anywhere.

Let us not forget that the best in the economy comes to the fore only when every sector of the economy is exposed to the discipline of a free and competitive market. Government cannot replace market forces except to intervene temporarily to check undue rises in the price of any commodity brought about by external circumstances. Therefore, gradually price controls have to be knocked off and replaced by market forces. In a competitive world it is the more efficient who promote development. It is these producers who, compelled by competition, would make optimum use of human and material resources, which alone can bring down costs and prices. I would also like to suggest that development, to the extent possible, should be promoted by existing enterprises to enable them to reach the optimum size at which the cost of production is the least. Most of our enterprises are too small by international standards and are using technologies which are outdated. Technological change which will improve productivity both of labour and capital is required to ensure the highest outcome from each unit of labour or capital. In that situation we shall be able to complete in international markets without much effort and be able to regain our share in world trade.

Freedom of the market is not confined only to products but also to factors of production. What I have specially in mind is remuneration of managerial personnel. For one reason or the other, the government has cut down the pay and perquisites of top managers who in fact are the most critical element in industrial development. This productive class of people has been subjected to restrictions which have led to considerable frustration and even brain drain. For instance, in 1978, the pay and perquisites of the top management were reduced from Rs 2.23 lakh to Rs 1.32 lakh per annum. I fail to understand why business executives should not be eligible to housing facility at 10 per cent of the pay just as civil servants are. The approach needs to be modified and companies must be given liberty to buy managerial services at prices which the market commands, subject to broad guidelines.

As I said earlier, development of industry at 10 per cent per year would require considerable finances. My assessment is that an investment of at least about Rs 70,000 crore will have to be undertaken in the next ten years in industry, assuming that the resources are utilized in the optimum manner. Finance, whether it is in the government sector or in private hands, has ultimately to come from savings. Mere taxation does not generate additional resources; it only transfers resources from the people to the government kitty. However, there is one resource which comes almost from nowhere. That is deficit financing. The vote on account which was presented to Parliament on 11 March leaves an uncovered deficit of Rs 1235 crore in 1980–81. I think the Finance Minister has been conservative in his calculation. A much larger deficit is in fact possible considering that some of the industries are already facing a mild demand recession.

In a long-term perspective, it would be wrong to seek to enlarge government revenue by pitching up the tax ratios. I do agree that the government needs more money to fulfil its multiple responsibilities. However, the additional revenue should be secured by widening the tax base rather than raising the rates of taxation. For instance, if an additional Rs 4,000 crore worth of industrial production is secured by provision of electricity and coal, government would be better off to the extent of at least Rs 2,000 crore or so from the additional tax revenue. If industry grows at 10 per cent per year, by 1990 the government's tax revenue will be up by Rs 30,000 crore. It is such measures which would be more helpful in the long-term development of the country than the shortsighted approach of hiking taxes for raising revenue.

I would like to be more specific on this point. The marginal rate of income taxation, in my view, should be brought down to 60 per cent and the rate of corporate taxation limited to 50 per cent, for all companies. In suggesting this, I am not asking for any concession. I am only basing myself on the rates of taxation in most other countries. I am inclined to believe that the lower rates of taxation which prevail in a country like Japan, are factors which have assisted faster development of the economy. Taxation has to be conceived in the national context. It is hardly material to the people whether it is the government that brings about development or the private sector. What is important is that development takes place. If higher taxation acts as a barrier to development, it would be self-defeating.

I am also aware that there are areas where additional taxation is possible. Take, for instance, import tariffs. I do understand why government should regulate through an administrative mechanism like import control. It would have been better if imports were regulated through a simple tariff mechanism. What is costly is purchased in smaller quantities. Naturally, by raising tariffs, government can get additional revenue which at present takes the form of an unnatural profit on the part of the importer, whether it is the STC or the private sector.

Similarly, government can achieve a better budgetary balance by reducing the number of non-productive expenditures. This aspect needs to be carefully examined by a committee of secretaries and quick action taken on the means by which greater economies in expenditure can be achieved.

My purpose in suggesting these kinds of fiscal measures is to highlight the fact that any policy system which hinders development, whether in the public or in the private sector, is not in the national interest. With the modifications in the taxation system that I have suggested, the corporate sector would be in a position to generate internal resources, as also to float new issues. Nevertheless, institutional finance will remain important. Even today, it meets about one-third of the total investment needs of the corporate sector. However, one of the handicaps is the option given to institutions to convert a part of their loan into equity. This causes considerable management uncertainty and also upsets the debt equity ratio. Many potential shareholders are deterred by this prospect, as also entrepreneurs. My suggestion is that the conversion clause which has proved to be a handicap in industrial development should not find a place in loan contracts. In any case, for industries in which the debt equity ratio is less than the maximum that is stipulated, namely 2:1, the convertibility clause should not be insisted upon at all. Neither should conversion lead to increasing the share of financial institutions in the capital of a company beyond 30 per cent. This would create greater confidence among entrepreneurs and induce them to undertake larger investment.

I am quite aware that domestic finance may not be quite enough if growth is pushed up to the high level of 10 per cent per year. A supplementary source would be the Eurodollar market. The loan would be on commercial terms and a mechanism will have to be devised to tenable repayment in foreign exchange. This does not mean that the borrower should himself have to find foreign exchange resources for the servicing of the loan. What it means is that the development financed by foreign loans should conform to a certain scheme of priorities which will automatically enlarge our export earnings. This is not at all difficult and if a systematic approach is made to the problem, we should be able to resolve it on a very low-risk basis.

You may probably feel I am a little too optimistic. However, if our planning is not ambitious enough, I do not think it has any place in our development scheme. Of course, a 10 per cent growth in industry will call for tremendous effort on our part and great understanding on the part of the government. But I would certainly say that industry is willing to put in its very best to take the country forward in its march towards industrialization. It is up to the government to utilize these forces for the betterment of the country and to provide our people with new opportunities for a better life.

Address at an AIMA Conference , New Delhi, 18 March 1980.

COMMERCE AND INDUSTRY : DEVELOPMENT OF OUR ECONOMY

I feel privileged to have been asked to be the Chief Guest this evening at the Annual Session of the Indian Merchants' Chamber—seventy-third in the series. This Chamber—an offspring of the Swadeshi movement—has developed into a premier business organization in India. Its contribution in helping to stimulate informed opinion has been outstanding. The present stature it enjoys is due as much to its founding fathers as to the succession of eminent presidents.

There are many 'firsts' to the credit of the Chamber, and I am happy that after the close of the session, the presidency will be taken over by my young and talented friend, Smt. Sharayu Daftary. She will be the first lady to adorn the chair of any chamber, to the best of my knowledge, in this part of the world. While wishing her every success, I take the liberty of enjoining on her that she should bring to bear on the assignment that sure feminine intuition which will open up new horizons of service not only to business interests, but also to the community at large.

It is often said that we are living through a time of difficulties and problems, national and international. In one sense there is hardly any time which has been free of troubles or of potentialities to be exploited. Every generation has sought a golden age that has passed or is yet to come. It is only occasionally that people are fired by an enlivening impulse, fully alive to the passing moments, eager to enjoy as much as to serve, looking forward to meet the new challenges of the morrow.

Let us confess that today we are not possessed by this spirit. On the contrary, there is too much lamentation all round compounded by a sense of drift in thought. We hear everywhere that there is a 'climate of disillusion' and that the 'political will' to back development is lacking. Maybe our developmental effort has fallen short of expectations and is not commensurate either with our needs, physical resources or human talent. Are there no objective considerations which should give us heart to look at the present and the future with at least a modicum of confidence and optimism? All said and done, is not our economy today far stronger and more viable than thirty years ago?

As I see it, there is a kind of persuasive death-wish which exaggerates failures and discounts successes. Successes are even frowned upon. There are some so-called intellectuals who find in successes not stepping stones to higher endeavour, but schisms that will divide society. Take the green revolution which has been spreading and the white revolution which is in the offing. There are Cassandras who bemoan this on the ground that the benefits have accrued only to a few and who declare without any statistical support that the poor have become poorer. A moment's reflection would clearly indicate that however gluttonous the few rich are, they cannot obviously consume the substantial additions to our food production over the years. The same kind of abandoned reasoning is applied to the achievements of the corporate sector, forgetting that the expansion and diversification of enterprises whether small, medium or large are a national achievement, not a failure.

So, I suggest that there is need for a proper appraisal of both our failures and successes. A rational and reasonable objective must be to desist from making the same mistakes and to garner the points of strength in the body politic. It is in this perspective that I shall endeavour to place before you some thoughts on economic policy—the kind of reorientation which is desirable to meet the demands of today and tomorrow in greater measure.

First of all, let me start with some general propositions.

— In a democratic political society like ours, it is axiomatic that policy should seek to maximize human happiness through personal freedom as well as economic independence. This, in itself, eschews both monopolistic capitalism and bureaucratic socialism. For good reason, therefore, we have opted for a mixed economy. All the same time, while we have enunciated the mixed economy concept in formal terms, we have not, I am afraid, applied the spirit in which it was evolved. In these circumstances, we are over-run by avoidable controls and a maze of legislative measures based, paradoxically enough, on a sentimental approach to development and an excessive suspicion of human nature. It is time we became realistic.

—Our policies and legislation must take into account human beings as they are, not in terms of a theoretical conception of what they ought to be, much less on the basis that they are wicked. If there is acceptance of people as they are, it goes without saying that they are first and foremost interested in the welfare of themselves and their families.

Then, in recognition of this fact, let policies be attuned to harnessing the horse of egoism to the carriage of progress or development. It implies equally that there are traffic regulations in order that the freedom of the individual does not infringe upon the equal rights of others.

— Development is not a once-for-all exercise. It demands sustained effort, a plodding kind if you will. In this view of things, while altruism certainly has a place, rhetorical sentimentalism must be ruled out as the latter has not done any good to man or beast anywhere, any time. It is only then that we will be able to erect a more solid economic structure which alone can stimulate the necessary production of goods, in terms of quantity and quality, to meet the demands of the people.

— Obviously, self-sustaining growth requires institutional change. I do not mean thereby the traditional method of changing the ownership of the means of production from private to public hands or vice-versa. What I have in mind is that we must concentrate on changes in social structure, education, birth rates and the like. Government must then prune the already overburdened legislative lexicon which is negative in character and which is being strangled by its own intensity, and divert the energies of the sizeable army of public officials to socio-economic developmental areas.

— Even though the Planning Commission has visualized a growth rate of over 5 per cent in the next plan, some people argue that whatever policies may be adopted the growth rate in India will be around 3.5 per cent, as the experience over three decades of planning has shown. This is tantamount to saying that rapid growth is not possible at all. In my view it will not be unrealistic if we set a higher growth rate target than even that visualized by the Planning Commission. Once we set out on the course of development in all sectors of the economy simultaneously—industry, agriculture, and so on—and there is an appropriate balance of one with the other, rapid growth is automatic. Unlike many other countries, India is in a favourable position in that we have physical resources and skilled manpower which in combination can overcome shortages in financial resources. In any case, in my view what is technically feasible should be financially possible.

— While rightly, the futile debate on the role of the public and private sectors has died down, and the contribution of both has come to be more widely recognized, there is still pre-occupation with the concept of concentration of economic power. This concept, I suggest, is misplaced not only in the Indian context, but also against the background of the advances made in science and technology. It is axiomatic that certain industries must be large in size to operate in a viable fashion and to pass on the benefits of large-scale production to the community. Moreover, only such large-scale undertakings can compete in international markets where the participants are normally big.

Having made these general observations, let me now get down to the specific economic issues facing us. While the Cassandras mouthing tragic forebodings ought not to be encouraged, it is at the same time necessary that we as a nation dedicate ourselves afresh to the tasks ahead of us. The point to be borne in mind is that we are capable of achieving much more than the 3.5 per cent growth we have had on an average in the last three decades. Now, while capital output ratio goes up over time, its increase from 3.6 in the first plan to 6.2 in the first three years of the fifth plan is as much owing to inefficiency as due to the trend factor. This is against the background of increase in investment from 11 per cent in the first plan to 21–22 per cent in recent years. Inefficiency is the result of wrong allocation of resources, delays in completion of projects, under-utilization of capacities, and more than anything else, all-pervading indiscipline. How else does one explain steel, fertilizer, multi-purpose projects taking as long as ten to twenty years to complete when the time required, by the experience of other countries, is five to eight years?

In about forty-eight hours from now the central budget will be presented. I wonder if we have not on such occasions failed to capture the essence while chasing inconsequential things. To begin with, an important step in planning is how to dovetail the present with the past and the future with the present so that there is a basic continuity. Far from doing this, the hardy annual exercise of the budget has come to take such spins and turns, that one wonders if there is any fiscal planning in the country. With the five-year plan spelling out allocations and targets in detail up to State/project level, budgets should be framed in a sequential way. In other words, ad-hocism should be minimal. Any drastic change in rates or revision of the policy frame cuts at the root of fiscal planning in so far as it affects expectations, cash flows, savings, investment and so on. I am not opposed to changes in taxation per se, because exogenous factors, for instance, could induce changes in excise for unavoidable reasons. All that I am suggesting is that too much of experimentation is fraught with uncertainty that could, in the final analysis, be hurtful.

Take, for instance, the abrupt withdrawal of development rebate and the granting of initial depreciation allowance in 1974 and its substitution by investment allowance in 1978. Or consider the hike in individual income tax rates in the 1979–80 budget. To cite the case of a different type of tinkering, duties on thirty life-saving drugs were savagely increased in 1979–80 but were mercifully withdrawn in 1980–81. There was a change from specific to ad valorem basis of taxation in a year on certain items that played havoc with their prices. On a different plane, small-scale manufacturing units covered by the residual item 68 of the central excise tariff were enjoying full exemption under certain conditions upto a production level of Rs 30 lakh but the limit was reduced to Rs 15 lakh in the 1979–80 budget and the original limit restored in 1980–81. Extension of excise to 130-odd specific commodities and recently to residual items has only added to the existing confusion. Such examples of change and the adverse impact these changes exercise can be multiplied. I have deliberately kept out the maze of legislation that has grown around income, wealth, etc. and the debilitating influence they have on initiative. All this has had a corrosive influence on the moral fibre. Ad-hocism should yield to well thought out tax measures that last a long time.

My suggestion is that, when the country is poised for a big development effort as in the present plan with a total outlay of Rs 172,210 crore and public sector outlay of Rs 97,500 crore, the opportunity should be seized for a thorough appraisal of the entire range of fiscal and monetary policy issues. This is inescapable because additional resource mobilization during the plan is placed at Rs 21,302 crore. It is also open to doubt whether public sector enterprises will be able to generate surpluses of the order of Rs 9,395 crore. This could well place further strain on resource mobilization. As it is, tax revenues form 16.7 per cent of the GNP, to take a recent year, 1978–79, as against only 7.4 per cent when we launched on planning in 1951–52. The present tax base is admittedly narrow. What could be broadly termed as the industry sector contributes the bulk of taxation—corporate taxes, excise duties, custom duties, direct taxes—and this is placed at 70 to 75 per cent of total taxation.

My contention is that there is no proper or thoroughgoing discussion on fiscal policy issues. It is a truism to say that the tax base being narrow, rates of taxation have been unconscionably steep with deleterious effects on savings. The quantum of savings itself and savings taken as a proportion of GNP has no doubt gone up significantly over the years. But the point remains, if taxation had been less penal, given the restricted tax base, more savings would have been forthcoming and committed to a more risk-bearing type of investment. I am not suggesting that the budgeting exercise can be conducted in the market-place. I am well aware that in most cases advance notice cannot be served about likely increases in excise taxes and the like. I am only wondering if budgeting need be shrouded in such secrecy, if there cannot be a greater measure of prior discussion and consultation with various parties and interests than has been the practice so far. The need for a wholesale revamping of the tax structure is heightened by the magnitude of additional resources to be raised as well as by the likely shortfalls on different counts. In many countries it has now been accepted that a reduction in marginal rate of taxation is a means to stimulate economic activity and to generate more revenues for the Exchequer. Somehow, this economic credo has not yet entered the consciousness of our fiscal administrators.

I will digress briefly to discuss one of the sources of plan finance. Deficit financing has been placed at Rs 5,000 crore for 1980–85, when for 1980–81 itself, it may well be in the neighbourhood of Rs 2,500–Rs 3,000 crore. Whether it will be possible to restrict deficit financing to Rs 2,000–Rs 2,500 crore in the remaining four years in the background of the difficulties listed in tapping additional resources, it is too early to say. When we talk of deficit financing, we tend to forget that long-term market borrowings of a certain type from commercial banks could also have an expansionary effect on money supply. It will be far more meaningful to take a total view of budgetary deficits and market borrowings on the one hand, and projected increases to output on the other, and maintain a balance between additional demand for goods and services and their supply over a period. What is happening presently is that the supposedly small residual item is finally proving to be a much bigger budgetary mainstay than was expected. It is better to plan for deficits than be caught unawares. In the name of containing the ill-effects of increase in money supply, prices, etc., legitimate borrowing is choked off. I am surprised at the naiveté with which a correlation is sought to be established between money supply and prices, forgetting that there are other factors like supply of goods, under-utilized capacities, capacities coming to a stage of fruition, buffer stocks and the like.

More than anything, emphasis should be placed on completion of ongoing projects and fuller utilization of existing capacities. About 60 per cent of the present plan expenditure is committed to projects under way. All the same, when we are on the threshold of a big development effort, we should remind ourselves that the government's expenditure is about Rs 25,000 crore, to take a recent year, 1979–80, and that it formed 30 per cent of the country's income.

How much of government's expenditure is economically useful is a matter of conjecture. I am not referring to the traditional division between developmental and non-developmental expenditure alone. That much remains to be done to get the most out of government's investment, is a point that need not be laboured. Right from the preparation of project reports to the stage of their final working, there should be proper streamlining, so that delays are cut down, there is better coordination and capacities are used to the maximum. If this were done there could be a drop in the capital output ratio. In other words, we would be able to wring much more out of the investment we have made or are planning to make. I agree that we have to run fast to remain steady, in Alice in Wonderland fashion, or in this case to attain a modicum of growth. Where I differ from the pessimists is in that I do not intend giving up the battle even before it is joined. Despite large outlays on social services including the minimum needs programme, 30 per cent of the people will still remain below the poverty line as against the present 48 per cent. And employment will go up from 151 million standard person years to 185 million standard person years. There will be only marginal increments in consumption in per capita terms. How far the government will show the required capacity to implement a plan of this size and get results from investment and above all to increase availability of goods and alleviate human misery and suffering remains to be seen. Otherwise the growth target is well within the realm of realization.

The increased emphasis on import substitution in the sixth plan, against which background I am making these remarks, is inevitable, particularly in the context of the huge trade deficit of well over Rs 4,000 crore expected during the year. While there cannot be import substitution to the extent of shutting out all improved/upgraded technology, import substitution in areas where the country has built substantial industrial capacity or has natural advantages, as in steel, cement, aluminium or in a whole range of consumer goods, is proper. But what should not be lost sight of is that production standards should be high and costs should be competitive.

With the yawning trade gap, the strain in balance of payments should be lessened not only through import substitution but equally and vigorously through export promotion. The plan document, for instance, postulates an increase in exports from Rs 6,150 crore in 1979–80 to Rs 10,150 crore by 1984–85 and this increase is spread not only over the traditional agricultural commodities and minerals but also over a whole range of industrial goods, engineering goods, chemicals and textiles. The increase in exports stipulated in the plan document is far more than what has been achieved in recent years, but is necessary to finance the growing imports. Only, it is difficult to reach in view of the restrictionist/contractionary policies of various countries. A viable policy of export promotion must be built not on subsidies but on competitive costs, delivery schedules, etc. More than anything we must plan for surpluses to be able to export. I am of the view that in the matter of export promotion we should emulate the example of some of the countries of Asia, though we may not link growth to exports, as some of them have done. It is worthwhile examining whether a larger inflow of private foreign funds, including diversion of petro-dollars, should not be tried. This is necessary to sustain the large volume of investment and exports.

To sum up, the opportunities for growth are immense but they have not been grabbed so far. We have been conditioned to think that the growth rate in our country can only be modest even as objective factors like resource endowment, technical capabilities, etc. are opening up new vistas. The acceptance of the sixth plan by the National Development Council, against which background some of these remarks are set, could be the starting point for a new awareness of our potential for growth. It could, in any case, provide a break with the past to the extent that notions and factors weighing down growth are discarded and we set out with confidence on a new voyage towards development.

Inaugural address at the 73rd Annual General Meeting of the Indian Merchants' Chamber, Bombay, 26 February 1981.

TOWARDS ACCELERATED ECONOMIC PROGRESS

I am thankful to you for inviting me to address you on a subject which I believe is of great concern to each one of us. 'Accelerated economic growth', the subject of my talk, has been the core of many elegant economic models, the major aim of the Planning Commission and the avowed objective of the government's economic policy. I would like to look at the issues in a simple and practical manner to be able to focus on the basic contours rather than the details.

It is disquieting that the Indian economy with three decades of carefully planned efforts should not have 'taken off'. Even smaller countries, which were less equipped to grow fast, have performed much better. What has really held us back?

When Pandit Nehru initiated in planning with his vision of a massive heavy industry to trigger a chain development, he could not have expected the slow moving giant which the Indian economy is today. The early decades of planning were charged with dynamism because the commitment to a 'mixed' economy was not without pragmatism. This is probably why, in spite of the heavy investment strategy of the second and third plans, industrial growth ranged between 7 and 9 per cent. In the subsequent period, growth petered out and the economy was caught in the 3.5 per cent trap, as it is commonly called. Investment was up; but the growth rate did not budge.

It is not usually appreciated that GNP growth, to be high, should depend primarily on industry rather than agriculture. This is so for the reason that agriculture cannot expand, even with the best of efforts, at more than 3 to 4 per cent per year. If GNP has to rise at 6 to 7 per cent per year, a 10 per cent industrial growth becomes a sheer arithmetical necessity. Industry has to be the critical area of development, whether it is for income generation, export promotion, import substitution or employment creation. It is precisely because industry failed to grow fast in the seventies that GNP failed to increase at a high rate.

The sixth plan projects a growth of 5 per cent in GNP and around 8 per cent in industry. Many consider these targets ambitious. And they are justified, past performance being what it is. If we continue with the same system as we had in the past, the chances of improvement are not great. But if the system is attuned to greater efficiency, to competition, the results will be far better even with the same rate of investment. What we lack is not skill, talent or resources but sheer organization.

Indeed, we claim to have the largest technical manpower reserve. And yet our telephones do not work, our electricity undertakings operate at only 45 per cent capacity, our trains do not run on time, our ports are congested, even our street lights and traffic lights do not always function. Our engineers who go abroad in search of jobs have done extremely well for themselves and the organizations for which they work. Why can they not achieve the same results in our own country? In my view, this is entirely due to deficiency of management and lack of discipline.

Take controls, for instance. Initially they were devised as a measure to nurture nascent industries, protect the consumer and achieve plan priorities. Controls proliferate and perpetuate themselves. They create vested interests. Now, a stage has been reached where there is no aspect of the economy that is free from the emaciating grip of controls. Whether it is production, distribution, import, investment or prices, controls have an all-pervasive presence. This delays project clearance, lengthens gestation periods, escalates costs, undermines the viability of enterprises and perpetuates a regime of shortages and consequently inflation. Leading intellectuals in universities and even in government are sharply veering to the view that controls, by and large, have outlived their utility and should be modified or removed to ensure accelerated growth. This is true as much of the private as of the public sector.

The present government is trying hard to salvage the situation. It is lending a pragmatic ear to suggestions to revive and restore the health of the economy. For example, the industrial policy recognizes the need for removing barriers and taking an integrated view of development. Yet, old cliches persist. The import policy has been liberalized, in spite of the difficult foreign exchange situation. The attitude towards private foreign capital has somewhat softened. These are positive indicators of the willingness to approach the problems differently. But, with small changes we cannot expect big results. We live in an interdependent world and to be able to compete in world markets we have to act with the speed that characterizes other countries. What we need is a new outlook and approach, willingness to give up outmoded procedures and rise above vested interests, whether they be in government or business.

It is obvious that if we want a persistent and continuous high rate of growth we must concentrate on two crucial areas. First, we must raise the productivity of our economy by promoting much higher capacity utilization; second, we must concentrate on accelerating capacity creation on a really large scale.

The productivity movement which was started twenty three years ago and then got derailed has to be put back on the tracks. Productivity consciousness has literally vanished. Concerted efforts must therefore be made to ensure that resources—financial, material and human—yield the maximum returns. This is a matter of management at all levels, whether in the public sector or private sector, whether in enterprises or government. It is a question of creating an ethos in which people become aware of their responsibilities without foregoing their rights. Labour and management, in this national endeavour, cannot be looked upon as separate camps opposed to each other, but as partners who have many things to share.

The other factors which restrain higher productivity, viz. infrastructure bottlenecks, have eased somewhat recently though in some parts of the country the situation is far from satisfactory. On current reckoning it would seem that sixth plan targets for power capacity and coal may not be achieved. Management failures on the infrastructure front are far too many and the improvement so far has been mostly peripheral.

Apart from these wider aspects, a productivity movement, to suceeed, calls for a complementary package of action in other problem areas. What are these? Inflation is one, the external trade deficit is another, stagnant investment is the third.

Take inflation. The two-digit price rise which persists is not entirely beyond control. There is in the price rise a relatively small imported as well as a large indigenous component, both of which can be corrected. Oil is the largest of our imports. No doubt, import substitution efforts are being made. Recent oil discoveries in another structure of Bombay High and the Cauvery Basin are very encouraging. However, it is disconcerting that though foreign private participation is acceptable, not a single agreement has been signed. Where does the fault lie?

Apart from oil we undertake totally avoidable imports of commodities such as cement, fertilizer, edible oils, paper, etc. to the tune of Rs 2000 crore a year. The import price is often twice the domestic cost. It is strange that while we do not mind paying a higher price for imports, we deny small increments to Indian manufacturers. This alone casts a shadow on new investment.

As for domestic factors, the prices of critical inputs have been raised sharply while the final products have not been allowed a corresponding increase to cover cost escalation. The consequent squeeze on profitability and production creates shortages which only aggravate the inflationary situation. Long-term price stability will be possible only if the price policy encourages and enables a continuous increase in supply. Price controls, if at all, should apply only to critical inputs without of course being unremunerative. At present, the anti-inflationary package concentrates on demand management via a credit squeeze. Curtailment of non-productive expenditure would have been more effective.

Higher production will not only ease the price situation, it will also generate adequate surplus for exports and facilitate import substitution. This, in turn, will reduce the pressure on the trade balance. More production presumes larger capacity; and larger capacity needs higher investment in a shorter time. Is this possible when entrepreneurs are busy getting one permit or another before they are ready to start construction of the project?

The present policy restrains the natural impetus to grow and is partly responsible for the stalemate existing today. 'Large houses', as they are described, have to seek special clearances lest they acquire too much economic power, though by international standards they are smaller than pigmies. This is precisely why we have to change our outlook. Regulations should not be for checking growth. Rather, government should direct industries to expand and penalize them if they don't, provided of course they are given the requisite facilities.

It must be realized that the faster we create capacities, the sooner we can use them and generate resources for further investment. In a sense, high growth is self-supporting. Hence our first task must be to drastically cut down the gestation period of projects. This is feasible. All that is required is that the different clearances are given at one point—a single window—within a prescribed time limit of, say, three months.

It is again a paradox that while our rate of national savings is high, the corporate sector is unable to acquire adequate finance. High taxes and unremunerative prices have affected internal resource generation. There are hardly any takers for new shares. The financial institutions themselves do not have enough resources and the terms they impose are also impractical. When all the savings institutions have been nationalized, it is the moral duty of the government to ensure that finances in requisite measure are made available to the private sector, at least for industries that have been assigned a specific role. The debt equity norms and promoter's contribution have to be redefined more realistically in the context of the current situation of high project costs.

Lengthy procedures and high taxes delay development. With a low growth there are shortages and with shortages there is black money in the system. Most people would agree that it is nearly impossible to eradicate this social evil. But we can at least minimize it to the extent possible. Abolish the capital gains tax and black money in real estate will disappear. Remove wealth tax and real savings will be stimulated.

Reduce income tax and more income will be disclosed, to swell government revenues. There are contradictions in the system which suppress growth and lead to undesirable distortions. If the system is modified growth can be high and inequalities less. The problems are pressing because aid, on which the country has depended for long, is becoming difficult. In a way, it may be a good sign as it should spur us to greater effort to remain independent of other countries. We have to find solutions to our external trade imbalance from within by exporting more and importing less, both of which presume higher production and investment.

Let me reiterate that no amount of planning or shifts in policies will achieve the results without discipline and hard work and commitment to the larger national good. Hopefully, the effort will begin right now. Time is the most scarce input in development and should not be allowed to slip by. We will either realize our national goal or just be left behind by the wayside.. I have no doubt that the government is aware of the need for change and that business is keen to respond. With this confluence of objectives, we cannot but succeed. Let the eighties be a decade of high growth, a decade in which poverty will be eradicated and the people's aspiration for a decent life fulfilled. All this is within our reach if only we try.

Address at the Gujarat Chamber of Commerce, Ahmedabad, 30 September 1981.

DEVELOPMENT CHALLENGES OF THE EIGHTIES : INDUSTRIAL STRATEGIES AND ADJUSTMENTS

I am happy to be associated with this meeting of the Forum for Financial Writers. I find financial writers to be not only nimble-footed in gathering specialized information but nimble-witted in transmitting the same in a manner that is comprehensible to the common people. Also, such meetings as the present one add another useful dimension to their work. The dust raised by Cancun has hardly settled and we find ourselves going over the questions raised there.

Following the Conference, there has been an overwhelming feeling of pessimism in certain quarters. My personal hopes for cooperative effort between countries, however, have not dimmed. Has not the meeting of eight developed countries and fourteen developing countries addressed itself to problems like eradication of hunger, reduction of trade barriers, strengthening of financial institutions in the context of flows of funds, and so on? Besides, they have pledged to carry on the talks preparatory to another meeting next year. To despair is hardly correct in the face of the fact that the meeting took place and attracted a galaxy of leaders, in itself a big advance over the earlier position.

What are the development challenges of the eighties and what are the adjustments that are called for? The stark reality is the dismal poverty of the people inhabiting the developing countries, particularly the low income oil importing countries, and the sharp differences in the living standards of the people in these countries and those living in the first world. About 2,383 million people, all belonging to the developing countries, excluding the People's Republic of China, had a per capita income of US $ 850 in 1980. Of these, 1,166 million people belonging to the low income oil importing countries had a per capita income of only $ 220. These constituted the poorest of the developing world. The middle income developing countries with a population of 735 million, excluding the oil exporters, had a per capita income of US $ 1,710. This is the level of income the poorest of the countries can hopefully reach by the end of the century, provided they put in hard and patient work and the international community lends a helping hand. As compared to this, the industrialized countries, with a population of 674 million, had a per capita income of US $ 10,660.

Per capita income in industrialized countries is 12.5 times that of per capita income in all developing countries, 42.6 times that of low income developing countries and 50.8 times that of low income oil importing countries in Asia. Not only are per capita incomes in low income countries pitifully small, but there are sharp differences even within this. The number of people living in absolute poverty is around 750 million. If nothing is done to ensure improvement in the living conditions of people living in low income countries over the next two decades, the numbers of the absolute poor will go up by 200 to 250 million.

It has been postulated that the world population, which was 4 billion in 1975, will cross the 6 billion mark by the end of the century. If it does not stabilize at about 8 billion, even rich nations may not be spared, let alone the low income countries, which will sink into a still deeper morass. The high per capita income in the industrialized countries is not because of their small population, but because of the high productivity levels reached by them in their farms and factories through the use of modern equipment.

Development presumes a deliberate policy of industrialization to reduce the pressure of people on land, to draw the unemployed and underemployed into the production stream. When raw materials or metals and minerals are processed within a country, they add to domestic employment and income. Historically, the prices of agricultural commodities and metals have been uncertain and volatile. Terms of trade are notoriously loaded against primary commodity or mineral exporting countries.

The need for fostering industrialization can be seen from the fact that per capita incomes in low income countries rose by less than half in thirty years, from US $ 170 in 1950 to US $ 250 in 1980, in 1980 price terms. On the other hand, the average income per person in the industrial countries increased by a whopping US $ 6,730 in thirty years, from US $ 4,130 to US $ 10,660, in constant price terms. As for the middle income countries, which progressed some distance in industrializing themselves, the increase in average incomes was from US $ 640 to US $ 1,580.

It is in this background, as you all know, that the UNIDO had suggested at Lima that the developing countries' share in total industrial production be raised to 25 per cent from the then existing level of 7 per cent, so that there is a structural transformation in the developing countries.

Is this target feasible? This would be like asking whether the low income countries should set out on the path of industrialization or not.

If the developing countries were to register a 7 per cent industrial growth, which is lower than the second development decade target, and the developed countries were to simultaneously increase at 2 per cent, as has been the case in recent years, the target may still be realized. Now, the important thing is that the differential in industrial growth rates will have to be around 5 percentage points for the developing countries to reach the target. Jan Tinbergen has expressed the view that, according to the 'Law of Fourastite', the share of industrial production in industrialized countries automatically goes down with a shift to the service sector, while it gets pushed up in developing countries. The Law is yet to work to the advantage of the developing countries. When the problem is posed, the Lima target seems forbiddingly high. However, if welfare or the per capita criterion is introduced, the target is ever so modest. Low income countries is only a statistical category, not an unalterable fact. Middle income countries, we should remember, were poor till recently, several of them having made striking advances only in the last two decades.

The theme was taken up by the Brandt Commission which warned that the problem of development brooks no delay. It recommended measures for tackling the problem of hunger, securing fair prices for primary commodities, including facilities for processing, enlarging trade opportunities for countries of the South following the Tokyo Round of negotiations, creating a better investment climate and transfer of technology to the needy countries of the South together with proper regulation of transnationals, reforming the monetary system through creation of SDRs and increasing the volume of development finance as also improving the terms for the same. Willy Brandt's efforts should be seen as a precursor to the exercise at Cancun. It is no exaggeration to say that these suggestions outline a programme for human survival, because poverty anywhere is a serious threat to prosperity everywhere. No country can insulate itself and lead a life of cocooned comfort.

I would like to concentrate on three or four issues, which call for adjustments by the developed and developing countries alike if trade and financial flows are to take place so as to facilitate industrialization of the third world. Let us take trade liberalization first. The fact is that the industrial countries are increasingly turning protectionist. Over the seventies, the exports of industrial countries increased by US $ 471 billion, of developing countries by US $ 226 billion, and of capital surplus oil exporting countries by US $ 140 billion, in 1978 dollar prices. For us, the important thing to note is that of the US $ 226 billion increase for all developing countries, oil exporters account for $ 118 billion and low income oil importers for a miserable $ 3 billion. It is clear that the low income countries experienced both slower growth of absolute exports and deterioration in export prices relative to those of other countries. The average yearly increase of 5.7 per cent in world trade in the seventies was hardly shared by the low income oil importing countries. The need for them to increase their trade is evident in the background of the deteriorating current account deficits following the two major oil price hikes. What they have to do on the energy front is to find alternate fuels, which is a different issue. That apart, they have to find ways and means to increase their exports just as the middle income countries did in the sixties and seventies. With improvement in physical and human capital resources, they have to orient their production to exports, as some of the middle income countries have done. I am not advocating a policy of export-oriented industrialization, which is a misnomer for a country with a market as large as India and with a population as deficient in the requirements of goods. But surely, greater attention could be paid to export promotion even as we undertake import substitution. I would not mind transnationals locating their factories in developing countries to promote exports, which would help to break trade barriers.

Almost 60 per cent of world trade, keeping the communist countries out, is within the developed countries, 25 per cent or thereabouts being within the developing countries, and the balance shared between the developed and developing countries. Will countries that are erecting protectionist walls ever consider suggestions about compensating the victims of protectionist policies through subsidization? In point of fact, it has been established that loss of employment in developed countries is not because of imports from labour-cheap countries, but because of factors connected with structural transformation, falling productivity in some industries and increased automation in some others like textiles.

The developing countries which are seeking to industrialize themselves will have to go in for more labour-intensive industries, leaving the developed countries to specialize in the more capital-intensive industries in which sophisticated technology is called for. This long-term structural adjustment, if pursued with vigour, can not only raise the levels of income in the developing countries but also reduce the prices of many consumer goods in the developed countries. As such, specialization along the lines I have mentioned, would be in the interest of all. However, short-term considerations seem to predominate economic thinking. This is precisely why imports from developing countries of commodities like textiles have come up against the protectionist policies adopted by the developed countries. This is directly contrary to the spirit of GATT, which sought to achieve international balance to the advantage of all the countries concerned. I hope that narrow self-interest will yield place to international social justice and that a better world economic order will emerge after the North-South dialogue gets going.

An equally important consideration is that the volume of trade within the developing countries, which accounts for 25 per cent of the total trade, should increase. The deficits of oil importers constitute the surpluses of exporters. To the extent that they use these sums for additional imports, it is a distinct gain. However, it is the developed countries and middle income countries which have benefited from the surpluses of oil exporting countries. There are several goods presently being imported by the developing countries, including the oil exporting and middle income countries, which could be supplied by the developing countries themselves at their current technological level. These should be identified. My suggestion would be that the Group of 77 or regional bodies should do a thorough study of this as the first step in South-South cooperation before the next round of North-South dialogue.

Remittances, project exports and sub-contracting provide another dimension. India has taken the initiative in starting joint ventures, which presently number over 200 in different countries, and this is another way of getting over the payments problems. Though the Summit at Cancun has not come up with a solution to this vexed question of trade, it is a happy augury that a beginning has been made.

I come to my next point. Financial flows are a significant source of support for balance of payments and domestic investment. Though the international capital market helped to recycle OPEC surpluses, the main beneficiaries have been the middle income countries. As these funds are available at commercial rates which are continuously increasing, the low income developing countries have not been able to take advantage of them. Call it aid weariness—official development assistance given to developing countries has increased by only US $ 19.84 billion between 1970 and 1979, while non-concessional flows including direct investment, bond lending, export credit, etc. increased by US $ 42.06 billion. The USA, which is already one of the smallest donors in terms of proportion of aid to GNP, has indicated further lowering of its aid. The United Kingdom has also indicated cutbacks. Only the Scandinavian countries have maintained financial flow ratios, under ODA, higher than 0.7 per cent of their GNP. However, the Arab countries, Japan, France, Canada and Italy have promised liberal assistance. How far this will make up for the shortfall is to be seen. Multilateral aid has been criticized on the ground that it is not possible always to translate it into viable investment. India gives the lie to this type of criticism. Overall, it will be difficult for infrastructural facilities to come up if there is a cutback in official development assistance. As it is, concessional aid per person in the middle income countries has been US $ 11.80 as against

$ 4.70 only in the low income developing countries. Structural lending facility, oil facility and similar such schemes could help countries to plan readjustment, but these are being withdrawn or reduced. It is increasingly clear that only bilateral aid will be available hereafter. In bilateral aid, there are the dangers of subtle exploitation, if the recipient country cannot stand up to pressures.

The prospects for tapping OPEC surpluses in a bigger way will have to be examined. It can be done by the formation of a regional bank with a soft loan window which not only gathers financial surpluses, but allocates the same in the region. Criteria can be evolved for this keeping the viability of the project in view. There can be bilateral inter-meshing of projects between the low income and oil rich countries. There can also be direct investment by oil rich countries, even if the required technology underlying the project will have to be acquired from industrialized countries. Policies and procedures in low income developing countries, in my opinion, will have to be suitably altered to facilitate this. To avail of short-term credit and invest the same in long-term projects is not correct. Straightforward direct investment would be better.

There can also be more direct foreign investment, export credit and bond-lending by the developed industrial countries to the developing low income countries. Most of the direct foreign investment is presently located within the developed countries. If the middle income countries are not counted, the low income countries would have attracted not more than 7 to 8 per cent of total direct foreign investment. The main vehicle for transmitting or providing direct foreign investment is the transnational.

Here again, the low income countries are at a disadvantage. Such countries as have been importers as well as exporters of technology have not suffered from the restrictive practices that are attributed to transnationals. Even the developed countries have often complained about how they have had to knuckle under the pressure from transnationals. You can well imagine the plight of less developed countries because they run into restrictive practices at many more points even if extraordinary happenings like outright political intervention and sub-resa activity by transnationals are kept out. Several of the middle income countries like Mexico, Chile, Turkey and Argentina have reported insistence by investors/technology suppliers on tied purchases of equipment and other inputs. An equally large number of countries have complained of restrictions on exports. There have also been limitations on local patents. Institutions like the United Nations, the Group of 77, the Andean Pact countries and International Chamber of Commerce have been exerting influence to reduce, if not eliminate, restrictive practices through a code of conduct.

Because of domestic awareness, as also the experience of other countries, some success has been achieved in providing a regulatory framework, in India, Latin America, etc. In fact, there is no inherent conflict between technology suppliers and technology receivers. If the low income countries are to increase their share in industrial production, inducting technology from transnationals is unavoidable in the light of international developments. That does not, however, mean, as I have always insisted, that there should be no regulations on their functioning. We have to learn to cope with them. Mutuality of interest forms the bedrock for successful technology transfer. In passing, I would like to add here that the private sector in countries such as India would play its part in collaborating with transnationals and absorbing technology to their best advantage.

India has done its bit, through joint ventures, to transfer financial resources, technology, etc. to several countries of Asia and Africa. This should be increased further as part of South-South cooperation. These concerns span a number of industries. The technical manpower and industrial facilities available here can be utilized to further programmes of industrialization in other low income countries. The surpluses of OPEC and the facilities available in countries like India can initiate a process of growth in the low income countries.

The point I would like to emphasize is that the growth of the world economy depends on complementarity between the developed and the developing countries. This complementarity is brought about primarily by the fact that the economic characteristics of the developed and the developing countries supplement each other. The developed countries generate capital on a large scale while the developing countries have considerable surplus labour. Besides, the levels of consumption in the developed countries have reached a point of near saturation and to keep the tempo of growth going they will have to depend on demand from the developing countries. It is in this context that the aid programmes of the developed countries can be considered as supporting their own development. In a period in which the world economy is in a recessionary phase, aid can become a more effective, and certainly a more desirable, alternative to military expenditure which has been used as a means of pump-priming.

To sum up, there is a paramount need to industrialize the economies of the developing low income countries and the Lima target was a suggestion in this regard. Industrializing the low income countries requires flows of financial and technological resources on a scale that would help the developed countries themselves in fully utilizing their industrial capacity and also in building up additional capacity. This is important particularly in view of the fact that many developed countries have reached a state of relative saturation of demand and will get the required impetus to activity if there is greater interchange with the developing countries. The movement of resources can be financed through trade surpluses and through official and non-official development assistance. In the ultimate analysis, there is a high degree of interdependence between developed and developing countries. To view the sale of labour intensive industrial goods by developing countries to developed countries as a threat to the latter is short-sighted and patently incorrect. Some adjustments are, no doubt, called for but they are not beyond human ingenuity. Above all, if a large number of countries are desperately poor, as is the case presently, it poses problems of a serious nature to the well-to-do countries as well. And that is what should be avoided.

Let me conclude by saying that I am not affected by the present climate of disillusionment. It is far more difficult to shake off old ideas and concepts that hold us in their vicious grip, be they about trade or aid or technology, than to accept new ideas. After the Second World War, the leaders of developed countries approached the problems of the world with high ideals of social justice. Several institutions were created to achieve the objective of balanced development. The concept of world social justice must not be permitted to be forgotten because of temporary problems in the developed countries. Unless we learn to share prosperity, poverty will catch up with us. What I say is an invitation to determined cooperative endeavour.

Address at the Fourth International Seminar of Economic Journalists, New Delhi, 7 November 1981.

POLICY LIBERALIZATION : WHAT IT MEANS

India has always welcomed foreign private investment and of late, the policy has been more liberal. Foreign investment, apart from supplementing resources, is also a vehicle for transfer of technology. In modernizing industry, making it internationally competitive and promoting a high rate of growth to cater to the domestic market and export needs, foreign investment has a crucial role to play.

Even though India has acquired and developed technological capabilities of its own in a number of industries, there are still many areas in which modern technology needs to be imported. Technical changes taking place all over the world necessitate updating and upgrading existing technologies. For these reasons, modern technology and foreign collaborations are allowed in a number of industries except those in which technology is indigenously developed.

In keeping with the economic objectives, foreign investment is generally preferred up to 40 per cent of the total equity capital. However, a higher percentage of foreign equity is permitted in priority industries if the technology is sophisticated and not available in the country, or if the venture is largely export-oriented. In such cases, foreign equity can go up to 74 per cent. In respect of wholly export-oriented units, even 100 per cent foreign equity is welcomed.

In recent years, the Indian government has provided various benefits to encourage foreign investment. These include, *inter alia*, the following.

— Investment by foreigners once approved by, the government, is treated on par with investment by Indian residents.

— Technology inflow is encouraged in sophisticated and high priority areas and import of such technology has been liberalized.

— Export production is now exempted from MRTP regulations.

— Oil exploration, both on-shore and off-shore, has been opened up to private foreign companies.

— Growth in capacity at the rate of 5 per cent per year is allowed, without prior government approval, to all core and other related industries.

— Royalty payment to foreign companies in excess of the 5 per cent benchmark, up to 8 per cent, is sanctioned in the case of export-oriented ventures and high technology areas. Similarly, the duration of the royalty payment has been extended from 8 years to 10 years in selective cases.

— Oil Exporting Developing (OED) countries can invest up to 40 per cent in the equity capital of Indian companies without any transfer of technology.

— Under a new scheme introduced by the government recently, 100 per cent export-oriented units can be set up anywhere in India. Such units enjoy the same facilities as are available to free trade zones. The period of manufacture under bond is normally 10 years, but can be reduced to 5 years if the specific item of production is subject to rapid changes in technology.

— Foreign investors are assured free remittances of royalties, technical fees and dividends. Similarly, capital investment by them can be repatriated at any time, together with capital appreciation, after payment of tax.

— Free trade zones are allowed to sell up to 25 per cent of their output in the indigenous market.

— Procedures for clearing applications for industrial collaborations have been further streamlined. An application for setting up an industrial venture in any part of the country will now be decided in just 70 days by a single government authority in the case of a non-MRTP and non-FERA company, and in 90 days in the case of an MRTP and FERA company.

The above policy framework is designed primarily to attract large-scale investment and technology inflows into India. I would like to emphasize that this liberalization and streamlining of procedures and administration come at a time when industry is on the threshold of a new era of high development.

India now offers excellent opportunities for foreign investment. Returns on investment in India compare favourably with those in other countries. This has been brought out by a number of studies made by the Industrial Credit and Investment Corporation of India (ICICI), a major financial institution, FICCI and other Chambers of Commerce. The study made by ICICI of the performance of 417 companies assisted by it shows that the return on capital employed for these companies was, on an average, 20 per cent for the year 1979–80. Another study made by the Indo-German Chamber of Commerce in respect of 30 major US companies in India revealed that the gross profits of these companies showed an average annual compound rate of growth of over 15 per cent from 1979 to 1980. Net profits after tax as a proportion of the net worth of these companies was nearly 20 per cent in 1980. A study undertaken by the US Department of Commerce has also come to the conclusion that the US companies have earned better rates of profit in their operations in India than in other countries including Canada and some West European countries.

FICCI, which analysed the balance sheets of 25 large public limited Indo-UK joint ventures with a minimum capital investment of Rs 5 million, brought out the high growth in their performance. The total assets of these enterprises went up at an average rate of 14.2 per cent, net sales by 14 per cent and profits after tax by 20.4 per cent, between 1975 and 1980. Net profit as a percentage of net worth increased from 14.1 per cent to 17.1 per cent, and dividend as a percentage of share capital, from 12.3 per cent to 14.9 per cent.

The results of these studies have shown that the overall level of profits of foreign controlled companies was much higher than in many other countries. India is a good investment risk. Appreciation in the market value of and in the demand for shares are a sure indication of these high returns. No wonder, therefore, that public issues made in India by foreign controlled companies, in many cases at a high premium, have been heavily oversubscribed.

As a result of the favourable investment climate in India, the inflow of investment from most of the developing countries has increased in recent years. The US for example, had invested US $ 351 million by the end of 1979. This has increased to nearly US $ 500 million as of today. Japanese private investment, which was at US $ 39 million at the end of 1980, has gone up to $ 54 million by the end of March 1982.

German private investment in India, which fluctuated between DM 170 million and DM 180 million per year during 1970–79, increased to DM 192 million in 1980. In 1981, West Germany emerged as the main investor in India, accounting for 49.80 per cent of the total Rs 108.70 million new foreign investment approved by the Indian government. The USA, with 20.70 per cent, ranked second, and the UK, with 6.50 per cent, was third. However, India's share in West Germany's total private investment in developing countries remains low, at 1 per cent. This needs to be increased. The bulk of the West German investment has been in machinery, followed by chemicals and pharmaceuticals, automobiles, technical and electronic products. West Germany is also one of the major suppliers of technology to India. Between 1957 and March 1982, out of a total of 6,828 collaborations approved by Government of India, 1,203 were Indo-German collaborations, accounting for nearly 19.76 per cent of the total collaborations.

It is now appreciated in almost all the capital markets abroad that the Indian economy has entered a new phase of growth and that policies have been attuned to enable foreign enterprises to harness the opportunities to the mutual advantage of all the partners in progress. The next two years will witness a tremendous upsurge in investment from different countries. And West Germany has already given the lead.

While investors who have invested in India are aware of the favourable conditions, still greater efforts are required to spread this knowledge in the investing countries. The most crucial aspect of foreign investment in India, which I am sure the foreign investor will appreciate, is that India is a stable democratic society, which may not be true of many other developing countries.

An article published in Financial Express: Indo-West German Co-operation Supplement, New Delhi, 22 September 1982.

STRATEGY FOR HUMAN RESOURCE DEVELOPMENT

This seminar deals with a subject which is crucial to the development of our society. As the background paper has noted, human resources not only contribute to development as a factor of production, they are also its ultimate purpose. Indeed, a society which, maybe due to mistaken political judgement, fails to reaffirm this purpose, can also be led to work for other objectives such as national honour, military might, grandeur of the state, and so on. On the other hand, by affirming that man is the immediate as well as the ultimate purpose of development we seek the reiteration of the sanctity of means no less than ends, of preserving the democratic process and the rule of law, whatever may be the strategy of development. As employers and businessmen we are often too busy to devote time to a subject such as the one chosen for this seminar. Nonetheless, it is of fundamental importance to all of us that human resource development in developing countries is dealt with within the framework of democratic values and the due process of law. I am, therefore, very happy that the AIOE and the EFI have utilized the Golden Jubilee Convention of Indian Employers to deliberate on this theme.

I may take this opportunity to point out that in our country employers have also seen adverse times during the colonial regime. The dignity, equality and respect we enjoy today have been earned and secured alongside the rest of our people and will last only if these values are guaranteed to all our citizens. We prosper with India and each one of us may look forward to scaling great heights so long as the country continues to develop. Moreover, there can be no worthwhile development if a majority of our people continue to be left out of the process. I believe that our industries will thrive more when an increasing proportion of our population is brought into the market nexus, made literate, enabled to acquire diverse skills, secures access to modern sciences and knowledge of the wider world, and sheds poverty, squalor, ignorance and superstition. As employers, we want to see this happen. Our long-term interests are entirely in harmony with the objective of the development of our entire population. In this respect there is no conflict between industry and the people.

It is now well recognized that economic development by itself does not lead to the kind of socio-economic progress we have in mind. If the rate of economic advance is as low as it has been in our country the chances are that it is confined to selected regions only and that its benefits do not percolate to the deeper layers of the society. In fact, if deliberate measures to correct this are not undertaken there is a possibility that the momentum of development may remain restricted to what I might call 'the developing islands' in an underdeveloped society.

A strategy of human resource development must take into account the geographical basis of the Indian economy and the fact that the country's different economic regions are endowed with vastly unequal natural resources. No doubt, a vast majority of our population lives in rural areas. But a mere rural-urban classification of population, as is very popular with some, is not relevant. Some rural areas are so well endowed with water, soil and suitable climatic conditions that they can easily claim a large share of planned investments for rural development. Nature, as well as the economic calculus, work on their side. They have natural advantages; they can also produce quicker returns on investment. If their claims are met, the results achieved will no doubt legitimize the planning decisions and, in turn, lay the base for even larger claims. However, the danger is that in this manner a small developing region may easily cut itself off from the rest of the country and start making demands which bear no rational relationship to the overall planning priorities of the government. Worse consequences may follow. If allowed to proceed uninterrupted, the planning process might get completely enmeshed in the politics of regional tensions. Widening regional disparities are partly unavoidable, for obvious reasons, but they need to be corrected before regional disparities begin to undercut the very purpose of development.

Perhaps it is no longer necessary to say that, in the Indian context, it is impractical to assume that industrialization will result in lowering the density of population in rural areas. No doubt, some rural to urban migration will continue to occur, but there are severe limits to this process. First, most of the migrants come to large urban centres which are already overcrowded and where the quality of life will inevitably deteriorate if this flow is not stopped. Second, the cost of urbanization is enormous and it will push the already high capital-to-output ratio to unacceptably higher levels. This can only lower the rate of growth besides restricting the availability of resources for the development of rural areas where they are badly needed. I may add at this point that while any further expansion of large industrial centres is clearly inconsistent with the strategy of human resource development, that of small and medium sized cities is not. Their development is complementary to the progress of rural areas. Indeed, if a larger number of cities do not develop, simultaneously neither would the surrounding rural areas.

Beyond this perspective, however, lies the domain of strengthening various economic activities for the majority of the population which will necessarily remain in rural India in the long run. How such economic activities, both in the developing as well as in the relatively undeveloped rural areas can be started and sustained is the hardest question to answer.

An even more intractable problem is one of numbers. It is certain that long-term solutions to our problems will prove unrewarding if the population growth is not stabilzzed. All of us will agree that if the population of illiterate, unskilled and unemployable people continues to grow, the question of helping them out of poverty, squalor and helplessness will assume daunting proportions.

Clearly, the population groups which are meant to be served are large, and the administrative agencies lack the manpower or the sense of urgency to produce the desired results. This should not surprise anyone, because long-term social problems cannot be dealt with in an urgent manner. What is required is a management approach characterized by expertise, professionalism, planning, empiricism, direction and determination, to produce steady results on a year-to-year basis. Our administrative system, though noted for many qualities, has not yet endeavoured to cultivate the qualities of management. Nevertheless, it is a job which by its very nature is largely earmarked for the government. Private agencies can only help in a supplementary role. The goal of human resource development should be accepted as a function of a committed public service, which deserves to be organized for the purpose.

In so far as industry is concerned, I do not have much to add to the background paper. The importance of recruitment and training are well understood. The government has endeavoured to expand the stock of trained manpower to meet the requirements of new and growing industries. In this respect, government policy has by and large achieved the planned objectives. Though highly skilled and skilled manpower may be in short supply in specific industries, there are hardly any complaints of general shortages. The pre-employment training imparted in Industrial Training Institutes is aimed mostly at skill formation that is just sufficient for employment; thereafter the responsibility for further training rests with the management concerned. Even if employers are not able to take more interest in improving the quality of pre-employment training, they should provide opportunities for trainers to get acquainted with more modern machines. They may also urge the government to keep in view the importance of updating technology at the training stage and help the institutes in whatever ways possible to improve the quality of the training staff. At present the links betwen the two are weak and deserve to be strengthened.

The main threat as well as principal challenge to people who work in the modern industrial sector is the thrust of technology. It has caused skill obsolescence on a vast scale in the past and will continue to do so in the future. The government now insists that Indian industry should become more competitive abroad and seek to survive and grow on its inherent strengths. There is no reason why industry should not accept the challenge, provided the government on its part and the unions on theirs, play constructive roles. It should be understood that industries and jobs which have been rendered obsolete cannot be indefinitely preserved under government proection. The practical questions which may be asked in this context are how, or in what manner, they can be phased out, how the affected people can be retrained and relocated, and how the new technology should be phased in. This has implications for labour policy as well as fiscal policy, both in the short run and the long run. The cooperation of unions is also essential. They should understand that technological obsolescence is inherent in industrial development and no society which aims to move forward can afford to retard this process. Given this understanding, it should be possible to work out the modalities of actual change-over on the basis of law and bilateral agreements. Indeed this is the ultimate limitation on the security of industrial jobs. Labour should be assured of job security subject to the overriding constraint that an industrial undertaking must always do everything possible to protect its competitiveness and profitability.

The background paper mentions the possibility of job enrichment as an important ingredient of the human resource development strategy. Frankly, I do not know whether, or how far, this can be practically done. Working conditions should, no doubt, receive higher priority. Safety and protection against health hazards are, without doubt, more important. Improved hygiene in workplaces as well as in workers' housing cannot fail to improve the quality of their work and life. Health care in general also deserves priority though I do not foresee how enhanced health benefits can be administered and financed under the present conditions. If resources for all these things must be found within industry, productivity must go up. Only if laboour contributes increasingly to the prosperity of industry, more be provided for its welfare. However, even as new ideas become fashionable in the West, and inevitably travel to India, it is necessary to know what are the more important things to be done and which should receive priority and what can wait.

Friends, I have made bold to offer comments and suggestions on a wide range of issues. Most of them may be better discussed by experts in a professional setting. However, the issues on which I have offered my comments are of general concern to all of us. In the end, I may restate that the theme of this seminar is of great and long-term interest to all employers. We would like to see an appropriate strategy being developed by the government at the core of successive five-year plans and also the means and administrative instruments for putting it into practice.

Address at the Golden Jubilee Convention of Indian Employers, New Delhi, 25 January 1983.

CHALLENGES OF THE NINETIES

I am grateful to the Delhi Management Association and the Association of Advertising Professionals for inviting me to inaugurate the seminar on 'Challenges of the Nineties'. I must say that you have chosen the subject well and the discussions at the seminar will help bring about a clearer understanding of the challenges with which enterprises will be confronted in the present decade. I would not like to restrict myself, however, to the challenges which will manifest in the fields of management and marketing. These are technical areas with which I am not too familiar and which I would not like to comment on. Rather, I would like to look at the environment that will emerge in the nineties, to which present-day marketing and management strategies will have to adapt.

The economy has been undergoing fundamental changes. When economic growth rose from an average of 3.5 per cent to an average of 5.5 per cent per annum, it had a significant impact on different sections of society, as also on industry and business which cater to its needs. The past few years have in many ways been dramatic—industrial production has increased at a rate of about 8 per cent per year; agriculture has also revealed visible signs of dynamism with a growth rate of over 4 per cent annually. As a result, the economy has performed exceedingly well and the living standards and life-styles of the people have improved.

These developments in the economy did not come about on their own. They were carefully engineered through a set of policies. These policies have affected marketing and management strategies at their very core. The reason is that, until the middle of the eighties, industry was protected not only from outside but also from within. Industrial licensing almost allocated markets among different producers and virtually eliminated competition which is usually expected in a growing economy. The MRTP and FERA imposed further limitations, diluting the role of marketing and professional management. But things have been almost transformed in the past few years. A set of measures which have been generally described as 'de-regulation' were adopted. I need not go into the specific measures which I am sure are very familiar to the participants here. Broadly, what they implied was infusion of greater competition which brought about business efficiency and thereby helped reduce costs and prices and improve quality. Competition is a double-edged weapon. It can help the efficient to grab a larger market share; it can throw the inefficient out of business. It is no wonder, then, that the set of measures which were adopted evoked a rather mixed response even from the business community.

The problem of sickness in industry is partly a reflection of the increasing competition that has resulted from de-regulation. It is not that industries do not become sick in other countries, but we have allowed the problem to grow for we have failed to accept the fundamental premise that freedom of entry also implies freedom of exit. There are surely social problems like unemployment which result from winding up enterprises when they fail. Even so, we have to allow the sick to die. In fact, I am convinced that the cost of maintaining a job in a sick mill through revival is more expensive than the cost of providing a job in a new industry. This, I am told, is even statistically proved. The problem of unemployment cannot be resolved by keeping these enterprises alive for a short time. Rather, unemployment has to be tackled through other means like 'unemployment insurance', or even the 'golden handshake'.

I have no doubt that the process of de-regulation will be continued further to impart dynamism to the economy and create efficiency in the system. Control gives rise to by-products like corruption. The freer the economy, the greater the chances of honest business and honest administration.

I believe that a change of government should not necessarily mean a reversal of every policy. What the previous government did was not all wrong; nor was it, right in every respect. The new government has to clearly identify the aberrations caused in certain sections of industry because some de-regulation measures have created an artificial situation. This is true, for instance, of what has often been described as screwdriver technology. But, by and and large, the direction of policy was right and if de-regulation is carried a step further, I am sure, the results would be wholesome.

De-regulation has become pervasive. We see it all over the world. Perestroika and Glasnost in the erstwhile USSR, democratization in East Europe, privatization in a number of Asian and African countries, are all manifestations of de-regulation, one way or the other. It is my firm view that there is no other path to traverse the decade of the nineties. Enterprises will have to have greater freedom. This may mean, for instance, that government has to set norms and parameters, leaving it free for enterprises to operate within these limits. Government clearances should be necessary only in cases which fall outside the prescribed norms and parameters. This would mean infusion of a much greater degree of freedom and competition in the economy.

A competitive environment is good for business, provided business knows the tricks of the trade. Management and marketing are crucial elements of the business strategy. It is precisely because public sector enterprises did not quite catch up with management and marketing expertise that they were not able to compete with the private sector and had to be protected through price and purchase preference. In the new environment of competition that is emerging novel strategies will have to be adopted for survival and progress. Only those enterprises which take the lead will succeed.

Development really involves bringing more and more goods within the reach of more and more people. In the past few years per capita income has gone up at a rate of more than 3.5 per cent per year. In certain segments of society, this growth may have been higher. As a result, over the years, a new class, which has generally been described as the middle class, has emerged, with purchasing power and the desire to buy a variety of goods. It is numerically a large class, nearly half the size of Europe. It is no surprise that we are now one of the world's largest producers of scooters, television sets, radios, watches and other durable consumer goods. This middle class has created a market for consumer goods which just did not exist a few years back. The emergence of a middle class has not only given rise to a market for consumer durables, but also led to greater employment, particularly for educated and skilled workers.

I must add here that contrary to what many people think, the middle class is not located only in urban areas. There are a large number of farmers who have joined the middle class and given a push to the demand for durable consumer goods. The locational diversity of the middle class adds another dimension to marketing strategy.

The spread of television has created a new medium for reaching this middle class in urban and rural areas. It has, in fact, started a wave of consumerism which has been partly responsible for the fall in our savings rate. The visual impact created by television has been the cause of success of a number of companies producing household goods like detergents, toothpaste and textiles. There is sometimes a misconception in the minds of people that advertising is a waste of money and that it merely pushes up the costs of goods. This is far from true. In fact, in my opinion, advertising through various media improves the quality of products and increases production, which leads to greater efficiency and a reduction in costs. In addition, it increases employment, particularly of educated persons, thereby tackling one of our big problems.

The domestic scenario, thus, has changed dramatically and will change further in the nineties. With a GNP growth rate of over 6 per cent per year, in the next ten years our economy will emerge from the low income group to enter the middle income group in the world assembly of nations. This growth will have to be financed not merely by domestic savings but also by foreign investment. We have possibly neither realized the importance and contribution of foreign investment, nor done any marketing on our part to attract it. Even much smaller countries like Thailand and Malaysia receive foreign investment to the tune of over one billion dollars a year. Foreign investment in India so far has amounted to only about one hundred million dollars. It is important to realize that foreigners have enough of a choice before them to invest in any country which offers them security and good returns. If we need foreign investment, which I feel we do, we have to welcome it openly in the areas where it is required. Simplification of procedures will also facilitate the inflow of foreign investment. I hope the government will take a constructive view and adopt a policy which will divert foreign investment to India. I am underlining this because it could be an excellent vehicle for 'state-of-the-art' technology and export of goods produced here.

We are at a stage of development where speedier internationalization will have to take place. To what extent it materializes will depend on the set of policies the government adopts. But I have no doubt that there is no alternative but to enter the international mainstream and to run with the other countries of the world. The scenario of the nineties, as I see it, is one of high growth supported partly by foreign investment and technology and characterized by a high element of exports. The signs are already visible. In the last three years, for instance, exports have been growing at a rate of more than 38 per cent per year. This will have to continue and go up even further. Already, the government has indicated that large business houses have to shoulder this responsibility and export a larger part of their production. As I understand, today large houses export only 5 per cent of their output. In the next five years, possibly, they will have to export more than 10 per cent of their production. This involves a strategic change which will expose Indian industry in an increasing manner to international forces. The very fact that we have to enter the world market means that we have to build our image as producers of quality goods. The foreign market is a different kind of animal than the Indian market. For this reason, in the beginning at least, it may not be possible for us to build an Indian image on our own. We may have to take assistance from marketing and public relations firms which specialize in this field. Let me tell you that even Japan has been seeking assistance from American public relations and marketing companies to sell its products in the US. This has helped them realize higher market prices than they would have got on their own. In the context of the subject of the present seminar, this would also be a challenge to our marketing and management professionals.

Here, I would specially like to refer to the changing international market matrix. Europe has become unified and by 1992 will become a single market. There are also other trade blocs which have come into existence like the Free Trade Area in the US, and the ones which are in a formative stage like the Pacific Rim bloc in the Far East. Strategies for marketing will need to undergo definite change in the context of these new international arrangements.

How do we react to Europe 1992? Surely, exports are likely to face stiffer competition than before. Equally, there would be better opportunities for higher exports due to the expanded market. To meet this challenge we shall not only have to produce the kind of goods that Europe will need but gear ourselves to the strategy of international marketing.

International trade is subject to additional risks arising from exchange rate fluctuations. Management of exchange risk now assumes special importance. In the past three years, for instance, the rupee has depreciated by more than 50 per cent against the dollar, and to a greater extent in terms of the yen and the mark. This exchange problem will continue even if we succeed at the end of the decade to make the rupee a convertible currency.

The broad thrust of my thinking is that the Indian economy is opening up. This is true of the world economy as well. The old strategies of marketing and management cannot hold good in this new environment. Industry and business have to grasp these changes that are taking place if they have to survive in the brutally competitive environment which is emerging. With fast communication, distances have been eliminated and the world economy has become more inter-related and unified. We have to be in tune with this phenomenon. The government on its part has to adopt policies which will make such adaptation easier, so that business and industry can learn faster to imbibe the spirit of change and challenge. We have gone through such metamorphoses before and I have confidence that we shall overcome the challenges of the nineties with success.

Inaugural address at a seminar organized by Delhi Management Association and Association of Advertising Professionals, 12 January 1990.

INDIAN EURO ISSUES

I am indeed happy to be here before you to deliver the inaugural address for the seminar that your institute is conducting on Euro Issues.

Friends, you are all professionals, actively associated with industry and involved in taking significant business decisions. As you know, when I was managing a large conglomerate of industries, approaching the capital market was quite a different proposition. There has since been a sea-change and I am here to share with you some of my thoughts, not so much as an active leader of one of the largest business groups of northern India, but more as a keen observer of India's economic renaissance.

Time was when the Indian economy was quite insulated and operated oblivious of world trends. India's international trade has since gained greater significance, due to the opening up of the Indian market. In order to compete effectively in the current context, the fundamentals of Indian companies have begun to get related to global economic trends.

Government of India has recently initialled the General Agreement on Trade and Tariffs (GATT). We have thus joined the world community to achieve a common economic order. This will throw open tremendous opportunities to developing economies like ours and reciprocally, the Indian market will be open to the other member countries. We are all aware that the prime object of this common world economic order is to benefit us economically, to create a level playing field across international trade to ensure availability of inputs and resources. It is thus expected that this decade will see India emerge economically strong in world trade.

Since 1991, the Indian government has introduced a series of measures designed to open up the economy and to make it competitive for integration with global markets. Opening up of the economy has brought foreign investors into India and has made them take an interest in India. The international investing community has followed these moves with interest—an interest generated by the sheer size of the

Indian economy, the improvement in the economic fundamentals and the presence of a large number of well-managed companies. By opening up the economy and allowing foreigners to share in the prosperity of good companies, we would in effect be creating a more vibrant corporate sector.

Internationally, the capital market is no different from any other market. It exhibits its own dynamics. As far as my memory goes, international issues were quite common in the West even during the last few decades; investors from the US were known to trade in securities not listed in the USA in the form of depository receipts. This was also in vogue in the UK to enable British companies to trade in securities not listed there.

When term loan credits in foreign currencies started dwindling in the last few years on account of India's adverse forex reserves and other uncertainties, different avenues had to be explored. International lenders of debt not being forthcoming, the possibilities of international investors in equity became an obvious avenue in view of the persistent demand for foreign exchange. This marked the beginning of what we today know as the 'Indian Euro Issues'.

Government of India in 1992 decided that companies with a good track record may be permitted to issue equity or convertible debentures abroad. Further, the benefit of a flat 10 per cent tax available to foreign investors on capital gains and dividends on such investments was extended to investors in these issues.

In the Indian context, the high domestic interest rates are resulting in a flight of fund-seekers abroad, as the international market operates at much lower interest rates. The relatively low 'issue expenses' and much fewer 'negotiations' add flavour to the Euro issues and this has caught the fancy of Indian fund managers.

Scores of foreign merchant bankers are camping in India to open India's window to the world of international finance. There are also expert agencies available who take up the overall responsibility for handling these issues, including important functions such as advisory role and research. The onus will then be on the issuing Indian companies to perform and acquit themselves creditably. Serving the investor is always a function of performance and therefore it is the financial skills of the Indian corporate fund managers that would decide which is the best mix.

As we generally know today, the raising of money abroad could be in the form of GDRs (global depository receipts), Euro convertible bonds or Swiss convertible bonds—we know that Air India had entered into cross-border aircraft leasing in 1985; and IDBI had an underwriting facility for an international issue in 1986. There are various other such attractive options today. For instance, we read about irredeemable bonds, bonds with step-up coupons, deep discount bonds and zero convertible bonds, to name a few in the Euro convertible bonds. It is up to the ingenuity of finance professionals to go on improving upon various securities that would meet the needs of investors.

The Euro convertible market is a mature market. It is a major source of capital for corporations the world over. Over 500 issues have been made since 1987 in these markets and approximately US $ 60 billion was raised in the last seven years despite the market having been subdued for nearly five years till 1992. The issue volume in 1993 was about US $17 billion. I understand that the investor's demand is fundamentally strong, particularly for dollar-based instruments.

Asian issuers represent an important sector of the Euro convertible market. About 55 per cent of the issue volume in 1993 was contributed by Asian issuers, with issuers from Hongkong, Japan and Thailand constituting over 85 per cent of the issue. In the very first year, India has taken 5 per cent. Some of these countries have grown economically strong in the last few years and the Euro convertibles issued by companies from these countries have been received very well. India has just entered the phase of rapid economic development and we will see international capital markets being more and more attracted towards Indian companies.

Although the market is driven by considerations of falling dividend yields, high share prices, etc., the international equity market has not lagged behind the world over. In 1993, the total new issue volume galloped and reached a level of US $ 80 billion more than in the preceding five years. This pattern has also been seen in India in the last two years, with international equity issues reaching US $ 350 million in 1993 as against US $ 250 million earlier.

Indian companies that go through such issues gain an international presence and image. The fascination of most corporate issuers of capital who have gone into the Euro market to raise funds is still confined to bourses like Luxemburg or Dublin in Europe which would be almost similar to listing with any ordinary stock exchange in India. One of the benefits that a listed company enjoys is that it gets regularly analysed and promoted by some of the world's leading names in financial analysis.

Gone are the days when an external agency could monitor and regulate the flow of capital in Indian corporate houses. Professional managers have the freedom to choose the sources, provided there are proper and growing returns. Input of capital finance in Indian enterprises should not result in trading in money. Money has to flow into the core sectors of the economy to generate trade at international levels and employment. The terms should match international norms. Indian finance managers have the habit of calculating the cost of equity as something equivalent to dividend cost. All of you are aware that this cannot survive in the context of international finance.

India is rich in finances of labour and knowledge. Indian managers and entrepreneurs have the ability to set up and manage large enterprises. We have all been doing this, although in a controlled atmosphere and with far less options than what the Indian manager has today. There are now practically no controls on the market front, and the growth of trade and the reduction of the trade deficit in the last year are indicators of the capability of the Indian manager.

I wonder if the full potential has been tapped. Capital is still dear in India, that is, dearer than it is abroad, and surely, this difference counts. All of a sudden, now, the Indian manager has access to international markets and finance as well. A beginning was made some time back by a few companies. There are many in the pipeline, both in the public and private sectors. In a nutshell, there is a mad rush. I wonder whether we are alive to the realities, i.e. whether we have enterprises in India which can absorb this volume of money overnight and produce adequate returns for the international investor.

I am not for a moment saying that we should pursue investment decisions dogmatically. These have to be reviewed frequently and adequate safeguards have to be built in to monitor and evaluate the performance of the business. This is important, as in the long run, it is the business that generates wealth for the stakeholder, be he a shareholder, a lender, a supplier, a customer, or an employee. More and more data will have to be made transparent to investors. Today, we may get away by not sharing business-wise financials with investors. That will not be the situation in the future. More and more investors will assess the business manager on the basis of performance rather than on past track record. Investors will dump and exit, the moment they find an industry or a business unattractive.

'After-market performance', which is the equivalent of 'after-sales service' in product marketing, is equally significant. This is closely watched in terms of effective discount and the prices on the Indian stock markets.

So far, the entire marketing effort seems to be reflected in the price of issues. Companies have so far accessed only the European markets, and the Asian markets which are part of the Euro dollar market. The largest market in the world, the US, has remained untapped until now. The reason for this is that securities regulations in the American market are more stringent. Adhering to their accounting requirements and disclosure norms would necessitate a change of the entire price mechanism.

Indian management apprehension was of destabilization arising from Euro issues. Sufficient safeguards, such as the company buying back its own shares at a fair value or at market price, when necessary, are not presently available. There is also a concept of non-voting equity shares which is only now in the offing in the proposed amendments to the Companies Act. This would certainly give a boost to Euro issue equity.

Recently, it has been observed that raising of money abroad through bonds would technically increase the country's debt. But so great is the demand by Indian companies to raise funds from the international capital market coupled with the interest shown by international investors, that it remains to be seen whether the regulations now proposed by the Ministry of Finance will lead investors to look elsewhere for their money.

India has an ambitious plan for the next few years in terms of trade. We can correct our current imbalance in trade only by healthy trade surpluses. Financial inflow can help India achieve this in an accelerated manner. All of us have a role to play in this process. Raising of resources today is the subject for discussion. I am sure this group here will address these issues in more detail. For my part, I would conclude by saying that we should turn this opportunity to the advantage of the Indian economy in a great measure.

Inaugural address at a seminar on Euro Issues organized by the Institute of Company Secretaries of India, New Delhi, 29 April 1994.

DIMENSIONS OF DEVELOPMENT : INDUSTRY

DYNAMICS OF INDUSTRIAL GROWTH IN INDIA

I am grateful to you for the opportunity given to me of meeting you and sharing with you some of my views on and hopes for the dynamics of industrial growth in India.

The immediate problem after independence, fifteen years ago, was one of social improvement and economic progress. Economic policy was gradually transformed to encourage and promote industrial development. To achieve results in the shortest time and to ensure the most productive use of resources, avoiding possible economic wastages, a planned system of development was adopted. The plan is merely a rational scheme which outlines the investment to be undertaken and the production targets to be reached in a period of five years. The plan is not doctrinaire in its nature or rigid in its working. Excepting industries of strategic importance, the field of private enterprise is almost unbounded.

Under the system of planning the economy has gathered force to move at a rapid pace. The responsibility for development is shared by the people and the government according to their capacity and ability to promote economic and social progress. The main limitation on private enterprise is the size of resources at its disposal. The area of development is vast, and if the full potentialities are not realized, it is because of the physical limitations on the ability to undertake investment.

It was possible for us, because of our friendly relations with all countries, to spend only the minimum necessary on defence. But recently there has been trouble on our northern borders with China and we have been brought into an unwilling conflict with a powerful neighbour. It is difficult to predict the intentions of the enemy. But our country is determined to face it at any cost. In this endeavour we are assisted by friendly countries like the USA, the UK, etc., to whom we are deeply grateful.

This conflict has upset our plan calculations. But my own view is that we will be emboldened. It will step up our efforts and bring out hidden resources and energies. It will, in fact, prove to be an impetus to economic progress.

The results achieved in the first two plans give us the confidence that our methods are appropriate, that our policies are working in the right direction, that our efforts have been fruitful, that our ambitions will be fulfilled in the greatest measure, and that we shall be able to reach higher levels of development in a very short time. Nevertheless we are conscious that our domestic resources are not fully adequate to reach the final objectives, and we have to seek assistance from friendly foreign countries. We are being helped and our development has assumed the vitality and the force which will enable it to sustain itself in the future.

In the first two plan periods our industrial production nearly doubled. I would like to indicate the rate of growth achieved in certain important branches of industrial production which are a measure of our inner dynamism and indicate the changing pattern. The production of steel ingots during the first two plans increased from 1.4 million tons to 3.5 million tons. Currently the production is estimated to be more than 4 million tons. The production of machine tools increased from $ 0.7 million to $ 11.5 million and is currently estimated to be $ 17.8 million. The production of cement trebled, that of sulphuric acid increased three-and-a-half times, of nitrogenous fertilizers fifteen times, and of automobiles more than three-and-a-half times. Generation of power is higher by two-and-a-half times. These are quantitative indices which give an indication of the achievements and the propensity for growth in different branches of industry.

Also, the gamut of industrial production has widened. New goods have been manufactured for the first time which will make the economy increasingly more dependent on domestic resources, techniques and efforts. Production of industrial machinery has been undertaken with a view to lessen the pressure on imports. Cotton textile machinery, cement machinery, sugar machinery, paper machinery, cranes, chemical machinery, etc., are now being produced in the country. The installed capacity is not adequate to meet the indigenous demand in full. But the size of production is growing and it will eventually make the economy self-reliant in its requirements of machinery and equipment. This will obviously take time, however.

There are other items like precision instruments, surgical instruments, watches, earth moving equipment, certain chemicals like hydrogen peroxide, carbon black, industrial explosives, etc., drugs like sulpha drugs and penicillin, plastics, automobile tyres, industrial gases, etc. which have been produced indigenously for the first time. This has given strength to the industrial base and made it less dependent on external factors.

But even this production does not wholly depend upon domestic supplies and materials. Many of these have to be imported from other countries for which we have to pay in foreign exchange. The programmes of expansion also create additional demand for foreign exchange for the import of necessary capital goods. These two claims on foreign exchange will together constitute a total demand of about $ 12,000 million in the five years of the third plan. Against this, our exports would be of the order of $ 7,770 million.

The growth of Indian industry is facilitated by various factors. There is enough consumer demand; there is the zeal to progress; there is a class of entrepreneurs willing to take risks and venture into new fields of production; financial institutions like the banks, stock exchanges, Industrial Finance Corporations, etc., have developed and are effective instruments for mobilizing the resources of the country; the public is investment conscious and the shares of many companies have been subscribed manifold (in the first half of 1960, 109 issues were over-subscribed, the amount applied for in respect of these issues aggregating $ 461 million or nearly five times the amount offered); government policy encourages the development of industry; there are large deposits of natural resources; there is a protective market.

Industry is also subject to certain limitations which reflect, in great measure, the stresses of rapid development. There have been shortages in critical industries like power and transport. Development of some of the engineering and chemical industries has been slower than is necessary. These stresses also reveal the areas for further development. There is great potential for development in engineering industries like machine building, intermediate goods which at present have to be imported, fertilizers, electrical equipment, precision instruments, etc. in chemical industries, pharmaceuticals, and paints. Large deposits of oil have been discovered and their exploitation will promote the development of oil refining. There is immense scope for the production of power generators which will relieve the local shortages of power.

In other words, there are problems and there are prospects. Investment in terms of foreign exchange is in these conditions made necessary and profitable, because foreign exchange is a major limitation to industrial development. To implement an investment of $ 2,836 million in large-scale industry, minerals and transport in the private sector in the third plan, the requirement of foreign exchange is estimated at $ 1,050 million; and to implement the total plan of $ 26,000 million, the foreign exchange component is estimated at $ 4,200 million. This amount of foreign exchange cannot be found from the reserves which have now reached a minimum limit. Nor can it be met by increased exports, because the latter depend upon the conditions in other countries, the level of tariffs and the amount of import quotas fixed. Our efforts, therefore, are hindered. We have to seek aid from foreign countries. We have also been helped by private foreign investors. In the last six or seven years the inflow of private foreign investment has rapidly increased, as the vast opportunities for productive investment and the high quality of Indian entrepreneurship got to be known abroad. In 1960, the net private foreign investment was more than $ 110 million. The total outstanding investment in the private sector from all sources at the end of that year was $ 1,450 million.

I have mentioned these facts and these figures because they indicate the extent of financial needs and investment profitability. Vast opportunities exist; it is for you to make use of them, to gain from the conditions that prevail, to share in the development of the largest democracy of the world, which believes in and respects the freedom of individual enterprise. Because of the shortage of capital, investment in India earns a higher return, and a progressively rising return. For, there is no problem of paucity of demand. The process of development itself creates perpetual and increasing demand and natural potentialities for expansion. India has set itself the task of industrial development. We hope to reduce the economic distance between ourselves and more industrialized countries like the USA, the UK and Japan. We cannot expect to reach their standards in a short time. But we are striving to develop the economy and achieve better international balance. Our objectives become difficult if they are based on indigenous effort and resources alone. We need help from our friends abroad. With their assistance our efforts will be more productive and the goals will seem nearer.

Address at the Indian Chamber of Commerce, New York.

THE ROLE OF BUSINESS IN SHAPING GOVERNMENT POLICIES

I am happy that I have been provided with the double opportunity of being a guest of the Administrative Staff College, about which I have heard so much, and of meeting you all to share some thoughts with you. Please do not look upon my remarks as mere conventional gambit, for the gathering here is after my own heart. You represent a cross-section of both the public and private sectors, administrators and organization men. And you want to know each other's minds so as to reduce the areas of misunderstanding and increasingly appreciate each other's problems and stand points in the right perspective. This, I believe, is good.

It was suggested to me that I should give a talk on the role of business in shaping government policies. While so doing I am to cover generally the subject of relations between government and business and the positive role played by commercial and industrial associations in shaping public policy. I shall present before you this morning a few themes that are woven together by one thread, namely, that only by working together—government with business, government departments with other government departments, business with business and any number of combinations of these—can we successfully solve our manifold problems. Both in the larger and particular sense, this cooperative endeavour is a unique characteristic of political democracy and free society. There can be no doubt that though we are a young democracy, we share the points of strength as well as weakness of older democracies. I wish to put forward to you, not in a spirit of artistic chauvinism, but as a serious thought, that in a democracy the best way to serve the common cause is to be ourselves. No group need be apologetic about being different, or having a distinct point of view. On the contrary, all of them must have a chip on the shoulder. Only then can we contribute to the common fund of knowledge, policy, philosophy, and what-not. However, I must make it clear that this attitude, though honestly aggressive in a sense, should not weaken the common cause. It should be the endeavour of all of us to develop to our highest capacity, so that growing beyond the limit of our own narrow fields, we are able to give something to others.

How does business opinion shape government policies? Before I go on to discuss the elements or composition of government policies, let us consider what is meant by business opinion. Is there one such comprehensive opinion? Anyway, what is business? Let us agree that business connotes a wide amalgam of those engaged in industrial activity, trade and commerce, including banking, insurance, shipping and distribution. What about agriculture? Are we to include the views of farmers in this category of business opinion? Perhaps not directly, but to the extent that the well-being of agriculture is important to industry and to the country as a whole, no business opinion worth its name can ignore the problems of agriculture. Therefore, it must follow that business opinion coming from such diverse and sometimes conflicting interests will amount to a reflection of trends of thought or a general climate of business sentiment. On this basis, I am prepared to admit that business opinion is unlikely to be clear-cut on many general issues. Nevertheless, this is not to say that sectional opinions in business cannot often be usefully combined to present a general picture. This is what the Federation of Indian Chambers of Commerce and Industry, of which I have the honour to be the President this year, has sought to do since it was established in 1927.

The Federation, today, has in its membership over 170 industrial and commercial associations, including chambers of commerce. The breakdown, roughly, is 50 chambers of commerce, 80 industrial associations and 40 trade associations. As may be expected, there is hardly any interest or region which is not covered. Besides these we have about 400 companies on our rolls as associate members. There are 10 overseas members, that is the Indian chambers of commerce functioning in Burma, Ceylon, East Africa, Hongkong, Japan, the UK and USA. it would be useful to go back to the years before Independence and to take a quick look at the methods adopted by the Federation and other commercial and industrial bodies to put forward the viewpoint of the Indian business community before the then government. Let us admit without hesitation, even with a sense of gratitude, that by and large, the British provided us with a good administration. Their fault was that they did not stimulate the conditions for economic development. Yet, through the sheer force of entrepreneurial ability, backed by national political sentiment, the pioneers in business ventured along such advanced lines as iron and steel manufacture and shipping in the first two decades of the century. Even before World War II, India was self-sufficient—no doubt at the relatively low levels of consumption that prevailed then—in cloth, sugar, cement, jute, etc. The Federation launched upon its eventful career in one of the most formative periods of our economic and political history. The hesitant steps towards protection under the aegis of the Fiscal Commission, the evolution of the present exchange value of the rupee with the sterling , the establishment of a central monetary institution, to mention only a few, were the initial steps on which the present economic arrangements in our country are based. In all these questions, the Federation took an active interest; its contribution to complex questions such as the ratio controversy is well known. It has been a fervent advocate of the reservation of coastal shipping for national shipping companies and other measures which will enable the country to have her own mercantile marine. Later, the Federation was among the first to draw pointed attention to the implications of the accumulating sterling balances and was persistent in its demand that those legitimate credits accruing to India should be utilized wisely and carefully for strengthening the industrial economy of the country. These are only a few salient instances of the useful work done by the Federation in the past. Politically, the last twenty-five years or more may be called the period of the Indian National Congress. Economically, the period may be considered as that of the Federation which aligned itself with the political movement for Independence and translated national aspirations into economic terms.

Since Independence, the setting has changed in a fundamental way. A national government and planning have provided conditions which were lacking before 1947. Entrepreneurship has therefore a wider field and greater opportunities. At the same time, it has to face many new problems, both tangible and intangible, the latter being the unmanifested manifestation of political democracy. Almost overnight, private enterprise which was for a long time identified with the national movement came to be placed on probation. It is no longer taken for granted. At every turn it is asked to prove its social utility to the economy. It is not merely enough to point out, howsoever reasonable it may be, that in all the free world private enterprise is the greatest or most powerful agent of production, its specific merits being quick appraisal of needs and the willingness to take risks, and that it constitutes the chief source and nursing-ground for managerial skill and technical ability. As I said, private enterprise has to prove its claims again and again.

I should not be misunderstood to mean that the government's attitude, or for that matter the attitude of the public, towards private enterprise is hostile. On the contrary, as I said earlier, private enterprise in India today has far more opportunities. Why then, you may ask, as I have asked myself so often, should there be this continual challenge which private enterprise has to face? I believe the milieu has changed. Our Constitution in its Directive Principles has to a degree stimulated a revolution of rising expectations. It has been assumed, perhaps with justification, that this revolution cannot be met successfully unless the infrastructure is strengthened and basic industries are established—by infrastructure I mean social capital like roads, power and irrigation facilities. Now the argument runs that private enterprise by itself cannot augment social capital or establish basic industries of the magnitude that is necessary. Therefore, as a logical consequence, we have the Industrial Policy Resolution defining the areas of the public and private sectors and what is common to both. There has been, as you know, considerable controversy over the public versus private sector issue. The Federation has consistently taken the view that this issue is as unnecessary as it is fruitless. The controversy between the sectors as to which is superior is like the controversy as to whether man or woman is superior. What John Ruskin said apropos the 'battle of the sexes' is true of the controversy of the sectors: 'We are foolish, and without excuse foolish, in speaking of the superiority of one sex to the other, as if they could be compared in similar things. Each has what the other has not, each completes the other and is completed by the other: they are in nothing alike and the happiness and perfection of both depends on each asking and receiving from the other what the other only can give.'

Our stand has been that since so much has to be done in the economic field, both the sectors can effectively contribute. We are not against the government undertaking whatever activity it chooses to shoulder. Our only contention is: let there be no rigid demarcations. And I must say that in actual practice government policies have been flexible. We have instances of industries like aluminium and fertilizer, supposedly reserved for the public sector, which have been thrown open recently to the private sector as well.

When we talk of government policies, the question arises: who formulates them? True, there is our Constitution with its Directive Principles. Then we have the Avadi Resolution of the Indian National Congress on a 'socialistic pattern of society', subsequently rephrased as the 'socialist pattern' or 'socialist structure'. Do they in themselves constitute the economic philosophy of the government and do they permeate every legislation and procedure that is laid down? To my mind, they represent an attempt to think in broad terms, with a view to synthesizing the conflicts that thinking in compartments necessarily engenders. I should not like to be quoted as saying that government policy is ambivalent, that it is an odd mixture of incompatible wishes. I sincerely feel that the government, like any other group in society, must have clear objectives, if only to move ahead in an orderly way. The fact that in all probability no one does all that he is expected to do, which often is not really calamitous, is no argument that some broad objectives should not be kept in mind for accomplishment.

Earlier I had raised the question, who determines government policy? The electorate? Parliament? The cabinet? The administration? Pressure groups? In a democracy like ours, with a federal constitution, it is indeed difficult to locate the exact seat of power. It will be quite fair to assume that everyone contributes to the formulation of policy and to that extent there is often, as is inevitable, confused thinking and lack of clarity in legislation. My point can be quickly made. About a year ago, the Lok Sabha Secretariat brought out a brochure reviewing the activities and achievements of the second Lok Sabha. The second parliament alone passed more than 300 Acts of which 5 were amendments to the Constitution and more than 100 related to fiscal matters and finance. There were 20 Acts concerning labour. By and large there was not a piece of legislation that was passed which did not directly or indirectly affect industry and trade. To these must be added the pieces of legislation of our state governments. We must also keep in mind the spate of regulations, directions and orders formulated by different ministries of the central government and different departments of the state governments. Each piece of legislation, to put it bluntly, has its fair share of unintelligibility, confusion and uncertainty. Take the Companies Act for instance. There are 658 sections, a number of sub-sections, and then clauses to these sub-sections. In all, it contains nearly 4000 provisions. If the Act can claim that it has achieved an appreciable measure of clarity, the length would be justified. But all those who know law will agree that the enormous length has only added to the confusion. I have referred to orders and directions all of which require form filling by industry and trade. Too many authorities in government ask for different kinds of information, sometimes even the same information and statistics from private industry. Some time back, a joint study was undertaken regarding the reports to be submitted by the textile industry. This study went into the issues of elimination of unnecessary reports or information, reduction of frequency of reports, reduction in the number of copies of reports, simplification or consolidation of existing reports, elimination of unnecessary details, delay or cost of reporting and elimination or modification of specific procedures. The study found that there are nearly 312 forms and returns prescribed by various government agencies for the textile industry. However, you will be interested to know that this joint study, in which industry was represented, came to the conclusion that many of the reports could not be eliminated for they were in the interest of the industry itself. I will not go so far as to say that I entirely agree with this view, or that simplification or modification cannot be effected apropos the returns to be submitted from time to time by different industries including the textile industry.

It will not be an exaggeration to say that especially to a foreigner we seem to be living in a welter of confusion and arguing distractedly with the impersonal forces of legislation and regulations. Yet you and I know that things are not as bad as they seem. Older industries have expanded; new industries have been set up. No doubt, our development could have been quicker, but the fact remains that there has been recognizable economic development.

The Federation is represented in over 65 advisory committees and councils set up by the central government. To mention the more important ones: Advisory Committee on Capital Issues, Board of Trade, Central Advisory Council of Industries and its Committees, Coal Transport Advisory Committee, Customs and Central Excise Advisory Council, Direct Taxes Advisory Committee, Iron and Steel Advisory Council, National Shipping Board, Oil Advisory Committee, Purchase Advisory Council, etc. There are also other consultation channels. It is not unusual for ministers of the central government to have a heart-to-heart talk with a committee of the Federation or of industrial and trade associations. The office-bearers of the Federation meet ministers and senior officials of the central government from time to time in order to discuss in an informal manner major decisions or proposals of the government. Sometimes we write to the Prime Minister and/or call on him for discussions. Invariably the response is sympathetic. The Planning Commission, too, in the process of formulation of the plan, holds a series of discussions with persons representing particular industries in order to decide upon the various targets for the plan period.

In general, therefore, it would seem that considerable opportunities already exist for frequent consultation between government and business. Is the liaison, it may be asked, as good as it ought to be? Do the authorities take follow-up action on the suggestions made or even on the decisions taken? Do representatives of the government come to the meetings of these advisory councils which they themselves have convened with preconceived judgements or conclusions? The answers to these questions will depend upon whether one is an optimist or a pessimist. I, for one, feel that if representatives of the commercial bodies go to these meetings well informed, they can undoubtedly make an impact. It is in this connection especially that I have taken the stand that our commercial and industrial organizations require to be strengthened so that the difficulties that confront business are dispassionately analysed. It is no good if businessmen, like politicians, hold 'opinions and impressions'. These have to be reduced to facts and figures, so that the policies of the government can be dissected in an informed manner and we are able to show what impact the policy in question has on the working of business, and how, if business is affected adversely, it will also affect employment, government revenues, etc.

The Federation has been endeavouring to function along these lines. Some of you might have heard that even before the official second and third plans were brought out, the Federation published its own plans and our targets almost anticipated those of the official plans. Further, the Federation organizes seminars and conferences on subjects of national importance. The main object of such meetings is the provision of a useful forum where different interests can express their points of view and make suggestions embodying a maximum amount of agreement that can be transmitted to the government. In August this year, for instance, we will be holding a seminar on the problems facing industrial undertakings in the public and private sectors. You will agree that there are many problems which the private and public institutions alike encounter—problems such as capital resources, price control, transport and power shortages. The Federation also keeps in close touch with international organizations. It sponsors bodies like the Indian National Committee of the International Chamber of Commerce, the latter being a world organization of businessmen enjoying consultative status category 'A' with the United Nations. For the first time the International Chamber of Commerce will be holding its Congress in New Delhi in February 1965—its twentieth Congress, in fact. The Federation is a member of the Afro-Asian Organization for Economic Cooperation which has its headquarters in Cairo and enjoys consultative status with the Economic and Social Council of the United Nations. The All India Organization of Industrial Employers (AIOIE) which deals with industrial relations and other labour matters is affiliated to the International Organization of Employers, and the Federation's Secretariat functions as the Secretariat of the AIOIE.

There are many major unresolved problems, and I am convinced that joint consultations and discussions are the only way to solve them. Our political institutions, cumbersome though their working might appear to be, ensure the widest possible participation on the part of the citizenry. Frictions there might be. Mistakes might have been committed. But in a democracy, the community has the right to uncover mistakes, and if it is vigilant, uncover them rapidly enough for the mistakes not to develop into grievous errors. Even more important, in a democracy government and business can walk hand-in-hand notwithstanding intermittent quarrels and occasional attempts to shove and pull at each other. Despite the uncertainties of today, I look forward to our economy pushing ahead on the two essential wheels of lively private expansion and vigorous public investment. Speaking for myself, this is no mere pipe-dream.

Address at the Administrative Staff College, Hyderabad, 21 June 1963.

PROBLEMS OF PRIVATE AND PUBLIC INDUSTRIAL UNDERTAKINGS

I am very happy to have this opportunity to welcome you all this morning to the seminar on the Problems of Private and Public Industrial Undertakings. It is for the first time that problems confronting private and public undertakings are being discussed from the same forum. This is unique, and even of historic significance, for it simultaneously emphasizes the identity and complementary nature of the roles of industrial undertakings in both the sectors. Apart from our developmental programmes which call for a dynamic approach, we have to reckon with the innumerable problems of organization of human and material resources to meet the menace on our northern borders. Our economic system must be strengthened as well as made more adaptable to meet the twin challenges of development and defence. This involves numerous adjustments and adoption of new techniques so as to utilize most effectively domestically available and imported resources. Till lately there has been, according to me, an unnecessary and fruitless controversy over the position and share of the two sectors—private and public. The area of development in a growing economy like ours is so vast that the responsibility of development must be shared by the people and the government in terms of capacity and ability. In the circumstances, it will be futile on the part of anyone to adopt a doctrinaire approach. Our common objective must be to divert the energies of the nation to tasks connected with the most productive use of our limited resources. Those who are in the thick of managing industrial enterprises have to realize that no sector is ever as efficient as it believes itself to be, nor is any sector ever so inefficient as each believes the other to be. They can all learn from and contribute to each other. Progressively, economic development has to take the form of cooperative effort between these two sectors. Efficiency must be the norm by which we judge and value the functioning of both public and private industries. In so doing, let us not forget that efficient management will keep social objectives in view and ensure that its activities will give satisfaction not only to all those connected with the undertaking in different capacities, but also to the public at large.

Some of the major problems which we have come to discuss have been highlighted in the background paper which has been circulated. May I refer to the dimension of the problems and the context in which we have to face them? The problems are not independent of each other, nor are they confined to any one specialized area amenable to easy and readymade solutions of yesterday. Some of these problems are ingrained in the organizational structure. Others merely reflect the strains of development. I shall refer first to the latter. It is in a system of democratic planning that we are seeking development. Despite differences in approach and emphasis, it is generally conceded that our plans are fairly well designed. The fixing of targets and the prediction of results have given a sense of purpose to our effort. In statistical terms, the record of progress which our economy has made during the last decade or so is appreciable. Our national income has increased by over 40 per cent; our industrial output has nearly doubled; new types of goods in many sectors including the engineering and chemical sectors are being produced. To this extent, the economy has been made less dependent on imports. There have been other gains—psychological, if you choose to call them that—of great import. Our minds are being drawn out of traditional grooves; we have grown to face new fields of awareness and new challenges of attainment. At the same time, it will be dangerous not to have a clear conception of planning, its points of strength and weakness. The mere fact that we have a plan does not carry with it an inviolable guarantee that we have decided upon the correct kind of technical relationship between different economic activities. It will be equally wrong to pursue the original plan when conditions change. In the best of circumstances, a plan has to be drawn up on many uncertain factors, internal and external. Therefore, the plan framework can at best be a guide to action. In actual fulfilment, there will necessarily be adjustments based on changing situations. Judged by reference to these criteria, it seems to me that our approach to planning, particularly during the last two years, has not been flexible enough. This may explain why there is appreciable idle capacity in an important industry like engineering, and why the production of major items like steel ingots, cement, machinery, machine tools, heavy electrical equipment, fertilizers, etc., has fallen far behind the annual targets. We must, I feel, make an objective evaluation to see whether all our investments have produced optimum results.

I might make a reference to some of the outstanding problems faced by the undertakings in the two sectors—problems peculiar to each and common to both. As far as the public sector undertakings are concerned, there has been discussion both in and outside parliament about the manner and method of their working. Particularly, anxiety has been expressed about the low returns on the capital employed. Investment in industrial and commercial concerns as on 31 March 1963 of the central government alone amounts to over Rs 900 crore. These investments represent the savings of the community of the present generation, and, if misapplied or mismanaged, can constitute a draft on the savings of the generations to come. Therefore, it is only appropriate that everybody should want the public sector undertakings to be run efficiently and well. It is generally acknowledged that their lines of decision-making and communication are lengthy and slow. I would strongly recommend the adoption of procedures which will help public sector undertakings to operate as business does. It is obvious that to reduce costs, to earn a profit and to provide funds for further development, they have to have a good degree of independence. There have been learned treatises on the subject of the control which parliament ought to exercise. It is a complicated issue. The fact, however, remains that the managers of these undertakings and the concerned ministers are hard put to explain to the sovereign parliament in simple language the intricacies of business decisions which have been taken in the past to meet particular situations. This, to a large extent, seriously impairs the efficient working of public sector undertakings. I would, therefore, suggest that detailed and informed discussions about the working of the undertakings take place at the level of the board of directors. Businessmen of proven ability should be associated in greater measure with such boards so that informed internal control may be exercised over organizational and business problems, thus obviating the necessity for intervention either by the ministry concerned or parliament. At the managerial level as well business talent should be attracted. This, to my mind, will improve the working of these enterprises; they will be less prone to public discussion and function in a normal way. In this connection, it will not be out of place to mention that private sector undertakings, which are undoubtedly more democratic in structure and organization, are run by directors who are responsible to the shareholders on matters of general policy and not on day-to-day working. This arrangement has worked well, and I do not see why it should not be adopted by public sector undertakings.

Private sector undertakings, however, have their own problems. The biggest problem faced by them is the various controls of the government, their inadequate coordination and the not so effective organizational approach on the part of the 'authorities'. I have used the word 'authorities' because few will deny and many deplore that no one is certain as to who has to be approached in government. We are only too familiar with the position. At innumerable points, right from the stage of inception to the stage of production and distribution, industry is brought into continuous contact with various government agencies. On the one hand, there is interminable consultation between the centre and the states, between the different departments in the same ministry, the Planning Commission intervening at almost all stages. Then there is the other extreme where each authority functions as a zealous votary of the maxim of Peter, who declared, as you know, that he would cut off his left hand if it were conscious of the intentions of the right. As a result, the sharing of responsibility is uncertain and complex; there is virtually no agency that can be located to bear the blame or to which we can go for relief. I submit that the overall administrative organization which determines in large measure our own success and failure at the industrial level is also our concern. The general aspect of administration is highly important because industry is subject to it.

There are common problems of organization and management that confront public and private sector undertakings. I feel that in the working of enterprises a systematic exchange of personnel between the public and private sectors will be rewarding. It would enable both the sectors to streamline the present techniques and even improve upon them. This exchange will evolve a common system of management and organization based on sound working principles and suited to the social and economic conditions in the country. Management has become highly scientific and sophisticated. Increase in productivity cannot be achieved merely by using more mechanized techniques. These must be accompanied by utilization of manpower resources in an economic manner. This necessitates study of the working methods with a view to encourage the greatest economy of energy. In most of the western countries time and motion studies have been made to employ labour scientifically; we have a long way to go in this direction. By no means can we emphatically aver that all of us have uniformly shown depth of vision and excellence of execution in all departments of industry. It is understandable if there are marginal differences between one industrial undertaking and another in efficiency and productivity. But, are there not wide divergences on account of differences in attitudes, delegation and allocation of responsibility, office methods, mechanized handling, packaging techniques, machine utilization and other factors? There may be some external reasons which set limits on each undertaking reaching higher levels of productivity and efficiency. Even so, in respect of internal factors, the differences should be brought down to the minimum.

In this connection, I appeal to my labour friends for their cooperation. Undoubtedly, labour has an important part to play in any programme of promoting industrial efficiency. Too often, however, labour disputes hinge around work load and remuneration unrelated to output. This is unfortunate, for it weakens the common effort to overcome common enemies as represented by inefficiency and high costs. While saying this, I would like to add that the principles of work study lend themselves to application at senior executive levels as well. The need to make management better is as important, if not more, as getting the workmen to work better. It is only when an analytical study is made that the scope for improvement in the higher ranks of management comes to light. Indeed, persons holding responsible positions should exchange views on the basis of their practical experience. It would be necessary, however, to guard against over-expectation and impatience vis-à-vis these exchanges and to accept that satisfactory results can only come slowly and thereby perhaps more enduringly.

I cannot help feeling that for some time in the past, there has been a creeping 'unsought, unconscious and unsuspected' lassitude in our thinking. There has been a tendency to mistake appearances for actuality with the result that we have tended either to exaggerate or to minimize the seriousness of our problems. I sincerely feel that we must go through a process of dehypnotization, and this can be accomplished by all of us in every walk of life once the obvious fact of the need to improve our techniques of organization and management is fully appreciated. I know that nothing is more difficult than acceptance of the obvious. Nevertheless, I plead that management must become our first concern. While organizational patterns may be diverse, as they must be, they have, at the same time, many common characteristics. As industrialization goes apace, organizations grow in size as well as in number. It is inevitable that there should be greater sub-division of functions, and we have to secure a more intimate connection between them.

There has to be a conscious drive to improve management techniques and promote higher productivity at all levels. Our costs of production at present do not compare very favourably with international prices. We have to rationalize the operative methods in industry and achieve higher efficiency with the same resources. We cannot continue to live, much less prosper, without competing in the world market and becoming more, not less, of an industrial nation. As it is, we are buying one-and-a-half times more than what we are able to sell. We have to export more of our traditional items, but more important, export new products. International commerce is a competitive fighting front and there is no place there for the weak or inefficient. Therefore, we have to put in unstinted effort to get to a position of strength in personnel, organization and functioning so as to bring down costs and improve the quality of our industrial goods.

We are acutely aware of our problems and want to solve them because of our anxiety to progress. Realization of problems is in itself a test of our willingness and our effort to do better. Though we have an uphill task, let us march ahead, not just trudge along, with confidence in our capacity and destination. We have come here with unbiased minds and uncommitted to any individual motives. This will make our work more objective and useful. I am sure, our combined thinking will help towards better understanding of the intricate problems and that we will be able to find solutions of both immediate and long-term value.

Address at a seminar on Industrial Problems in Private and Public Sectors in India, New Delhi, 1963.

INDUSTRIAL POLICY : PERSPECTIVES AND PLANS

I have been asked to speak on the subject of investment for productivity. As you will appreciate, it is not possible to restrain oneself to the confines of this narrow topic, and I hope I may be allowed the opportunity to transgress a little to other related ideas.

Improvement in productivity implies larger output per man employed or higher production per unit of capital invested. I hardly need to elaborate that this improvement in productivity not take place solely because labour works harder or because capital is used more intensively. Normally, labour and capital are combined in a certain proportion depending upon the technology that is used. When productivity improves there is usually a change in technology, or what may be called technological progress. It is this advancement in science that enables larger output from a given amount of labour and capital.

Improvement in productivity is thus inextricably bound with the adoption of new techniques, or improvements in the techniques already used. The development of technology is an industry by itself and involves considerable investment. It will be futile for us to rediscover what has already been invented by other countries. We have, therefore, to keep our doors open and expose our industries to technological developments that are taking place in the rest of the world. If we shut our doors to foreign investment and technological collaboration, we shall be denying ourselves the advancement of knowledge, which makes it possible to get larger output from given resources.

This point is often not appreciated and industrial and economic policies are shaped on the belief that we can be self-sufficient even in technology. This is an extremely short-sighted view and will fail to impart the dynamism that is necessary to keep our industry viable and competitive in international markets. But what is even more harmful is that we may not be able to get the possible larger output from the resources that we invest.

What I have said applies primarily to the benefits that technology can give to an enterprise and the improvement it can bring about in output, costs and prices. But productivity is not a micro concept alone. The productivity even of an enterprise depends, to a large extent, on the way the whole industry and the economy are managed. In modern times economic activity is extremely specialized. It will be futile for any enterprise to produce all the components which go into the final output. It should be possible for most undertakings, particularly engineering enterprises, to farm out orders, decentralize production and create a large group of ancillaries to support the parent unit. It is on these lines that production has been organized in many competitive economies, like Japan and the USA.

This trend of ancillarization has not actively caught up in our country. There are a variety of limitations which have stifled this trend, and, to a large extent, compelled parent units to manufacture components even on an uneconomic scale.

First, our entrepreneurial base is rather small. Entrepreneurship cannot be fostered merely by providing finance or allotting a shed in an industrial area. Entrepreneurship is something in-born which has to be drawn out through proper training. My suggestion is that the management institutes, in collaboration with financial institutions, should locate potential entrepreneurs and organize training courses. These new entrepreneurs will spearhead the progress, first of ancillary industries, which themselves can grow later into medium and large enterprises, through a process of vertical development.

The second major obstacle to the development of ancillaries, and industry generally, is our industrial policy itself. Though well-intentioned, a variety of controls, restrictions and regulations have been imposed, which discourage new enterprises from venturing into industrial activity. The Industries (Development and Regulation) Act, Companies Act, FERA, Income-Tax Act, capital issues control, industrial licensing, import licensing, price controls, banking regulations, terms and conditions imposed by financial institutions, have created such a complex policy framework that it is not easy for an entrepreneur of small means to start a new industry. I think it is time that government gave thought to this problem and simplified industrial policy and procedures in a drastic manner. The old policy was devised for a particular situation, which has undergone very drastic changes. Today, the problem is not one of selecting investment proposals or rationing foreign exchange, but one of stimulating investment, which has dropped to very low levels.

My own suggestion in this respect is that it should be possible for government, considering the improvement in the foreign exchange position and the demarcation of areas between large, medium and small industries, to revise in a very constructive manner both industrial licensing and import control. Just by simplifying these two policy measures industrial progress can be greatly expedited.

The third factor which comes in the way of the development of small and medium industries, as also large industries, is the state of the capital market. In today's world no entrepreneur can rely on his own sources for all the finances that he needs. He has necessarily to depend on the financial institutions and the banking system, apart from the new issues market. But the terms and conditions imposed by these institutions and the rigorous disciplinary measures adopted by commercial banks have squeezed the amount of funds available to industry to finance production and investment.

Another important factor that constrains the development of small and ancillary industries is marketing. I have mentioned on many earlier occasions that small and ancillary industries will not be able to fulfil their role unless an arrangement is devised by which their products are marketed by large-scale enterprises. One problem that comes in the way of this is the MRTP Act. A number of commodities, like television sets, electronic calculators, sewing machines, shoes, etc., can be marketed on a large scale throughout the country and abroad only if the sales part is looked after by large undertakings which have a network of sales and are capable of advertisement through different media.

I have mentioned some of these problems which affect decentralized production and improved productivity so that we may realize that there is a harmony of interest among large, medium and small industries and that they have to grow together, complementing each other's efforts. This progress has to be brought about by using modern technology, which is more productive and can generate larger output with the same capital and labour. Personally I do not see any conflict between modern technology and employment. It is wrongly believed sometimes that modern technology replaces labour and, therefore, is anti-employment. In fact, by generating greater surpluses for investment modern technology can expedite the process of growth and bring about a higher standard of living to a larger number of people in a shorter time.

What I have said so far indicates policy action that is required to promote productivity and production. However, we have to look at this problem not in isolation but in the context of the situation of industry today. My assessment is that we are heading for trouble. In a number of industries production is not picking up at all. We have what the Keynesians describe as the unemployment equilibrium. This is so, for example, of a variety of consumer goods industries. Simultaneously, we have another set of industries which are not growing for lack of investment. In spite of the demand, investment is not rising because new units are not commercially viable. If things are allowed to drift, we may be faced with shortages of very critical commodities, like cement, fertilizer, paper, etc., in a year or two.

The basic reason why investment is not forthcoming is that the cost of projects has gone up severalfold and the return on investment has become negative. The capital cost per ton of paper today is Rs 12,000 compared to only Rs 3,300 in the case of old units. Similarly, in the case of cement the cost of a new project is three times higher, in automobile tyres five times higher, and so on. Naturally, the high cost of capital projects is reflected in the cost of production by way of depreciation and interest charges. For example, in paper, depreciation and interest amount to 36 per cent of the production cost in the case of new units, as compared to 11 per cent in the case of old units. A similar phenomenon may be seen in other industries as well.

I am convinced that unless this disparity in the costing pattern of new units is compensated in some way, new investment will not come up and growth will be stifled. That would be a very sad day for our country and for the new government, and I would, therefore, urge the authorities to look at the problem in a constructive way and adopt quick solutions to put industry back on the growth path.

Personally, I would say that two basic measures are required to give a fillip to new investment activity. First, the excise duty rebate scheme should be adjusted in such a manner that new enterprises are able to avail of its benefits to the extent of increased incidence of depreciation and interest charges. This can be done by fixing the rate of rebate and the period for which it is made available in such a way that the advantage to the enterprise is equal to the increased cost of production. These rates and periods could be specified for different categories of industries depending upon their capital intensity. Second, new enterprises which are capital heavy should be given an interest subsidy or charged a lower rate of interest by the financial institutions. The rate of interest today is excessive. Interest on bank credit is 16.5 per cent, on the IDBI bill rediscounting scheme about 16 per cent, on long-term loans from institutions about 11.5 per cent, and so on. Even the interest on long-term deposits with banks is 10 per cent. In comparison to this, the rate of dividends is low, only about 6 per cent, on the market value of shares. The market value itself has been declining, making it unattractive for the public to invest in equity. I would, therefore, strongly appeal to the authorities to review the whole structure of interest rates and bring down the excessive burden of interest in the cost of production.

I am concerned about these problems because today's investment determines tomorrow's income and employment. If investment today is shy, income tomorrow will be low and unemployment high. It is within the power of government to change these conditions, improve the climate and induce people and enterprises to go in for large investment.

What I wish to emphasize is that improvement in productivity is not a problem of merely making labour work more or using capital more intensively. It involves better organization of industry and more productive methods of operation. Unless the picture is looked at in totality we may merely be tinkering with small and insignificant issues. To tackle the problem effectively government has to liberalize policies and make development more competitive, free, economic, efficient, and based on modern knowledge in the field of engineering, management and organization.

The last few months have been a period of transition for our country. I hope that the new government will also bring new thinking to the old issues. If we continue with policies of over-control, our industries will not get out of the vicious circle of low productivity and high costs. There is great complementarity between the public and private sectors and between small, medium and large industries. This complementarity only emphasizes that different industries have to grow hand-in-hand to ensure a smooth transition from a low growth to a high growth economy. I do hope that government policy will follow this line and promote best results.

Address at a seminar held at Vigyan Bhawan, New Delhi, 20 August 1977.

INDIAN INDUSTRY : LOOKING AHEAD

It is an exciting pastime to speculate about the future. When things are in bad shape, it becomes a soul-searching exercise. We are now passing through a phase of rising prices, growing scarcities and great political uncertainty. Therefore, 'looking ahead' is serious business. It must take the shape of an objective analysis of policies and programmes relating to economic growth.

During the past three decades or more we have tried many experiments in the realm of economic management. Despite all the sophisticated arguments in favour of what we have done or not done, our country still remains one of the world's most deeply impoverished nations. The erudition of India's planners and administrative elite has naturally provoked the criticism that 'the Indians are better talkers than doers, better planners then executives'. I for one do not feel offended at this criticism, for the simple reason that it is well deserved. Once this is generally accepted, I firmly believe that we can see to it that our policy ideas do not deteriorate and grow flabby as has happened hitherto.

This is my first proposition as I attempt to look at the environment for industrial growth in the 1980s. Whether this proposition will turn out to be true is anybody's guess. In my moments of optimism I see the light at the end of the tunnel, and believe that we can write a new and brighter chapter in our economic history.

The background paper poses several questions and also provides relevant statistical material. It begins with the statement that India now ranks among the first ten industrialized countries in the world. This gives the impression that we have acquired a new status. Actually, it is not so, for since 1919 India—undivided India of course—has had a seat on the Governing Body of the International Labour Organization by virtue of being one of the ten countries of chief industrial importance.

While saying this, I am not for a moment ignoring facts, namely, that India today, geographically and economically speaking, is much smaller than it was in 1919. Nevertheless, we now have broader growth of the industrial sector and it is reflected particularly in the development of basic, capital goods and intermediate industries. The share of these industries has also grown relative to consumer goods industries. I am aware that in all growing economies, the share of consumer goods industries comes down. Be that as it may, are the basic needs of vast sections of India's people met at all? What is the per capita consumption of basic necessities like food, clothing, fats, sugar, etc. here? Consumption, which was never high, over the last 10 to 15 years has been coming down. Almost 40 to 50 per cent of the people live below the poverty line. If the needs of the mass of the people for consumption and consumer goods had been met, the ratios of different kinds of industries may have been different. However, I am not concerned so much with relative ratios as with taking such steps as will alleviate poverty.

When there is a multiplicity of goals or objectives to be served, there will undeniably be conflict between different considerations governing policy decisions. There are political considerations that impinge on policy; there are social pressures that have to be taken into account; there is also what may be called the purely economic aspect. That there should be conflict between these different pressures is understandable and is not something unique or special to India. These seemingly irreconcilable conflicts get resolved in terms of 'trade-offs' between the contrary pressure groups. It is often our inability to realize this which makes us raise slogans and shibboleths to the level of great principles. One such area is employment creation. We are all agreed that mass poverty of the type prevalent in India is debasing and will have to be eliminated in good time. Perhaps with some adjustment of policy, what is called the tiny, cottage and small sectors could provide employment to some more people. And yet the small sector is expensive and does not throw up the per-unit/per-employee surplus that bigger or technologically advanced units can and do. Neither will the consumer be able to get goods of quality at relatively cheaper prices, nor, equally important to note, will the employee or worker get adequate remuneration. Production in this sector of industry would not have a significant multiplier effect on economic activity. To the extent, therefore, that aggregate demand will not automatically increase, the tiny sector would be quickly exposed to sickness. There are obvious technological and other constraints also on tiny-scale production. All that I am suggesting is, apart from the cost consideration, which is rooted in the scale factor, and the technological constraint inherent in certain lines of activity, there cannot be a largescale switch-over to small-scale units.

The trouble, here, is this. We assume that industry and the manufacturing sector alone can provide employment to the teeming millions for whom we are anxious to secure a better deal. We forget what the agricultural sector itself could do to provide additional employment by bringing more areas under irrigation, and what additional employment irrigated land could provide as compared to land that is not irrigated. In spite of the present comfortable food position the need to increase the production of foodgrains, oil seeds, and commercial crops is pressing. There are also greater opportunities for employment in the tertiary sector. Construction of houses is one area that could absorb many more persons. The housing shortage is so endemic that if 4.5 million. houses are built yearly for the next ten years, the backlog of requirement and the future demand, which may be estimated at 44.53 million, could be met. As against 4.78 million workers estimated to be employed in building and supporting activities, as many as 30.5 million workers could find employment, both direct and indirect. Even under a less ambitious twenty-year target, there is additional employment potential for 21 to 22 million persons. There will also be necessary side-effects on cement, steel, and suchlike industrial units, the production of which would have to be increased, creating further employment. Similar happy results would flow from undertaking a massive programme of road-building. It will open up and strengthen the countryside on the one hand and provide considerable employment with consequential growth of the transport industry.

The important point to realize is that we as a people have to move on and not get lost in arid controversies as to who should do what. The essential complementarity of the private and public sectors is an accepted fact and there is little argument about it. However, when government's control is total, as it is presently in banking and insurance, or nearly total, as in power generation, steel, etc., has not efficiency suffered? The inability of the public sector to generate surpluses even on a modest scale, despite big price hikes, is by now well known. Let alone efficient running or surplus generation, the giant-sized public sector units have not been able to keep the economy moving. Their smooth working is in the hands of highly unionized, articulate workers who do not hesitate to hold the economy to ransom to drive home their power. Has the government really captured the commanding heights of the economy when the functioning of the different sectors of the economy is subject to severe pressures of the type we have been witnessing? If there were a number of units, some controlled by government, and some owned by individual shareholders, stoppage of work can never be so total or complete. It may indeed be wise to denationalize segments of certain industries to introduce an element of competitiveness, as also to reduce the danger of total stoppage of work. In France, for instance, do not the Renault and Simca factories co-exist and perhaps compete and raise efficiency?

We could take a look at another related field. To take the latest year, 1976–77, for which firm data are available, of total net domestic savings of Rs 14,052 crore, the household sector accounted for Rs 10,550 crore and the public sector for Rs 2,568 crore. Of this the non-departmental enterprises contributed only Rs 628 crore. The private corporate sector's contribution is even lower, at Rs 237 crore. If the various levies and taxes had not cut into their incomes/savings, the household sector would have done even better. Apart from that, a succession of indirect taxes, pushed costs further and set off a cost-push inflation. It has not exactly benefited the exchequer to the extent assumed because the government itself is a big consumer. As an employer government has to dish out extra emoluments by way of increased salaries and dearness allowances, due to the increase in prices brought about by the hike in indirect taxation. Thus a large part of the indirect taxation is in the nature of a zero sum game.

In the meantime it is instructive to notice that the household sector's savings as a percentage of Net National Product (NNP) came down from 12.5 per cent in 1976–77 to 10.4 per cent in 1977–78. There could be a further slideback. While there is no escape from a certain level of direct or indirect taxes, the mounting burden could deliver a final crushing blow. The steep increase in prices in recent months have a clear message to deliver. It is not exactly that the government has been proving to be a good conduit for directing savings into preferred channels, because government consumption has been reaching 'gargantuan' proportions, what with the increase in its non-developmental expenditure. Finally, government's draft on monetary savings has been increasing apace such that precious little is left for investment in the corporate sector, of non-FERA companies, for instance. It is not realized that both direct and indirect taxes get shifted, the former in smaller measure perhaps, and that they add to costs and prices, apart from reducing our competitiveness abroad. It is not that industry shirks its responsibility or bemoans every increase in taxes. Where increases are crippling and take away the incentive to save/invest, there is need to halt and ponder over the drift of things. Merely because the aggregate savings-income ratio has gone up to 16 or 17 per cent, it should not be assumed that the hump has been crossed and there is nothing wrong with the fiscal system. A lowering of personal tax and a reordering of indirect taxes could, on an enlarged turnover, push up savings to still higher levels, as they are indeed required to step up investment.

This takes me to the somewhat related field of increases in prices and investment costs. Even though administered prices have been increased all-round for good reasons, they have not been helpful in attracting new and larger investments. Not only has additional capacity to be created but the worn-out equipment in existing factories has to be replaced. The fiscal inducements presently being offered are not strong enough to attract capital of a sizeable order. Still worse, credit policies are such that it would not be possible to raise capital. How difficult it is for a unit established thirty years back to raise finances may be seen from the fact that a unit set up in 1947–48 would have to now pay for the same machinery a price that is 4.8 times higher. For all commodities, the price increase has been as high as 5.2 times. In the forty years since 1939, the consumer prices of all commodities have increased phenomenally. Let us consider for a moment the resolve of the leaders of the national movement in the thirties to limit the salaries of ministers of the old provinces to Rs 500 a month. Their salary presently would have to be fixed at around Rs 25,000 a month to provide them with reasonable sustenance as was available thirty years back after reckoning for the phenomenal increase in prices and taxation. I mention this to indicate several aspects including the irrelevance of fixing managerial remuneration without reference to the prevailing reality. More than anything else, in my opinion, the restrictive thinking concerning managerial remuneration will result in erosion of morality and character of the intelligentsia.

One way of getting over the problem of cost escalation for industry is to obtain newer and better technology and to go in for larger scale or size of operation. That per unit costs come down with larger size of operation and/or better technology is not always appreciated and is sacrificed for the so-called employment consideration. This is apart from the political overtones that import of technology assumes. While world trade or payments for technology in 1976–77 were US $ 7,000/8,000 million, India's payments were miniscule, at US $ 67.1 million by way of royalties, US $ 60.6 million by way of dividends and US $ 16.4 million by way of profits (of branches). One estimate for world trade puts the payments figure at US $ 11,000 million. This shows that India has been no more than a small importer as compared to countries like South Korea, Brazil and Mexico. I am sure that a bolder technology import policy will help India take longer strides. It is not enough that India with her vast untapped resources and skilled manpower is just the ninth or tenth most industrialized country. Much more could be done if we were to wrest the utmost out of the advances in technology, as technology is the most potent input in triggering growth. With the industrial base and infrastructure we have already created, we have only to set out a bold policy.

To sum up , I suggest that the environment for industrial growth in the coming decade will depend upon the following.

— How soon and how well we will be able to forge a national purpose and actively implement it.

— If providing greater employment is the assumed objective—a rational and moral one—we have to look to an improvement in the agricultural sector and a massive programme of house and road building. In other words, industry, even the tiny-sector industry, cannot be a big provider of jobs.

— The economics of production as between different sectors of industry must be objectively assessed, and it would be far from correct to assume that the tiny sector is the answer to the endemic problem of unemployment.

— Inasmuch as greater employment can be brought about on the lines indicated, it is imperative to ensure that the development of basic, capital goods, intermediate and consumer goods industry is stepped up. Here, the question is not whether the public or the private sector should be the agency, because the controversy has gone on far too long and has been unproductive.

— In the light of past experience and the requirements of the future, industrial harmony can be best brought about by de-nationalizing a segment of the industry presently in the hands of the government. This will not only bring about greater competitiveness and efficiency, but also will not expose the nation to the unreasonable demand of concentrated, unified, unionized labour.

— There is considerable need to reorient both direct and indirect taxation policies, for those which have been pursued until now have been counter-productive.

— Similarly, the short and long-term credit policy followed at present must be reviewed in the context of the needs and requirements of our growing industrial sector.

— A more liberal technology import policy will help us to keep abreast of our competitors in the world markets.

— The remuneration to managerial personnel must be so fixed as to be realistic in more than one sense—with reference to the prevailing and increasing cost of living on the one hand, and on the other, the need to ensure that this intelligentsia is not encouraged to adopt unethical practices.

I have placed before you some of my thoughts—rather, my version of the changes that are required to be made to reduce unemployment and improve living standards. No doubt, changes of one sort or the other are always taking place. What is required to be done is to bring about a conscious and deliberate change to break the back of underdevelopment. It is essential that we keep in mind the mistakes of the past and the experiences of other countries which have a better performance record than our own. This is what history teaches us—to look at the present as a link between the past and the future, and to see how man's future lies in the direction of his increasing liberation from self-imposed shackles. Let us then begin shedding these shackles.

Address at the ICICI symposium on 'Indian Industry', Bombay, 9 November 1979.

ON THE CONCENTRATION OF ECONOMIC POWER AND THE ROLE OF THE MRTP ACT IN DEVELOPMENT

When Shri Kapoor of the National Investment and Finance Weekly invited me to participate in this meeting I readily agreed because I thought I may be able to understand new ideas on the MRTP Act after its operation for the past five years and also to share with you some of my own impressions. I feel there has to be a review both in government and outside as to whether the objectives of the Act have been achieved and how the Act has actually affected industrial growth. The Monopolies Commission has made an endeavour to interpret the provisions of the law in the context of the parameters of our economic situation. This is as it should be. I believe that continuous reassessment and re-examination of major policy instruments is necessary to see that the framework within which development takes place is such as responds to the needs of society.

Let me trace a little of the history of the MRTP Act so that we can see the issues more clearly and gain an insight into how it has influenced the course of industrial development. You may recall that way back in August 1960 the Prime Minister, the late Shri Jawaharlal Nehru, reviewing the outline of the third five-year plan, had commented: 'an advance in our national income and in our per capita income has taken place and, I think, it is desirable that we should enquire more deeply as to where this has gone'. Accordingly, a Committee headed by Professor P.C. Mahalanobis investigated the question of distribution of income and wealth and concentration of means of production. Based on a study made by Dr R.K. Hazari, the Committee came to the conclusion that

> the social significance of the concentration of economic power that exists, has grown over the plan periods in the hands of a comparatively few individuals; and it has become possible because ownership and investment of personal funds is not required for acquiring operation control over large segments of the non-governmental corporate sector

and recommended that

> the sooner the government sets up the necessary machinery for collection, examination and analysis of all relevant data on the subject, the easier it would be for it eventually to formulate the necessary policy that would combine industrialization with social justice and economic development with dispersal of economic power.

To conduct a more specific inquiry into the question of monopoly and concentration of economic power the government appointed a Monopolies Inquiry Commission on 16 April 1964 and its Report was published in December 1965. The main recommendation of the Commission was the setting up of a permanent Commission to look into monopolistic and restrictive trade practices, mergers and amalgamation and expansion of dominant enterprises. The government's decision on the Report of the Monopolies Inquiry Commission was contained in a Resolution dated 5 September 1966 placed before both Houses of Parliament. In accordance with this Resolution the Minister for Industrial Development and Company Affairs introduced in the Rajya Sabha the Monopolies and Restrictive Trade Practices Bill in August 1967 which became law in December 1969.

However, the concept of monopoly, or rather 'larger house' had already gained currency. The Planning Commission in July 1966 appointed Dr R.K. Hazari to conduct a study on licensing with the object of reviewing the operation of the licensing system and to suggest modifications. The terms of reference included the impact of licensing on avoidance of monopoly and prevention of concentration of wealth. A more detailed inquiry was subsequently made by the Dutt Committee, which reached the conclusion that a disproportionate share of licences and financial assistance went to large industrial houses and that influential parties and larger houses were permitted to pre-empt capacity. The concept of 'larger house' was formally introduced into the licensing system on 18 February 1970. However, the concept was loose and is now made to conform to its counterpart in the monopolies regulation. Thus, there is dual control over larger houses and concentration of economic power, by the Ministry as well as the Monopolies Commission.

I am fully aware it is too late to raise the fundamental question whether concentration of economic power, however interpreted, is really against our economic and social values. The Directive Principles of state policy enshrined in our Constitution provide that the operation of the economic system should not result in concentration of wealth and means of production to the common detriment. But in the actual implementation of acts and policies the full spirit of the Directive Principles has not been respected. If I may draw your attention to the second half of the Principle I have just quoted, what is emphasized is that concentration of wealth and means of production should not result in common detriment. This is really the touchstone by which we must judge or evaluate concentration of economic power, or monopoly for that matter.

Here, concentration is not necessarily bad. In fact, the advancement of technology and economies of scale often lead to expanded size of production, and consequently are bound to result in what one may call concentration of economic power. But the question is whether it would be worthwhile from the national point of view to restrain or break up enterprises so that we may dissipate economic power while simultaneously reducing the pace of development. In short, the choice really is between the emotive concept of economic power, in the sense it has usually been used, and economic progress. I, for one, have never been able to understand why concentration of power has been equated with the size of the undertaking or the size of the group. If by concentration is meant the capacity to influence decision-making in the economic field, it is probably more relevant that the Monopolies Act should cover trade unions and public sector undertakings, both of which, at the moment, are outside the purview of the Act.

We often hear debates in Parliament and outside where the Honourable members refer to a big house or a big enterprise as if it was some kind of evil or disease inflicted on society. We have almost become allergic to the very words 'big house'. It is enough to condemn anyone by calling him big and to make anything acceptable by calling it socialistic. We have become slaves of phrases and slogans; we are reluctant to look into the essential meaning behind these phrases and slogans and to evaluate facts in terms of national interest.

Is this confusion accidental or is it deliberate? The concepts of monopoly and concentration of economic power are clubbed together although they mean and imply entirely different things. In my way of thinking the concept of monopoly and restrictive trade pactices is essentially an economic concept. It implies a conscious effort on the part of an industrialist to gain for himself a larger share in the market with the sole motive of increasing prices and raising profits. It may imply collusion when entrepreneurs fix prices jointly so that competitive forces are eliminated and industry gains merely because of its monopolistic practices. No one in this country, including enlightened businessmen, would hesitate in condemning such unfair practices. In fact, I would be the first one to do so.

Let us also be clear that monopoly does not mean a single producer or a limited number of producers. In a country like India, which is in a developmental stage, many new industries are making their appearance for the first time on the industrial scene. By the very nature of circumstances these industries would seem to be monopolistic for the simple reason that production may be undertaken by one or two units. But to call these monopolistic would not only be unfair but unreal. In fact, the profitability of these undertakings, considering the state of demand, may sometimes be lower than the profitability of many other undertakings. One has to recognize the conditions and circumstances which give rise to such apparent monopoly, but which is not in effect a monopolistic undertaking.

All that I am saying is that the concept of monopoly is one of pure economics. Monopoly is condemned for the reason that under conditions of competition it is possible for the economy to function more efficietly, to reduce costs and prices and to make more productive use of resources. Indeed, our own policies including industrial licensing, foreign exchange control, price control, etc., have limited the areas of competition and tended to foster a monopolistic atmosphere. I know that a certain degree of control and regulation is inevitable in a developing economy which has to have a certain order of priorities in economic development, which has to ration its scarce foreign exchange or even internal resources, and so on. However, as we develop, it is undoubtedly necessary that we expose ourselves more and more to competition rather than tighten the degree of control. It is only in a competitive atmosphere that the opportunities for economic monoply are eliminated and the operation of the economic system is it its best.

The other problem is one of concentration of economic power. This concept has no economic basis at all. It is primarily a political concept, though it has found its way into the monopolies legislation. I fail to see how a big house or a large enterprise, simply because it is large, can operate against national or social interest. In fact, I can quote a number of instances in which the scale of operations have contributed to national development in far greater measure than a more decentralized industrial structure. Industrial development has a logic of its own, governed by economic factors. There is something called efficiency which makes all the difference to the success or failure of an enterprise. For broad comparisons we can take profitability as an index of industrial efficiency. But it is only a rough and ready measure which can be used to evaluate the performance of enterprises, at least in the private sector. From a study made by the RBI, I find that gross profits as a percentage of sales increase with the size of undertakings. For example, for companies with paid-up capital between Rs 5 lakh and Rs 10 lakh profitability was 4.4 per cent in 1971–72. With increase in size, the profitability went up to 8.3 per cent for companies in the size group of Rs 50 lakh to Rs 1 crore and 12.8 per cent in the size group over Rs 5 crore.

These figures are quite revealing and indicate clearly that large undertakings enjoy economies of scale and utilize resources more effectively than others. I am fully aware that this way of looking at the problem really distorts the logic of industrial development. There is an optimum size in each sphere of productive activity. What is more, in the present situation in which firms tend to specialize, there is considerable decentralization of production, and the parent industry or undertaking is supported by a number of smaller units manufacturing spares and components. It is also necessary for industries to diversify either horizontally or vertically or both to ensure that the group is composite, that the risks are balanced and that there is integration of processes and full use of entrepreneurial and managerial skills. It would be folly to brush aside the technological developments which make it possible for us to get a higher amount of output for the same amount of invested resources. Greater integration of processes has been taking place all over the world in response to technological progress. We must also recognize that industrial enterprises which produce a single commodity are often exposed to very severe ups and downs. To even out the business cycles, it is, I think, legitimate that enterprises diversify so that the fluctuations in any one product are counteracted by the trends in others. We must also accept that the costs of manufacture of any unit continues to rise and the only way to keep the costs down would be by increasing the size of operation or by setting up new manufacturing facilities in the enterprise. If this is not done the costs and therefore the prices will go up. The only other alternative is for the unit to become sick and close down.

In a competitive economy where the opportunities for entrepreneurs are unlimited, the growth of any business house does not stand in the way of the growth of any other. There is no pre-emption, there is no foreclosure, there is no concentration which can be prejudicial to public interest. But in a complex industrial environment and limitations on entry into industry, foreign exchange, technology,, finance, etc. as we have it, there is almost a forced growth of the more successful entrepreneurs, which results in concentration of economic power.

We have now had considerable experience of the working of the Monopolies and Restrictive Trade Practices Act as well as the Licensing Policy which has been modelled in that spirit. In the three years prior to the introduction of the concept of 'larger house' and the MRTP Act the rate of growth of industrial production was 6 per cent per year. In the three years after these concepts became policy measures the rate of growth of industrial production has fallen to 3 per cent. It would be rash on my part to say that this fall has been due only to the new values which have crept into our policy armament. But I would not, at the same time, brush aside the argument that at least a part of the fall in industrial development has been due to the stringent regulations which have prevented large houses from putting up new industries. Two examples which come to my mind are those of cement and paper. I can say categorically that if adequate licences had been given to the larger houses for the establishment of cement and paper industries, the present shortages of these essential commodities and of many others, which have crippled our economy, would not have occurred at all. My feeling is that this whole conception of large house, monopoly, concentration of economic power, and what not, has come in the way of rapid development which would have otherwise taken place. It is like declaring a batsman out even before he has taken his stance.

I would like to emphasize, lest I be misunderstood, that I am not advocating concentration of economic power. All I am saying is that the growth of the economy, and of the industrial sector in particular, should not be sacrificed in favour of the rather uncertain objective of dispersal of economic power. The evils of concentration can be, and have been, taken care of. The financial institutions already nominate Directors on the Boards of assisted concerns. The Monopolies Commission keeps a watch on the possibility of collusion, on mergers and on monopolistic practices. Industrial licensing is also modelled on lines that would prevent concentration of power. I am only posing a question as to whether this vast armoury of weapons to check concentration has really achieved the dual purpose which was stated in clear terms by the Mahalanobis Committee, viz. ecoomic development and dispersal of economic power.

I hope this group will discuss these basic issues objectively. A reconsideration of our industrial policy, free from bias and prejudice, is absolutely necessary. The only criterion that is relevant, to my view, is public interest and social good.

Address at a seminar organized by the National Investment and Finance Weekly, Vigyan Bhavan, New Delhi.

ROLE OF THE TEXTILE INDUSTRY

We are meeting at the beginning of a new decade, a new year, and with a new government.

The winter rains have hopefully pulled us out of the nightmare of drought which had threatened the very basis of our economic performance in agriculture. The massive Indian general elections, the biggest democratic and human decision-making process in the world, have taken us out of the political uncertainty and instability which had gripped the very entrails of our national and public life in the recent past and threatened to paralyze the essential quality of our nation.

Through a remarkable and dramatic, but clearly democratic, process we have given to ourselves a new government at the Centre. In terms of parliamentary returns this is a massive mandate to give to the new leadership. It is a sacred article and act of faith with which the people have entrusted the future to what we expect to be a stable, strong and sensitive government with dedicated and sincere determination to steer the country onto the path of growth.

The economy has been reeling under mounting two-digit inflation and a breakdown of the infrastructure of power, energy sources, transport system, credit supply for production purposes, governmental inaction and even incompetence. The base line indicators of economic survival still are the realization of the triple national goals of removal of poverty, elimination of unemployment and under-employment and attainment of satisfactory growth.

In all these critical areas we have lagged pitifully behind and the people of India had begun not only to question but even lose faith in the process of planning and other cherished ways of governance of our national life as enshrined in our Constitution. Indiscipline, indecision and inactivity, let us hope, are things of the past. We have to put the seventies behind us as we enter the excitement of the eighties.

Even after three decades of planning and industrialization, the basic needs of over 35 per cent of our masses, who live in squalor below the poverty line, are food, shelter and clothing. I therefore feel particularly strongly when I speak to my colleagues in the textile industry. Economists who have analysed the history of the industrial revolution and the process of industrialization anywhere in the world have highlighted the role of the textile industry. In fact, the process of economic and industrial development in a free economy has been summed up under the banner 'Textile First'. Ours is an industry which from the very beginnings of human creativity and enterprise, has given the basic structure, dimension and direction to the process of growth. It is based on a cash-crop of agriculture and entails the application of human skill for conversion into goods for the common man's use. Qualitatively and quantitatively, therefore, textiles form an essential part of civilization and economic progress.

I would like to talk a little about the economic scene at the macro level before I address myself specifically to our textile industry in its setting in northern India. As we look at the decade of the eighties, and its strategy parameters and variables, we immediately think of inflation which has given a big jolt to the assumptions of policy-makers all over the world and particularly in India. Inflation is the worst form of taxation as it fritters away the fruits of productive effort and hard labour. More than anything else inflation hits the poor the hardest. The battle against inflation, therefore, is likely to take up at least the early part of this new decade. Industrialists and workers, but more so the government, will have to generate a climate in which the economy may start to improve, a climate in which the 'slack' of wasted factory capacity, the increasing reserve army of the unemployed and the increasing immiserization of labour and the common man can be reversed. Unemployment is one of the greatest and most explosive problems which is of concern to economic systems all over the world. We have to find jobs for the existing unemployed as also for those who will be seeking employment in the very near future. It is estimated that almost 85 million jobs would have to be created in India alone in the next decade. The employment potential of industry, and particularly of the textile industry, cannot be overemphasized in this context. But then there is a tragic paradox. Industry is expected to employ more and more and pay more and more to its employees. Yet it is hamstrung by constraints and a negative policy framework.

The State suspects the bonafides of industrialists, the working class disregards the obligations of higher productivity, and the consumer regards the entrepreneur as an exploiting Shylock. These three corners of hostility can hardly be said to generate a healthy economic climate.

The State has been curtailing and/or containing so-called monopoly houses in terms of lofty pronouncements and prospects. How much monopoly or monopolistic and restrictive trade practices can a public institution like the State regulate if it, in its own right, or professed right, creates its own monopolies to do so? I think that the issue is not so much what is public sector or private sector, or what is small-scale sector and what is large-scale, or what is beautiful and what is otherwise, but what is imperative. We have to break the strangulating paradox of self-imposed constraints and have a policy based on economic and managerial judgement flowing out of judicious awareness and extension of social benefits. The non-performance of industry should not be blamed on the private sector alone. If and where necessary, and I might tell you that it is necessary in the majority of cases, public sector undertakings also should be restructured and revamped.

The new government should take positive and new initiatives to destrangulate the economy from the shackles of curbs and constraints. Let us generate a new momentum in which the unprecedented, yet democratic power vested in the government is galvanized with the dynamism of industry and private enterprise. There should be overwhelming priority for boosting investment, and improving operational efficiency in the public sector which is responsible for the infrastructure of power, coal, railways and industrial relations. There is need for bringing about policy formulations which pull down the barriers and road-blocks to cooperation among the various sectors of the economy, agriculture and industry, small-scale and large-scale, labour-intensive and capital-intensive, domestic needs and export imperatives. We will have to redress the distortions and imbalances which we have unfortunately visited upon ourselves through lack of perspective and will.

As for the textile industry, due to two good cotton crops in succession, the industry has had a brief spell of recovery. It would have been much better but for problems like power-cuts, increase in the tax burden, increase in input costs, and the general escalation in production costs.

With regard to cotton production in the northern region, I feel that we should develop new higher medium staple cotton varieties which are early-maturing and high-yielding. Our region has rich potential for substantially increasing cotton output. More intensive research and development in cotton is called for and the governments at the centre and the states should give greater attention to this.

While the government has announced an integrated textile policy, I think the approach should be flexible and pragmatic. Taking the total requirements of fibre, whether cotton or man-made fibre, the government must continue to have a multi-fibre policy. In my opinion, if we are to raise the per capita consumption of cloth, it is possible only through supplementing cotton with man-made fibres. The government has recognized the need for a multi-fibre policy, but the policy continues to change from time to time. It is necessary that there is continuity of policy.

Another aspect of the integrated textile policy on which I would like to comment is the prohibition of expansion of weaving capacity in the organized sector. We must certainly encourage the handloom sector. At the same time, I do not think that the increased requirement of cloth can be met by the handloom sector alone. The sixth five-year plan projects a substantial increase in production by the handloom sector from the current level of 2,300 million metres to 3,700 million metres, i.e. a 60 per cent increase by 1982–83. I do not believe that the handloom sector would be able to achieve this target. I will not be surprised if a shortage of textiles develops in the next few years. Apart from several other reasons, one of the important reasons for textile mills becoming sick has been that units have not been permitted to increase their capacity. Unless a unit expands or diversifies, with the continuous increases in costs it will either become sick or prices will go up. Textiles is one of the most important industries from the point of view of exports and an increase in prices would make it non-competitive in the world markets. I am, therefore, of the view that a small percentage of increase must be permitted in the organized weaving sector every year.

I need not over-emphasize the urgent need for modernization of the industry. It is a pity that at a time when the industry is recovering and the mills are keen to modernize their plants quickly, the implementation of the soft loan scheme by IDBI has been slow and rigid. The difficulty in the availability of indigenous textile machinery and the long waiting period quoted by the manufacturers is a matter of serious concern. The government should seriously consider allowing import of such equipment, while taking measures to accelerate the growth of the domestic textile machinery industry.

Modernization is a continuous process, the fruits of which will not only accrue to the mills, but ultimately to the masses. Hence, I think the soft loan scheme should be placed on a permanent footing to enable the industry to plan for a sustained renovation and rehabilitation programme. I am sure that the new government will address itself to improving the situation, giving it top priority.

In general, managements and labour, whether in the private or public sectors, should agree to a moratorium on strikes and lock-outs for the next two or three years, so that there can be sustained production, industrial growth and economic revival. I would also very strongly suggest that in the organized sector of the industry, any further increase in wages should invariably be linked with improvement in productivity.

I would exhort fellow industrialists in the mill sector to continue their active awareness of the social and national obligations of business and industry. We have been loyal and patriotic co-builders of an India of our dreams. We take pride in being Indians and in things Indian. Let our industry toïl further and strengthen the economy of which we are a part and serve the people still better.

Research and development is a continuing process and no industry can survive in the modern world without innovation. I am glad that NICTMA is growing fast. Its membership covers a large number of units in northern India. I have no doubt that NICTMA will serve not only the textile industry of the north, but make its contribution to research and development for the whole of the Indian textile industry.

When one sees the great strides made in the development of textile machinery in the rest of the world, one does feel disappointed that India has made no significant contribution in this field in spite of the fact that the Indian textile industry is now more than 125 years old. I do hope that NICTMA will work to this end and make important contributions towards research and development in this field.

Inaugural address at the Fourteenth Annual General Meeting of Northern Indian Cotton Textile Mills Association, New Delhi, 15 January 1980.

CORPORATE STRATEGY FOR MODERN INDUSTRIAL ORGANIZATIONS

In the modern industrial world it is necessary for any corporation to plan for the future and it is for this reason that I have chosen to speak on the subject corporate strategy for modern industrial organizations. The concept of 'strategy' had dominated military thought for many centuries before it became part of the language of management. In a famous statement, Clausewitz said, 'Most battles are won—or lost—before they are engaged, by men who take no part in them; by the strategists.' In business the importance of strategy rose in direct proportion to the rise in the risk of losing a business battle—even before it was fought. In other words, the more business came to depend upon long-range planning for success, the more strategy-conscious it became.

The Need for Corporate Strategy

To understand why long-range planning became essential in the first place one can point to the following developments of the last fifty years.

The pace of technological change

Technology now brings about changes not merely in degree but in kind. Electronics, for example, has changed office management, communications, banking, etc., in a manner that has very little in common with the mechanical/electrical technology that it replaced. Manufacturers as well as users who had not anticipated such changes found themselves being sidetracked even though they had earlier been leaders. 'Industries in space' are another example. Very few understand the impact that space-manufactured products might have on earth-based industries. Only those who prepare themselves in advance to tackle such drastic developments can possibly hope to do so. The rapid spread of robots in Japan and America is yet another instance. Howsoever attractive it might seem, there is little doubt that managements cannot successfully put robots to use without developing a comprehensive strategy that accounts for robots in the first place.

In India, technological changes may not be so drastic but they are nonetheless decisive. Even in an old industry like textiles, corporations have been known to go out of business because they have not anticipated changes in technology.

The inter-dependence of world economies
Although the two world wars clearly indicated the inter-dependence of world economies it was the so-called 'oil-crisis' that really drove the message home. It is now clear that major economic changes abroad will be quickly transmitted to us in this country. It is equally clear that unless we have somewhat anticipated them and developed ways of coping with them we shall continually be caught off-balance.

The social responsibility of business
Very few managers will now disagree that to remain viable over a length of time business will have to operate within the framework of social accountability. It will have to systematically and conscientiously discharge its responsibilities towards such goals as employment generation, price stability and environmental balance. For a large corporation, only long-range planning can indicate the industries that most readily fit in with its anticipated social responsibility.

Role of the government
The governments of almost all nations have come to have an important say in their respective economies. Despite certain trends to the contrary, it will be naive to imagine that the role of government will disappear. Not, at any event, in this country. Indian managements, particularly of large corporations, will have to plan so that they remain in step with their government. To the extent that governments plan, or ought to plan, over a long period, corporate managements will have to follow suit.

If I may, I would like to dwell a little longer on this last matter. While it is obvious that a large corporation's strategy in India must fit in with the strategy of our government, it is not equally clear if the government *has* a strategy. We have the five-year plans, no doubt, but very often they lack the ring of true practicality. The figures of growth, savings, taxation, deficit financing, etc., which form their foundations are often meaningless assumptions and everyone perceives them to be as such. The details of the industrial plans are very often contradictory. They fail to indicate to a serious manager what exactly is required of him or the corporation managed by him.

There is another aspect. To be effective, a government's strategy must take account of all that is happening in the world outside. In a regulated economy such as ours this becomes all the more imperative. As I have already said, today the economies of the world are interdependent as never before and a slip-up on the part of the government in assessing the strategic implications of a development abroad is bound to jeopardize the working of all the corporations that it regulates. Therefore, before we expect corporations to have strategies, it is essential that the government itself should have a strategy. The first task is for the government to have a careful look at the world economic scene today and form a judgement about its anticipated and possibly dramatic transformation during the next twenty years. It can then make up its mind about the salient aspects that it perceives and advise the nation and its corporations, both public and private, on what requires to be done. The statement of such strategic objectives must be specific and unambiguous. Above all, it must not be contradictory.

For corporations in regulated economies there lurks another danger. The more the central authority takes over strategic planning, the less equipped the corporations become to do so. Over a period, the strategic planning function atrophies at the corporate level. Considering the task to be futile, managers simply cease performing the strategic planning function and get diverted to other affairs.

In our own conditions it is difficult for enterprises to evolve and adopt strategies of their own. This is so for the reason that the policies of the government in the fields of industrial licensing, import licensing, payment of wages, supply of materials by canalized agencies, determination of prices, generation of resources internally or mobilizing resources from banks, institutions or the capital market, are extremely uncertain or conform to criteria adopted by the government. It is not open, for instance, to the enterprise to choose its degree of diversification of investments, the debt-equity ratio, the current ratio, etc., all of which are stipulated by one government agency or the other. In short, the degree of freedom available to corporations is extremely limited and the adoption of an individual strategy becomes naturally difficult.

As things stand, large corporations concentrate more on acquiring licences than on developing a rational strategy. There is no doubt, however, that as time goes by we shall be exposed to steadily rising pressures from the outside world and our habits will have to change. The corporations, sooner or later, will have to shift attention to their own backyards and depend for their direction more on their planning than on short-cuts and the hapless processes of acquiring such manufacturing licences as they can somehow lay their hands upon.

For the remaining part of my talk, therefore, I shall assume that all is well, that a purposeful government strategy exists and all that remains to be done is for the corporations to develop one for themselves.

Management of Corporate Strategy

The management of corporate strategy, in India or elsewhere, can be broken down into three segments:

1. Strategic appraisal of the environment
2. Strategic appraisal of the corporation
3. Making of the strategic plan and its implementation.

I shall try and elaborate these, especially with reference to the conditions prevailing in large Indian corporations.

Strategic appraisal of the environment

At best a difficult and complicated task, it is made even more complex in India due to lack of data. Our civil servants' age-old tendency to be secretive and mysterious does not help matters. Information, at a premium anywhere in the world, becomes an infinitely precious commodity because of this filtering process.

Our corporations are not very successful in gathering data from the public at large either. Considering the size of investment in industry our efforts at market research, opinion surveys, and futuristic studies are non-existent. Most of us are happy to deal in a sellers' market, even a stagnant one, rather than explore new avenues of industrial opportunity. In short, we lack that all-consuming curiosity which makes managements in other countries continually explore new consumer needs, and develop new products to meet them. All said and done, therefore, our appraisal of the environment right now is limited to the guidelines and licensing priorities declared by the government. Personally, I do not think that this is sufficient.

Strategic appraisal of the corporation

Here the picture is somewhat better, inasmuch as most managements have a fair assessment of their strengths and weaknesses at least in such functions as finance and marketing. Strategic evaluation of human resources, however, still remains weak. At times it does not even exist, the assumption being that as and when we need somebody we can advertise and recruit from among the competitors.

I should emphasize here that the quality of a corporation's strategic development can be only as good as the quality of its human resources. While in the short run one can hope to secure gains through a sellers' market or through fortuitous circumstances, for continued success one must ensure the existence of managers trained in strategic thinking, men who have a dynamic rather than a static view of industry.

Making of the strategic plan and its implementation

It seems to me that strategic planning in large corporations would vary according to the following: (i) the size and complexity of the business, (ii) the extent of professionalization prevailing in the corporation. Size affects long-term planning because the larger a corporation, the more difficult it is for it to change its course. This holds, by and large, whether the corporation is large by investment or by manpower.

Apart from size, the complexity of a corporation is another factor. A single-product processing company, for instance, is much easier to plan for than a multi-product engineering or textile company. Pharmaceutical companies that are not only multi-product ones but also depend on research are yet another category. Export-oriented companies that have to take account of manufacturing costs the world over are a class by themselves as far as the Indian scene is concerned.

A company's strategic planning must obviously fit in with the nature of its business. It need not be any more elaborate than its business suggests. It is important, however, for a management to first clearly understand the business it is in, in the well-known sense that Peter Drucker has laid down at length.

In fact, according to me, defining the objectives is the heart of the matter. Does one want to diversify? Within the same industry or a different one? Does one want to go deeper into the industry one is presently in? Does one want high technology products? Are exports essential to one? These are some of the questions that must necessarily be asked while clarifying the objectives.

Flowing from the corporate objectives, the objectives of virtually every department, every manufacturing facility, will have to be laid down. Only after all this is done will one know if the strategic plan holds together coherently or not. If the strategy of a government cannot afford internal contradictions neither can that of a corporation.

Through all these details and difficulties, however, we need one common touchstone, one accepted yardstick, to guide our efforts. Strategic planning for what? While a number of alternate concepts have lately been mooted, the rate of return on investment, to my mind, still remains the only acceptable guideline for strategic decision-making. However, in any long-term planning a corporation must consider diversification in order to have stability and shock-absorbing capacity in periods of depression in one line of product or the other. It is especially relevant to strategic decisions whose impact is by definition long-term.

This brings me to a fundamental point. The story of corporate strategy does not end with planning. To achieve an acceptable rate of return, as well as other desired results, a sense of strategic management must enter the thinking of every manager. Indeed, a top management that is content with only the planning process is in for a big surprise. It will soon discover that the organization has simply shelved its strategic plan and carried on quite as before.

A question very often asked is, how do we organize strategic planning? Clearly, there cannot be a single best method of doing so. I have heard of many systems being practised abroad. In this country the task was largely performed, to the extent that it was performed at all, by the managing agencies until they were abolished. Since then everyone has devised his own ways of keeping up with the task.

A point to remember here is that strategic thought is not the monopoly of any one level in the organization. Anyone who is in contact with the day-to-day business reality and is perceptive enough would have something to say about the future direction of the organization. It is useful, therefore, to involve all such persons in the planning process. This may be done by way of committees or by some other suitable method. The participation of managers at all levels is also necessary from the point of view of implementing strategy. It is only when they are involved in the planning process that managers can be expected to implement it wholeheartedly.

The most important aspect of any business, apart from the strategy which I have talked about, is the development of human resources. Failures take place in business because sufficient attention is not given to what one may call the development and management of human resources. If human resources are considered to be important, which I do, then an organizational effort must be launched, and sustained, to look after it. This effort may take the following form.

1. A suitable place in the organization hierarchy for those who are entrusted with assisting in the task of optimizing the contribution of human resources. Usually, it is the personnel department that is entrusted with this task.

2. Installing a personnel department, however, is not sufficient. The personnel effort of the corporation cannot work blindly or in a vacuum. The management has to answer several other questions before a genuinely effective effort can be launched. These may be summarized as follows.

(i) What are the appeals, intellectual and emotional, that move people to constructive action?

(ii) How is it that individuals are most rapidly assured a true learning experience—whether it be in job training, organization knowledge, or group collaboration?

(iii) What are the provisions that bring a reasonable sense of security to people in employment?

(iv) What are the fears, tensions and frustrations which are likely to confront men at work, and how can these emotions be minimized and channelled into constructive attitudes and efforts?

(v) What are the kinds of satisfaction of a long-run nature that men normally seek to realize in our kind of society?

(vi) How are the policies of corporations conceived and operated so that necessary, rightful human desires, procedures and aspirations are ministered to through personal relations and the social system of the organization?

When the above questions are thought through the management would have settled its basic philosophical approach to the task. In my experience this is a most complicated area and one where a general consensus is most difficult to obtain.

3. Assuming that a basic philosophy has been arrived at and wholeheartedly adopted by the entire corporation, suitable policies and programmes are required to convert the philosophy into action. At this stage the professional skills of the personnel department must be given full and free play. The tendency to assume that the personnel management function is nothing more than commonsense which everyone is already in possession of is a naive oversimplification. While the management of men is every manager's task, the function of personnel management has its own set of tools and techniques and its own body of growing research. I would go so far as to suggest that a corporation's concern for its human resources is manifested directly in the quality of its personnel and the use that is made of them by the top management.

A problem that crops up in this respect pertains to the conflicting theories that have been advanced in the past fifty years or so by different schools of academics.

(i) There is the Group Behaviour Theory that uses the tools of Theory X and Theory Y and Sensitivity Training.

(ii) There is the Individual Behaviour School that concentrates on individual psychology.

(iii) Organization Development theorists feel that employees should sit down and reason together, that they can manage themselves better than their managers can.

(iv) Labour Relations theorists see the problem in terms of government laws and plant organization politics.

(v) Personnel Management theorists suggest that if recruitment, training, compensation, etc., are well looked after, all problems will be solved.

(vi) Finally, Industrial Engineering people see the problem in terms of work design, machine design, etc.

What happens is that corporations come to be dominated by one or two theoretical approaches at a time, neglecting the others, and thus court failure.

While no comprehensive theory of human relations management yet exists it is certainly possible for managers and personnel managers to devise a proper mix in the light of the circumstances of their particular organization. This calls for sophisticated and well-trained managers, who are not always available. Corporate top managements should nonetheless encourage a reasonable amount of experimentation until something clicks.

In countries like India another aspect that adds to the problem of managing human resources is that the higher level managers very often come from a social stratum that has nothing in common with those whom they manage. With this kind of schism existing in virtually all organizations the problem of communication between levels takes on a dimension that has no parallel in the industrialized countries of the West. Indian managers will have to innovate on their own and devise ways of bridging this 'human gap'.

We have raised cadres of new managers from the business schools. But now we are up against their (and others') value systems. While new managerial techniques have been introduced, the managers' minds remain confused. Where we once looked to America we are now attracted to Japan, but we still have to develop a thoroughly indigenous ethos that can bring out the best in our vast reservoir of human wealth.

I believe that top managements must spend a great deal of time on the development of human resources, which to my mind is the key-factor of any successful organization, be it an industrial organization, a social organization or a government.

Let me conclude by again emphasizing that strategic planning and strategic management is, above all, a way of managerial life. It must permeate all levels of the organization extensively before actual plans can get off the ground. The planning process itself must lead not only to a plan but to a measure of organizational development so that, at the very least, it imparts among the corporation's managers a heightened sense of the tasks facing the corporation.

Address at the Management Conference, New Delhi, 7 January 1982.

WHY INDUSTRY MARKS TIME IN INDIA

While the first phase of industrialization in our country was completed by the middle of the 1960s, the second did not begin at all. The period since has been one of stalemate.This has aggravated the problem of unemployment.Certainly, agricultural production has risen considerably following the introduction of new farm technology.But agriculture cannot be a solution to the employment problem, though such a claim is often made. A high rate of industrial growth is basic to all progress. It promotes more productive employment, the export of value added goods, the supply of materials such as steel and cement for construction, and tractors and fertilizers for agriculture. And by expanding the range of available consumer goods, industry helps raise the standard of living of the people. These objectives were underlined in the last three plans but were not achieved in a substantial measure.

Faster Growth

Economic development assumes faster growth of industry than of agriculture. For instance, in the first plan industrial growth was more than four times the growth of agriculture. In the subsequent plans this ratio came down to about 1.5 or so. If national income has to increase by more than 6 per cent a year, it is necessary that industry grows at over 10 per cent annually.This is the experience of fast growing countries like South Korea, Singapore, Taiwan and Hongkong (the NICs).

Why is industry not able to maintain a high rate of growth? Of course, there are problems like shortage of power and, in some cases, even of raw materials. But, in my view, the biggest hurdle is the lack of adequate demand for industrial goods.In many industries there is adequate capacity to produce more. But the capacity remains idle because industry is not able to sell. This is particularly true of the durable consumer goods industries which, incidentally, have a high employment potential.

The size of our market has remained small on account of fiscal and financial measures which made saving a virtue and consumption almost a crime—precisely what Keynes so vehemently fought against.Two such measures deserve special mention.The first is the increase in the rate of interest. In the early fifties the interest on bank credit was 7 per cent, by the middle of the sixties it had risen to 10 per cent and in the next two decades it rose to 17.5 per cent. On term loans the financial institutions charge 14 per cent.

Interest hurts in two ways. First, the rate of interest raises the cost of production and the cost of distribution.Taking the debt-equity ratio at 2:1 and the ratio of production to investment at 1:1, the interest burden would amount to over 15 per cent of the cost of production. Second, a higher rate of interest can lead to reduced activity in many sectors and consequently lower the demand for industrial goods. A number of activities are particularly interest-sensitive—construction, purchase of durable goods like trucks and refrigerators, for example.

The rates of interest in other countries are much lower. Currently Japan charges only 4.13 per cent on bank credit, the US 7.5 per cent, Hongkong 6.25 per cent.And there is pressure in all these countries to reduce the interest rate further. Our interest rate has got stuck at 17.5 per cent.

The second major factor which keeps demand low is the sharp increase in excise duties.When industrialization began, excise was hardly 5 per cent of the value added in manufacturing. Even by the middle of the sixties it had not exceeded 28 per cent. Since then the government has been raising excise duties, possibly in the belief that indirect taxes are wholly passed on to the consumer. This belief is not correct. Passing of the tax to the consumer means that the price paid by the consumer is higher than it need have been. Consequently, the demand is reduced.

Excise revenue now accounts for over 45 per cent of the total and 40 per cent of the value added in manufacturing. The tax element in prices is extremely high. In synthetics, it is over 200 per cent, in truck tyres over 60 per cent, and so on. This and the high interest rate account for the bulk of the costs; the rate of industrial growth will remain low unless corrective steps are taken.

Some steps in the right direction have been taken. A reduction in direct taxes, for instance, which incidentally has helped raise revenues. Industrial policy has also been liberalized. There is now urgent need to reduce the cost of production in order to enable enterprises to modernize and improve productivity. This can be done only if industries are allowed to eliminate surplus labour. Labour that is thus retrenched can be suitably compensated.

As argued earlier, for industry to grow rapidly it must be supported by adequate demand. Demand can be stimulated as in other countries by reducing the rate of interest, providing consumer credit and reducing prices through modernization of production and reduction in excise duties. What is the scope?

Interest Cuts

First, the interest on bank credit and on loans by financial institutions should be reduced by at least 3 per cent immediately and 5 per cent eventually. This will call for a reduction of interest on bank deposits by 1 per cent. Correspondingly, the interest on debentures and small savings will need to be brought down.

Second, in respect of many durable consumer goods, there can be effective schemes for consumer credit which can be provided by specialized agencies such as banks, leasing companies, or by industry itself. Such a system of consumer credit has not developed in our country partly because there is a belief, especially in the Finance Ministry and the Reserve Bank, that consumer credit will mean diversion of resources from productive to non-productive uses. This psychological barrier needs to be overcome.

Third, excise duties on industrial goods must be brought down. This will not result in a reduction in the government's revenue. On the contrary, in most cases where price elasticity is high the reduction in excise rates would mean an actual increase in revenue, especially if production capacity exists or can be put up quickly. This is true, for instance, in respect of items like refrigerators, air conditioners, fans, two-wheelers, automobiles, synthetic textiles, tyres and other consumer durables. The consequent increase in demand will stimulate industrial activity and employment. This would help the government to mobilize larger revenue from direct taxes.

An article published in Times of India, 22 September 1986.

BUSINESS AND ITS ACCOUNTABILITY

Society is composed of various segments which interact. The nature of this interaction determines the harmony in social relationships. Each segment has its responsibility and accountability to others. Tensions arise when any one segment is either not aware of its responsibilities, or being aware, shows total disregard for the same. Business is no exception. It is very much a part of society. Its responsibility, and therefore accountability, is greater because it has a leadership role; it interacts with almost every other group directly or indirectly. Being a pace-setter, it can neither be unaware of its obligations nor disregard them.

In the course of its operations business interacts with the government, shareholders, employees, traders, other business concerns and consumers. Thus no section of society is isolated from its direct commercial activity. It is accountable to each of them for proper fulfilment of its tasks, though the nature of accountability may differ.

The most important task of business is its actual commercial activity. The manner in which it carries out this activity determines the degree of fulfilment of its major responsibilities. First and foremost is effficient production and distribution. It has to be ensured that production operations are efficiently carried out so that costs are minimized and production maximized, quality is maintained and prices are reasonable. It must plough back resources. And it must modernize and diversify. Research and development should receive priority. Likewise, the distributive mechanism should be able to serve the consumer well both in times of scarcity and abundance.

There may be constraints faced by business in carrying out these activities. For example, raw materials may not be adequately available. This may raise the costs of production. Similarly, inadequate finance may disrupt production, or the price policy may not enable remunerative prices, and so on. We did have such a situation in the seventies. Despite this it should be possible for business to function to the best of its ability.

The responsibility of business to various sections of society are naturally different. With the government, business has primarily a responsibility to cooperate to the full. Various platforms are available for conducting a fruitful dialogue on policies that hinder. Government–business relations are now looking up. There is greater willingness to understand each other. The effectiveness of this dialogue would be greater if business too, on its part, does not create grounds for complaint. It has a responsibility in timely payment of taxes, in maintaining costs, in ensuring that the benefits of cost reduction are passed on to the customer. These will go a long way in improving its credibility not only with the government but also with the public at large. In fact, it is the adverse image of business with consumers that often deters the government from taking remedial action.

Another section of society which is crucial and integral to business is employees. Trade unionism has not developed along the right lines in our country. Unions have been politicized and they do not always strive in favour of workers' interests. But the isolation of the workers from the management provides fertile ground for unionization, which in itself is not bad. At the same time, it is the responsibility of business to provide its workers with reasonable job security, facilities for increasing training on the job as well as outside, and other amenities such as housing, medical facilities, education of children, etc. There are statutory responsibilities in these areas. Business should, however, go beyond the legal requirements. This will enable it to establish relationships with employees which are essentially human. To this end, mechanisms have to be devised which provide for better and greater interaction between employers and employees. A genuine interest in the lives of workers and their families, provision of sports and recreational facilities, and above all, creation of fora for a meeting of minds, are necessary.

This does not, however, mean that employees on their part do not have responsibilities. Employees are accountable for giving their best to their work. They should realize that unless levels of productivity go up their lot cannot improve significantly. Human relations, whatever their nature, are not a one-way street. In other words, a socially responsible business is possible when there is a socially responsible working force. The two go together.

Business owes maximum accountability to the consumers. The recent rise in consumerism is a direct outcome of total neglect of this section of society. In developed countries there is an outcry against unsafe vehicles, impure food, poor quality appliances, and so on. Ralph Nader in the United States has become an institution in himself because of the constant campaign against substandard and unsafe products.

This is an aspect which business can ignore only at its own peril. Before that happens in India, let us take cognizance of this and other facts of life.

There is another point. A number of industries in the initial stages of development naturally seek protection. But this protection cannot be for ever. Over a period of time, industry must apply itself to improving product quality, innovation and generally become competitive not only in the domestic market but also in overseas markets. Competition is the best friend of the consumer. Unfortunately, the protective umbrella is sought to be extended from time to time. This is not playing fair. Apart from hurting the image of business it also results in the growth of a parallel market for smuggled goods. The same consumer who once prided himself on the use of 'swadeshi' has succumbed to cheaper imports. The consumer cannot be blamed. He needs, and indeed deserves, value for money. Unless business guards his interests, emotional approaches which held good during the struggle for independence are not going to help any longer.

These developments have also affected relations within business itself. Due to linkages, every enterprise is dependent on others for supply of raw materials or for the sale of its products. Often raw material shortages result in practices which cannot be regarded as wholesome. Imported raw materials sometimes find their way to unintended places or destinations. Obviously, in such cases, short-term gains triumph over the long-term interests of business. This is certainly bad ethics. Fortunately, such examples are few and far between, and nobody can claim that business, like other sections of society, does not have its share of black sheep. Government intervention is no answer to such problems. Business has to evolve ways and means of self-correction.

The section of society to which business is directly and legally accountable is the shareholders. Its obligations to the shareholders are to ensure that the funds provided are efficiently utilized, as also profits. Adequate provision has to be made for the future growth and health of the enterprise. This is not always done. The shareholders are sometimes not taken fully into confidence. This is partly because the management culture is not fully developed. The hangover of mercantilism still persists in some segments. Modern management practices have to be increasingly adopted. In any case, there should be no gap in communication as far as the shareholders are concerned. They must know the true position of the enterprise. This alone can build their confidence. Once they are satisfied that the management is giving them a good deal, the investment climate itself will improve. It should also be remembered that the small shareholders, often comprising retired salaried individuals or widows, are particularly vulnerable. To play with their hard-earned savings is, to say the least, highly irresponsible.

I have so far dealt with what may be called the direct responsibilities of business. There are indirect ones as well. These, in our circumstances, relate to population control, which is an absolute imperative because the gains of development are eaten into by the growing swell of population. Not only do employees have to be catered to, but also those living around factory premises and business establishments. Creation of work through rural development is equally necessary. More earners means more incomes and hence an expanding market. Even enlightened self-interest demands that business should pay more and more attention to this area. Pollution control too cannot be neglected.

It would be incorrect to say that business alone is accountable. Other segments of society too have their share of responsibilities towards business and society. Government must ensure that it creates an environment that enables business to perform to the best of its ability. This means that infrastructure should perform well, controls are minimum and justifiable solely on the basis of social accounting, taxes are reasonable, and above all, that there is trust in those who manage business. If business expands, the nation benefits. Employees have to give their best to their enterprises, ensure that their demands are reasonable, and that productive activity is not disabled for extraneous reasons. Consumers too have their responsibilities. In times of shortages, they should not resort to hoarding or fall prey to spurious products.

Within itself business has to conform to certain ethics without which operations cannot be smooth. In fact, it is not enough for any single segment of society to be aware of its responsibilities and accountability to others. What is needed is a responsible society in which all segments and sections cooperate and move forward together in the overall interest rather than protecting their own interests to the detriment of others.

An article published in the IMC Platinum Jubilee Souvenir, 4 October 1982.

INDIAN INDUSTRY : PERSPECTIVES FOR THE FUTURE

Over the last three decades the industrial scene has been substantially transformed. The process of planned development has accelerated the growth of the industrial sector, particularly in the first decade and a half.

The planning process made development more systematic. Basic industries were specifically nurtured through substantial imports of technology and capital. The public sector took root. A structure of industries, heavy as well as light, was firmly established. During the first fifteen years, the rate of industrial growth generally averaged 8 per cent. While agricultural output was somewhat slow, overall growth exceeded 4 per cent per year. A sharp rise in the rate of investment was kept up by external borrowings, which acounted for about 25 per cent of the investment. Employment in the organized sector expanded by about 11 million during the second and third plans.

In contrast, in the subsequent period growth has been slow. The growth rate has fallen. Fluctuations have become sharper. However, a happy feature has been a major improvement in agriculture, particularly food production. Indeed, foodgrains production has become fairly stable. From a net importer of foodgrains India has emerged as an exporter and we are able to maintain a buffer-stock of about 15 million tons of foodgrains to meet periodic shortfalls. Unfortunately, the rise in agricultural incomes has not provided an impetus to industrial growth. This is partly because of the hardening of agricultural prices, the benefit of which has accrued to a small proportion of rich farmers. As a result, a broadening of the market, which would have provided a strong stimulus to industry, has not taken place.

The problem was compounded by certain government policies relating to industrial licensing which became restrictive, MRTP regulations, the curb on foreign investment under FERA, and the proliferation in procedures which impeded initiative. A resource constraint, both internal and external, has been another handicap. High taxes, inadequate depreciation and the inability of units to generate internal surpluses for reinvestment have also impeded growth. The nationalization of banks has been followed by a shift in credit policies in favour of the rural sector which has inevitably reduced the flow of funds to industry. Term lending institutions have initiated a series of policies relating to promoters' quota, debt-equity ratio, the convertibility clause, and so on, which render difficult the raising of long-term funds. Thus, industry has been affected both ways—its profitability has reduced and its ability to raise resources has been constricted.

Additionally, Indian industry's exposure to the international environment has been limited. Protection from imports, a restrictive foreign investment policy and the accent on the domestic market blunted the competitive edge. Consequently, absorption of modern technology was far from commensurate to technological developments. This weakened the qualitative base of Indian industry.

These factors have led to uneconomic industrial operations, cost escalation and obsolescence of equipment. Curbs on expansion have affected the viability of units. Industrial sickness is widespread. International factors such as the oil crisis and growing protectionism in developed countries have further compounded the situatiuon by placing severe strains on the balance of payments.

We have today a gross national income of Rs 1,12,000 crore but a huge population keeps our per capita income at barely $ 190, much lower than most countries of the world. The rate of savings, though not low, has been at a standstill for the last five years, at 22 per cent. Happily, the rate of investment has improved.

In the years ahead Indian industry has to surge ahead. It has to make up for past setbacks. Exports have to be pushed up. And industry has to be exposed to the international economic environment. Exports are important not merely from the point of view of balance of payments. High exports alone will enable sustaining and speeding up the programme of acquisition of technology. Simultaneously, inflow of external capital will have to be augmented. The level of export earnings will largely determine our ability to qualitatively improve industry. Unless productivity, competitiveness and quality improve no major impact can be made overseas.

In the earlier decades external borrowings were available on soft terms. In the years ahead borrowings even from traditional aid agencies like the World Bank will be on harder terms and at variable interest rates. The servicing of our loans, therefore, will prove to be a distinct burden. It is, therefore, absolutely essential that the economy as a whole operates efficiently. The return on investment should be adequate not only to ensure that we pay our debts but also that the developmental process gets accelerated.

To achieve these aims, first and foremost, the economy has to be stabilized. Recurring cycles of inflation and recession have to be overcome. Unfortunately, inflation is sought to be tackled by a credit restriction. Ideally, it should be corrected by an appropriate interest rate structure which channelizes the flow of resources in the desired direction rather than by curbing the flow of funds itself. The latter results in denying funds for genuine productive needs and a diversion of long-term resources for current operations which is detrimental to investment.

The problem of technological obsolescence has to be faced squarely. A programme of modernization is imperative in order to raise the operational efficiency of the capacity already created. The need for modernization is pervasive and no industry can be considered an exception. Even our most modern industries do not have the latest technology and are eight to nine years behind. If the financial requirement for modernizing five industries is Rs 3,600 crore, as estimated by FICCI, the needs of the industrial sector as a whole would be far higher. Here again we will be up against the resources problem. To ease this problem corporate tax rates will have to be lowered to augment retained earnings. Depreciation based on historical cost is a major stumbling block. Several alternatives are available. Depreciation can be linked to the replacement cost of plant and machinery; free depreciation can be allowed; or accelerated depreciation can be permitted to enable industry to recover the entire cost of assets in the first two years. These deserve serious consideration. With the policy of administered prices in key capital intensive industries the problem has been further complicated because while returns shrink, costs rise.

Acquisition of the latest technolgy will not be possible unless we go in for the largest possible economic size.For this, industry itself has to adjust its concept of and attitude towards economic size. For example, the sugar machinery industry has the capability to set up 6000 TCD plants, but even new plants are only of 1500 TCD. Countries like Brazil are setting up 5000 TCD plants. Even in the power sector we are a decade behind, setting up 500 MW plants now, while countries like South Korea had set up 600 to 1000 MW plants in the early seventies.

Efficiency has to be of prime concern. This again calls for the best technology, regardless of cost. For example, we can buy the latest automobile technology to produce a million cars to meet the domestic and foreign demand. Indian consumers would benefit by this and exchange earnings would also be boosted. But if we opt for less we will only produce high cost cars in a protected market, and with hardly any export potential. Why then should we always choose the second best? Another risk is that in such cases obsolescence is faster. Why should we buy today's technology five years hence and at a higher cost?

Technological updating would involve additional infrastructural back-up. Therefore, adequate availability of power and other infrastructural facilities have to be ensured. However, it seems as if we shall have to live with a power shortage for quite some time to come. The power development programme needs to be accelerated and enlarged. Simultaneously, captive power generation has to be encouraged through appropriate means.

Fortunately, the foreign investment and collaboration policy has been relaxed in recent times. The process must continue. The recent liberalization, however, is restricted to sophisticated technology and high export-oriented areas. This may raise some problems because isolated pockets of high technology industries may prove uneconomic in the long run. There are close linkages between industries and if feeder industries are not updated or set up it may lead to a tremendous dependence on imports of spares and components. Import of high technology in one industry will automatically create a whole range of opportunities in entirely new areas which should not be missed. For example, if the heavy engineering industry is improved, the machine tools and hand tools industries would also have to be upgraded; otherwise, a large number of units will become outdated.

In addition, greater effort will have to be made to encourage in-house research and development. The total R&D expenditure incurred by the private sector was only Rs 72.4 crore in 1978–79, or 13.8 per cent of the total investment in R&D at the national level. The pace has to be stepped up. This is a responsibility which industry must shoulder. At the same time, policy influencing research activity can be further streamlined. For instance, the concessions available to R&D activity should extend beyond the immediate product line of companies. Similarly, import duty exemption should be given for equipment and raw materials required for R&D work. Greater exchange of scientists and technicians has to be arranged. There is no dearth of technical talent in the country. In fact, a number of scientists and technicians are forced to go abroad for lack of research opportunities at home.

Inflow of technology also provides the necessary stimulus for import substitution. By the end of the sixties import substitution petered out and the policies of the seventies, which curbed capacity expansion and technical inflow, resulted in reduced opportunities for import substitution. In the years ahead these efforts will have to be rejuvenated. What also needs to be borne in mind is that it is neither feasible nor desirable to replace each and every commodity that is imported. The comparative cost advantage has to be taken into account. Indiscriminate import substitution can result in high cost domestic production in lieu of cheaper imports. Emphasis has to be on effficient import replacement activity.

Another prerequisite to ensure smooth production is labour harmony. Strikes and lock-outs disrupt production. Most of the strikes are due to inter-union rivalries and have resulted in violence and damage to property. Unless labour harmony is promoted by effectively implementing regulations, the economy will not move forward. Industrial truce can be arrived at through the institution of a grievance machinery to settle disputes through conciliation and arbitration. Bombay is a glaring example of how massive losses of production, employment, exports and revenues to the exchequer can take place.

In conclusion, if we wish to emerge as a stable and growing economy with a special and unique presence in the international scene we will have to attune and dedicate ourselves to production and productivity. The economic environment the world over is so fiercely competitive that it leaves no room for slow starters and laggers.

An article published in the NCAER Silver Jubilee Souvenir, 9 December 1982.

TEXTILES : PERSPECTIVE EIGHTH PLAN

I must at the outset admit that I am a little out of touch with the textile industry since my retirement from business. I have, however, been thinking over these issues and also talking about them for several decades. I can now claim to be a more impartial observer, neither on the side of the industry nor on the side of government. As such, I can afford to be brutally frank even at the displeasure of my friends and colleagues.

The textile industry has been a mother industry. It has been the fountainhead for a number of other industries, some totally unrelated. It was so because with the resources generated by the textile industry and the expertise that it made possible, industrialists were able to venture into other lines. However, this mother industry has now become old and needs to be cared for.

The industry is complex. It is not simply the mill sector that we are talking about. There is a large powerloom sector, and a handloom sector which together add to the complexity of the problems. What is more, the industry has to cater not only to domestic demand but also the needs of exports. Many new countries like Hongkong, Singapore, Taiwan and Korea went into this immensely profitable line of business and having had their heyday, have now passed on to other industries. A new set of countries has now entered the export market, particularly China and Pakistan. It is surprising that India which has more than a century's experience of textiles is still unable to find its way. The reasons are not that there is something wrong with our industrialists or our government. It is because we do not have a clear perception about the future and as such we have not formulated precise plans for the different sectors of the industry.

The textile industry is still the largest industry in the country. It generates 20 per cent of the total value of industrial output, is the single largest foreign exchange earner, constituting more than 25 per cent of the total exchange earnings, and provides jobs to over 13 million workers. Of course, the bulk of the workers, nearly 10 million, are in the handloom sector which produces 25 per cent of the total cloth output.

The organized mill sector employs 1.2 million workers and produces about 25 per cent of the total output. It is the powerloom sector which now has the lion's share of 50 per cent of the output.

Although the textile industry is the premier industry of the country and also the oldest, it has failed to keep pace with modern technology. The automation in the industry is only 25 per cent in India as against 92 per cent in China and 84 per cent in Pakistan. We have also the lowest yield of cotton in the world, only 65 kg per acre as compared to 124 kg in Pakistan, and 264 kg in China. Even the world average is over 188 kg per acre.

With these handicaps, and the fluctuating cotton production, the textile industry has been moving through pronounced business cycles. The booms have been short and the slumps have been long. On the average, the profitability of the industry has been low and it has not been able to generate the resources required for modernization. The emerging picture is certainly not a cheerful one.

The subject of today's discussion is 'Textiles: Perspective for the Eighth Plan'. I personally feel that we have to take an even longer view, say, upto 2001 AD. In this longer perspective, we have to clearly identify the role that has to be played by the mill sector, the powerloom sector, the handloom sector, the cotton grower and the substitutes for cotton. The fuzziness in our policy has emerged precisely because we have not been able to define the role of each in specific terms. We want exports and for that we need the organized mill sector, and to some extent the handloom sector for specific requirements. We want employment and therefore we give encouragement to the powerloom and handloom sectors. We want to protect the interests of the cotton growers and therefore we have evolved a price system which will give them adequate income. But we have not seen the clear contradictions that exist and need to be sorted out before we can adopt a policy which will accelerate the natural trends which are ultimately bound to prevail.

I would like to present to you two perspectives about the future in terms of which we can devise policy. The first is about the role of cotton and synthetics. Cotton is probably the only crop for which there are industrial substitutes. The world over, synthetics have been considered to be the poor man's cloth. Only rich nations and rich people go in for natural fibres like cotton. We have totally reversed the roles and taxed synthetics so heavily that they have gone beyond the purchasing power of most of our people. There is a contradiction in this thinking because we are denying the country the opportunity to export cotton and earn valuable foreign exchange. As an alternative, we can produce less cotton and more of other non-substitutable crops like edible oils and pluses, which at present we are compelled to import. If we export cotton and produce synthetic materials, we shall be providing a much cheaper cloth to the large masses of the people. The same metre of synthetic textile costs three times more in India than it does in Thailand. Our own industrialists have set up factories there with the same technology and they can sell at only one-third the price because the taxation in Thailand is reasonable.

The fluctuations in the prices of cotton due to fluctuations in production of cotton create tremendous problems for the textile industry. These fluctuations would naturally get reduced with greater dependance on synthetic fibres.

With the introduction of synthetics on a massive scale, the demand for cotton textiles will come down and the price of cotton will be such as can compete in the world market. If necessary, the export of cotton could be supported by subsidies. This scenario would require that we expand our capacity in the production of synthetic fibres and the raw materials which are required for that industry. Eventually, it will work out to be much cheaper than continuing with the present strategy of massive production of cotton textiles.

Let us not turn a blind eye to the obvious problem that the textile industry at present is characterized by over capacity. A large number of mills are already sick. In Ahmedabad, which was considered the textile centre of India, only 5 or 6 mills are actually working profitably. The others are sick or dying. In a situation of over capacity, it is important that mills which just do not have a future are closed. In any case, no further expansion should be allowed in the textile industry. The existing machinery in many of the mills is outdated and only those mills which have an efficient management and the capability to compete in the international market should be given support to modernize.

The second perspective to which I referred earlier is about the reorganization of the mill sector itself. I believe that the days of composite mills are more or less over, except in the case of mills which cater to highly sophisticated demand or to the export market. By and large, the mill sector will have to primarily confine itself to spinning rather than weaving. I, for one, see this as an inevitable trend that is emerging in our country. It would be right to support and accelerate this trend rather than obstruct it and delay the process, creating problems for industry and the country.

The transfer of weaving to the powerloom sector and consequently the closure of some of the textile mills will create unemployment in the organized sector. This has to be viewed against the additional employment that will be created in the powerloom and handloom sectors. In the net, there will be more employment, not less. In any case, it would not be prudent to support an activity which is essentially uneconomic merely because its closure would result in immediate unemployment. The price we would pay in the long run is high and it can cause distortions which belittle our growth and our competitiveness in the international market. Besides, there are other ways of tackling unemployment, like, for instance, the much talked about 'golden handshake' or the unemployment insurance scheme.

While tackling the problem of composite sick textile mills, I would suggest that looms should not be rehabilitated and that only the spinning part of the viable sick mills should be revived. This would be cheaper and profitable in the long run.

If the powerloom sector handles most of the weaving part of the industry it will have to be modernized and updated so that the product is good in quality and production is low-cost. A massive programme of modernization of the powerloom sector will have to be undertaken, supported by the government.

What I have suggested is not intended to create more capacity or to generate more production but to ensure better quality and lower costs. There has been a complaint that in spite of the increase in per capita income there has not been substantial increase in the per capita consumption of cloth. There are two reasons for this. The first is that with the introduction of synthetics the life of garments has become longer. Today, only one-fifth of the total production consists of synthetic material. If this proportion goes up substantially to, say, one-half, it is quite likely that the per capita consumption will in fact come down rather than go up. The other reason for the fall in per capita consumption is the change in dress habits. Quite a large section of the population has shifted for instance, from dhoti to trousers or from saree to salwar kameez. As a result, the per capita consumption of cloth in terms of metres has, to some extent, dropped. The kind of division I am suggesting—the mill sector producing mainly yarn and cloth for exports and the powerloom and handloom sectors producing cloth for the domestic market—will bring down prices substantially and improve per capita needs, though not necessarily in terms of consumption of meterage. Of course, all this is possible only if the tax element in synthetic fibre and synthetic cloth is reduced drastically.

As I said earlier, these are not new thoughts. I am taking this opportunity to reiterate them in the hope that they may be seriously considered. The Hon'ble Minister for Textiles, Shri Ram Niwas Mirdha, has ushered in a new textile policy which goes part of the way towards the perspective I have mentioned. But the government has to do more than that to ensure that the emerging scenario of the textile industry crystallizes as quickly as possible and the different sectors of the industry become complementary and viable.

One other point to which I would like to refer is my disappointment at the lack of advancement in technology in spite of the industry being more than a hundred years old, in spite of the fact that we have a number of research institutes, in spite of the fact that we have a number of textile machinery manufacturing units, in spite of the fact that we pride ourselves on being the third largest technical manpower in the world. We are still very dependent on imported technology. This should be food for thought to industrialists and the researchers.

I am aware I have raised some controversial issues, but the textile industry is much too important for the country from the point of view of export earnings, employment and supply of a basic necessity of life, to be neglected. In this context, a longer term view needs tobe taken instead of resorting to short-term palliatives. From time to time various committees have gone into the problems of the textile industry and now there is a committee under the chairmanship of Shri Abid Hussain to review the textile policy. I do hope solutions will be found to the problems facing the textile industry, with a long-term perspective.

Inaugural address at a seminar organized by Parliamentary News and Views Service and Textile Association (India), 4 January 1989.

EXPORTS

PROBLEMS AND PROSPECTS OF EXPORTS

The basic problems, or to put it differently, the prerequisites for a programme of export promotion may be listed as follows.

1 Creation of export surpluses at competitive prices;
2 Acceptance by the general public of the sacrifices involved in promoting exports in line with the practices obtaining in foreign countries;
3 Ever-increasing vigour in locating foreign markets for traditional as well as new products;
4 Existence of a favourable atmosphere in foreign markets, particularly in the developed countries.

We must start from the premise that our requirements of foreign exchange will be on a much larger scale than was indicated in the third plan. This is because the lags in production in various sectors have made it necessary for us to place greater reliance on imports. Further, the defence effort makes and will continue to make heavier demands on resources which would lead to increased imports and maybe, in some cases, to a reduction in exports because of the use of certain resources which could have been used otherwise for making products for export markets. These are new factors which have to be reckoned with. What is even more important is that the export strategy must take full note of the fact that our export receipts have to be more than doubled by the end of the fourth plan to make the Indian economy more self-reliant. Considered in the light of all these, our export effort hitherto has not been commensurate with the needs. This is not to say that fairly vigorous measures have not been taken, especially in the last one year or so, to bring about a sense of dynamism in the export promotion programmes. The Board of Trade has proved its utility as a useful forum to bring together representatives of various ministries and of industry and trade to evolve appropriate solutions and to review their implementation. Our export performance in 1962–63 may be regarded as satisfactory taking into account the conditions that prevailed in India and abroad. Yet it cannot be said that all that is necessary and feasible is being done.

Even a casual look at our export earnings during the last decade or so will show that export receipts from certain items have been much higher in earlier years than the present levels. For example, in terms of value the export of jute manufactures was of the order of Rs 260 crore in 1951–52 as against Rs 155 crore in 1962–63. In 1950–51 our earnings from cotton textiles were as high as Rs 118 crore as against Rs 46 crore in 1962–63. Similarly, earnings from tea export in 1954–55 were Rs 148 crore as against Rs 129 crore in 1962–63. Earnings from manganese exports stood at an all-time high figure of Rs 30 crore in 1957–58 as against only Rs 8 crore in 1962–63. These few instances illustrate the complex nature of foreign trade, as also our potential. The higher earnings referred to here were due to increased demand abroad and other favourable circumstances which we ourselves did not engineer, though we took advantage of them.

It has to be conceded that the large earnings from jute manufactures in 1951–52 were the direct result of the Korean War boom when prices of jute goods rose to unforeseen heights. Similarly, in the case of manganese ore, the large export earnings in 1957–58 were partly due to high prices and partly due to the larger quantities exported which were more than double the present level. As for cotton textiles, both the quantum and value of exports reached an unprecedented level in 1950–51. We are facing newer problems in cotton textiles because of the growth of the textile industry in developing countries leading to shrinkage in import demand, intensification of competition from other suppliers and the existence of quotas and other kinds of restrictions in developed countries. The point that remains valid, however, is that we had exported larger quantities of some items and it should, therefore, be possible for us to think in terms of substantially augmenting our exchange earnings.

Of late the problem of supplying goods at competitive rates has manifested itself sharply. Until five or six years back exports took place without receiving any special incentives as such. But at present, over a considerable field of exports our prices are out of alignment with international parity and there does not seem to be any alternative to fostering exports except through some form of assistance. We must, however, underline the fact that most of our schemes of export assistance aim at the mere removal of disincentives. They only help in obtaining the requisite raw materials from abroad which are not otherwise available due to foreign exchange stringency. For example, the increased exports of art silk fabrics—from Rs 1 crore a decade ago to over Rs 8 crore during 1962–63—are due to the fact that the industry is obliged to export because its very existence and better utilization of capacity are dependent upon securing supplies of raw materials from abroad through schemes of export incentives. Inasmuch as the average realization on exports is only slightly above Re 1 per metre, it cannot be gainsaid that exports are being made at considerable sacrifice. The element of sacrifice is not less evident in the case of sugar where actual exports in 1962–63 were as high as Rs 18 crore although the price fetched had to be supplemented by higher domestic pricing. These illustrations serve to indicate the degree to which we are not competitive. Some schemes of assistance have necessarily got to be devised. But a problem which needs thorough investigation is the extent to which we should be willing to give inducement on a long-term basis for exports and the items which should receive such assistance. It seems to me that this problem has not received the attention it deserves.

From a long-term point of view it is of great importance to increase production all-round. Agriculture must necessarily play a very important role in the task of restoring competitive strength to our products. To give one instance, the average yield per acre of raw cotton in India is around 120 lbs as against 438 lbs in the USA. In such a situation, the percentage cost of raw materials in the prices of finished products is so high that countries like Japan and Hongkong which largely depend upon imports of raw cotton have a cost advantage over us for part of their supplies are procured under PL–480. Significant increases in production of other cash crops such as vegetable seeds and sugarcane can make an impact not only on releasing more surplus of exports but also in bringing down our prices to reasonable levels. As far as industrial exports are concerned, the problem is of coordinating our developmental programmes in such a manner that export industries can reap the advantages of economies of scale. They should be in a position to spread the entire overhead costs across internal sales. Export industries should also be given greater priority in pushing through programmes of modernization so as to produce goods in accordance with the exacting requirements of specialized markets. Special attention must also be paid to following an action-oriented approach to reduce costs of production, segregate all tax elements from the product which is exported, increase the productivity of labour and improve efficiency all-round.

Greater stress has also to be laid on increasing our earnings by exporting more of processed goods. For example, as a long-term proposition, serious consideration should be given to setting up large-sized pig iron plants so as to encourage exports of pig iron rather than iron ore which is now one of our major items of exports.

Among other problems which impinge on our export effort, mention may be made of insufficient appreciation by the general public of the need for sacrifice in selling goods at lower prices in the export markets. This arises partly because of the lack of an export tradition in the country, for in the past our economy was not oriented to the exigencies of earning more foreign exchange. We are still in the process of building efficient merchandizing methods. Our contacts with foreign buyers have to be far more intimate. This presupposes the need for taking concerted action by following coordinated programmes of carrying out commodity-wise market surveys. It is of importance that individual efforts to ascertain possibilities of selling more in different markets, not only traditional items but also new items, are not thwarted by niggardly policies in releasing foreign exchange for visits abroad. Such visits can go a long way in learning the marketing techniques of our competitors and in understanding their exact requirements.

Yet another problem which India is facing, along with other developing countries, stems from the trading policies being pursued by the developed nations. While there seems to be an increasing recognition of the need for giving export opportunities to developing countries, there continues to be a considerable gap between intent and performance.

In the light of some of the problems to which reference has been made, are we in a position to say what the prospects for exports are? Since various factors, national and international, intrude, the task of making projections even on a short-term basis about export prospects is not free from hazard. The only thing that can be said is that there is an ever growing awareness of the need to increase exports. Assuming that a vigorous programme of increasing domestic production with an eye on exports is initiated in a big way and special emphasis is laid on cost reduction, there is some hope of increasing exports to the desired levels. The problems are many and they cannot be tackled as a once-for-all exercise. The task of export promotion will have to be done on a continuous basis by all sections of the community. Naturally, governmental authorities have to play a major role in so far as the initiation and implementation of policies for adjusting developmental and production programmes are concerned. In the short run, the present schemes of assistance including those for enabling industry to have import entitlement for meeting its essential needs have a great value. But from the long-term point of view a bold effort is required to be made by imparting competitive strength to exports. At the national level, one can look beyond the present schemes of assistance and incentives only when we reach a stage at which internal production can be geared to release enough surplus for export after meeting internal demand. Until this happens the value of international action both in extending aid and in following appropriate trading policies to allow export opportunities especially in lines where developing countries like ours have comparative cost advantages cannot be over-emphasized.

At the ministerial session of the GATT last May, the Minister for International Trade rightly projected the idea of tariff preference on selected products of interest to less developed countries and the establishment by the GATT of a Working Group to examine this and other related matters would go some way in promoting the trade of developing nations. It is to be hoped that even before the convening of the World Conference on Trade and Development in March 1964, the developed countries will have taken some constructive measures so that the prospects of increasing our exports in several lines of manufactures and semi-manufactures become better than what they are today.

Article published in The Economic Times, Bombay, 9 September 1963.

EXPORT AND PRODUCTION PERSPECTIVES : 1980–81

I have been closely associated with the formulation of the background paper which will be discussed at length today and tomorrow. A number of ideas have been thrown up in this paper and I felt it would be worthwhile if I highlighted some of the salient features, at least those which are most relevant to this session.

Our development in the past twenty-five years has followed a certain route. The emphasis, mainly out of necessity, has been on self-reliance. In the present context it implies balancing our payments position without recourse to external assistance while at the same time, maintaining a high level of growth. It is natural, in these circumstances, that our imports will increase, in spite of our endeavour to speed up import substitution. The accent on exports, therefore, becomes inevitable and vital. Let me also add that export promotion is not merely a way of earning the requisite foreign exchange but of stimulating growth through all-round efficiency.

This session is confined primarily to 'Export Strategy'. A little reflection will show, however, that any discussion on the subject of exports cannot be compartmentalized. The issues are inextricably interconnected. I, therefore, hope that I shall be excused if I appear to transgress into other areas reserved for this afternoon and tomorrow.

The most fundamental premise, in my view, is that exports are but one aspect of the development process. This is not exactly how we have looked at exports in the past. The general impression has been that exports are surplus production which is sold abroad after domestic needs are fully met. This is why, there have usually been spurts in exports during periods of recession. This, I believe, is not the right approach. We have to make exports an integral part of our economic system; and the export strategy must be conceived as one of the main dimensions of development policy. For the purpose of discussion, however, it would be useful to confine ourselves to the export strategy as such, while keeping at the back of our mind the larger context in which it fits.

Export strategy should be conceived as consisting of two parts: a strategy for production of requisite exportable goods and a strategy for marketing these goods abroad. In the past fifteen years the government has adopted a variety of measures to promote exports on an increasing scale. Some of these proved successful. But their potency has worn off sooner than expected. Besides, the approach was, for the most part, ad hoc and piecemeal. What is required is a consistent and comprehensive long-term strategy. This is why we have considered a five-year programme which will enable building of the necessary infrastructure and production capacities to support the export plan.

The first task is to fix an export target. The background paper indicates that in 1980–81 exports can be of the order of Rs 6,285 crore, at 1974–75 prices. This target will go up to Rs 7,481 crore if prices rise at the rate of 3 per cent, to Rs 8,887 crore if prices rise at 6 per cent, and Rs 10,507 crore if prices rise at 9 per cent per year. Our share in world trade could increase from 0.53 per cent in 1975 to 0.67 per cent in 1980.

The task of achieving this target is undoubtedly challenging and will involve gearing up the economy in many crucial areas. An increase in exports will entail a corresponding addition to production over and above the improvement in domestic consumption. The overall production target will have to be broken down into sub-targets for different categories of goods. Once that exercise is done, investment will have to be initiated in these areas to ensure that adequate capacities are built up to meet both domestic consumption as well as export needs. It is estimated that the investment required to produce goods for additional exports in the next five years would be over Rs 1,800 crore. The vast bulk of this investment will be in the engineering and chemical industries and mining. Let me add that, to be effective, the production and investment planning will have to be taken a step further, to the micro level. Specific individual targets will have to be set for different enterprises, particularly in respect of some of the major export items. This linking of exports to production and investment is one of the important features of the Federation's study.

Export planning, however, does not end there. It is not merely fixing responsibility that can give results. There is an equal obligation on the part of the government to see that enterprises, whether public or private, which have to undertake investment and engineer production, are given the requisite wherewithal. The present state of industry is such that the required growth will not take place easily. There are a number of limitations which make it difficult for industry to secure capital, acquire the requisite technology, attain optimum size, get an economic price and secure a minimum cash flow. Various governmental regulations have affected the working of industry and reduced its competitiveness in international trade.

Let me clarify my point. Take, for example, the MRTP Act and Company Law. These two together have put industry in such a strait-jacket that it is unable to adapt itself to the rapidly changing world economic conditions. The size of enterprises is often less than optimum and technology is not modern enough. Both these stand in the way of reducing costs and prices, which is a good handle for increasing exports. Besides, the lowering of prices would stimulate demand internally, enhance production and generate larger employment.

Consider, again, corporate taxation. Our rates of taxation are excessive by international standards and have tended to inflate prices. The corporate tax inclusive of surtax is now about 67 per cent in our country, compared to 25 to 40 per cent in Korea, 15 per cent in Hongkong, 25 to 30 per cent in Taiwan and 45 per cent in Malaysia. Even in the highly industrialized countries the rate of corporate taxation is much lower—in the US it is 22 to 48 per cent, in the UK 52 per cent, in France 50 per cent, in West Germany 44 to 51 per cent, and in Japan from 42 to 50 per cent. I would like to emphasize that corporate taxation is an in-built item of cost for purposes of pricing. In covering the higher tax incidence, to earn the same net rate of return on capital invested the Indian exporter has to charge a much higher price than his counterparts abroad.

It is not enough merely to produce more; we have to produce more at minimum cost. It is from this angle that the government should review the impact of some of our policies to which I have referred.

The implicit handicaps which business in India face have been to some extent compensated by what are mistakenly called 'export incentives'. They may be more aptly described as 'support measures'. One of these measures is cash assistance. The impression has often been created that cash assistance is a bonanza offered to Indian exporters. I tried to understand the cash assistance scheme and found, to my surprise, that the total cost of such assistance incurred by the government in 1975–76 was only Rs 76 crore, less than 2 per cent of our total export earnings. I would hesitate to call this amount of support excessive. Of course, it is also true that cash assistance is not given on all exportable items on a uniform basis.

I have an impression that government has been hesitant to give the requisite cash assistance to exporters partly due to a consideration of loss in revenue, and partly due to the fear that exports may not go up. There is also a lurking suspicion that the exporter may make excess profits. Without going into the finer implications, I would venture to say that it would be worthwhile for the government to be liberal because the benefit to the country would be much larger than the cost to the government.

We should not forget that conditions in the world market change very fast and quite drastically too. At present there is no automatic mechanism by which cash assistance is brought in line with actual requirements. The decisions are delayed because of lack of adequate inter-ministerial coordination. I would, therefore, urge that a small sub-committee consisting of representatives of the Ministries of Commerce, Finance and Industry, as also export interests, be set up to review the assistance scheme as and when required and take instant decisions.

Many of our export commodities are still agro-based and are susceptible to wide price fluctuations. Undoubtedly, larger exports and greater domestic supplies would be possible only if productivity in agriculture is stepped up; at the same time, it is necessary to devise a scheme by which the prices of these goods remain stable. In the past twenty months, we have been able to achieve a modest price reduction while most other countries were in the grip of inflation. We can also expect stability of prices in the future mainly because the government has been successful in building up a buffer stock of foodgrains. I would suggest that this scheme be extended to other agricultural inputs like cotton or agro-based commodities like sugar and oil. Our recent experience in cotton and edible oil prices should convince the government about the desirability of such a step. Stability in the prices of a wide range of critical products will be a great advantage both for promoting exports as well as raising the level of development.

The second aspect of an export strategy, as I mentioned earlier, is marketing. In this field our failures have been even more distressing. Export involves aggressive salesmanship. We have to learn a lot from successful exporting countries like Japan. They have evolved special marketing knowhow and have created a wide organizational network. They adopt sophisticated sales techniques, undertake advertising, market surveys, etc. We have to adapt ourselves to meet these challenges. In this area a lot needs to be done by our own industry and trade.

The quality of goods has to be maintained; delivery schedules have to be adhered to; the packaging has to be according to international standards. Exporters should not think in terms of quick profits, but take a longer term view.

In a sense, our difficulties are of our own making. Government looks upon business with suspicion and compels it to conform to rigid and time-consuming rules and regulations which do not fit in with the constantly fluid world trade conditions. Equally, business attempts to dodge government rules wherever possible, only strengthening the suspicion that is already there. Mutual distrust has done greater harm than any other single factor.

I need hardly stress that export calls for a joint effort by government and business. If the cooperation from the two sides is full, it should not at all be difficult for us to cross the one billion dollar export mark, in the next five years. If each one of us realizes his responsibility and undertakes his tasks with dedication and diligence, export promotion would not be an insuperable problem.

Address at a seminar at the First Technical Session on Export Strategy, organized by FICCI, Vigyan Bhawan, New Delhi, 20 July 1976.

EXPORT POLICY

Export promotion councils were set up in the country with the main aim of accelerating the export effort. Some of these councils have been extremely successful. The Engineering Export Promotion Council is one of the finest examples. It has engineered a substantial change in respect of the volume, composition and direction of our exports.

It is a matter of great satisfaction that our exports have now outpaced our imports. Since Independence we had a trade surplus for the second time in 1976–77. This was not a mere freak occurrence. It symbolized a new trend in our foreign trade. In the first eight months of the current financial year also there was a trade surplus of the order of Rs 72 crore. These achievements are without doubt a reflection of the success of our import substitution and export promotion measures, which are the limbs of our national policy of self-reliant growth.

In the past twenty years or so our economy has grown in dimension and has also substantially changed in complexion. Industry, a vital part of the economy, has also undergone tremendous metamorphosis. It has not only grown in size but has also widened its base. As a result, trade has diversified. Now there is greater accent on exporting manufactures than primary products.

Our exports are still considerably concentrated, both in respect of products as well as markets. Fortunately, there are immense opportunities for diversification in favour of value added items like engineering goods. Equally there is great scope for exports to developing countries, especially those which are geographically proximate. New markets and new products have to be located, properly nursed and developed.

The most promising item of growth is engineering goods. Exports of engineering goods accounted for 8.6 per cent of our total exports in 1975–76. The estimates are that the share of engineering goods in total exports has now gone up to around 11 per cent. Scope for improvement in this field is quite large. Components of engineering items hold great promise for increased exports to developed countries. Further, new horizons are to be sighted in the export of consultancy services and joint ventures abroad. These will generate additional exports on a continuing basis.

Although India's experience in venturing overseas is of recent origin, the progress made so far is by no means insignificant. At present, 188 Indian industrial joint ventures are operating in a score of countries. Of these 83 projects have already gone into production and 105 are in various stages of implementation. These joint ventures have generated exports worth Rs 50 crore and earned the country Rs 4.25 crore by way of dividends, technical know-how and other fees. Apart from advantages like widening the market for capital goods, joint ventures also create a demand for raw materials, semi-processed manufactures, spare parts and components. The prospects for consultancy services and sub-contracting in the field of civil engineering are also good.

Our export efforts, however, are exposed to various limitations. The level of exports is governed not only by our ability to sell abroad but also the willingness of other countries to buy from us. International trade is not free. Most countries practise a protectionist policy. Almost all our export products come up against tariff barriers even in major developed countries. Besides, our exports have also to face non-tariff barriers. These take the form of quotas, discriminatory licensing, state trading, monopoly practices and so on. Many of our products, traditional and non-traditional, have become victims of these handicaps. The developing countries have been obliged to put, what are termed 'voluntary trade restraints', on a whole range of textile manufactures and items like steel, meat, dairy products, etc. Unfortunately, at present the international environment is not conducive to trade liberalization and domestic protectionist pressures are increasing to alarming proportions in many developed countries. This fact came up in sharp focus at the recent meeting of the Indo-US Joint Business Council. There is growing apprehension about the additional measures of anti-dumping on products originating in developing countries.

More recently, our exports have been hit by the depreciation of the dollar. The United States is likely to have a trade deficit of over $30 billion in 1977. The dollar has been allowed to find its market level in the hope that its depreciation would reduce US imports and increase exports. But it would be sad if this affects developing countries adversely. In the case of India, as against a realization of Rs 8.50 per US dollar at the beginning of December 1977, at the end of January it has gone down to about Rs 7.90. Many exporters working on small margins of 2 to 3 per cent have burnt their fingers and suffered incalculable losses. The problem requires immediate corrective action, for one is not sure whether the policy of 'benign neglect' being used by the USA as a possible self-correcting mechanism will succeed. This may or may not happen. It may then become a case not of 'benign neglect' by the USA but of 'malign neglect' by India. I suggest that action should be taken immediately so that the rate of exchange between the rupee and the US dollar is fixed by the Reserve Bank of India or the scheme of obtaining forward cover is liberalized so that exporters do not have to pay a large percentage in obtaining this facility. We must show readiness to quickly re-adjust our assistance and support measures.

Lately, there has not been sufficient stability in our export policies and programmes. Exports of a number of items such as cotton yarn, fruits and vegetables, spices, etc. were banned on the ground that these could not be undertaken at social costs. I venture to suggest that this policy is relevant up to a point. It is true that in India we cannot have export-led growth, for exports constitute a small percentage of our GNP. However, a sudden ban, especially in respect of items for which markets have been built assiduously, results not only in dislocation but also permanent loss of markets. What is worse is that in some cases they lead to accumulation of stocks and constitute a drag on augmenting production. This can be illustrated vividly with reference to sugar whose exports are currently banned. This year, sugar production is expected to reach an all-time high of over 52 lakh tons. Internal consumption will at best be around 40 lakh tons and if exports are not permitted, the industry will have to carry a burdensome surplus, if note is taken of the large carryover of 16 lakh tons of stocks at the beginning of the season. The stocks at the end of this season may well amount to a staggering figure, equivalent to eight months' consumption. This surplus will require huge finances and the stocks are liable to deteriorate in quality.

I am aware that presently sugar exports can be undertaken only at a marginal loss even when calculated on the basis of the levy price, but it is imperative to undertake exports to ensure that cane cultivation and production of sugar does not go down in the coming years. It may be mentioned that after long discussions, the International Sugar Agreement was concluded last year and for the current year, the total effective quota of India has been fixed at 6.5 lakh tons. If we do not undertake exports, our credibility in the international markets will go down. I would like to characterize the present ban on exports of sugar as 'sheer obduracy', which is not designed to protect either the long-term interests of the industry or of the consumer. In fact, if timely action is not taken the sugar industry which is in the doldrums may well become 'sick.'

I am afraid that because of the accumulation of foreign exchange reserves, the need for promoting exports has not been receiving the attention it requires. In my view, we should plan for higher levels of both exports and imports. In the current financial year, our rate of export growth, at around 10 per cent, will be much smaller than in the last few years. But for the sharp rise in exports of gems and jewellery the growth rate would be much lower, for declines have taken place in a large number of items. In the context of the favourable balance of payments position, there is talk of dilution of schemes of cash compensatory support. In fact, what is required is proper rationalization of criteria for cash assistance. It is well known that cash assistance provides compensation for a host of indirect taxes which go into production costs and are not refunded through duty drawback schemes of excise and customs. They also provide compensation for freight differentials and for initial promotional expenditure for new products and for developing exports to new markets. What is, however, not fully realized is that by giving support to the export effort, we not only help better capacity utilization but also create an environment for creation of new capacity and provide increased employment opportunities. In saying so, I am not pleading for a revival of the doctrine of export-led growth. However, it would indeed be disastrous to disrupt the export apparatus that has been successfully built. Let me illustrate this with reference to cotton textiles. What is required today is to give additional support because the price of raw cotton in the world markets has gone down much more than in India. We are being outpriced and this has begun reflecting itself in the falling exports of textiles.

There is yet another consideration to which I would like to make a reference. The GSP has provided increased export opportunities to many non-traditional products. However, under the Multilateral Trade Negotiations currently being held in Geneva many importing countries are proposing to reduce tariff rates which will attenuate the preferential margins that countries like India enjoy under the GSP. There is also the fear that anti-dumping regulations may be enforced more stringently and already many categories of steel-based items have run up against difficulties in the US market on this count.

It is well known that the selling prices in India are high because of the cumulative burden of indirect taxation, sales tax, octroi, etc. The Jha Committee has made an excellent analysis of the problems but complete identification of the burden is really not possible. Cost escalation takes place through a variety of taxes on inputs. I, therefore, strongly plead that a beginning should be made for instituting value added tax so that the entire burden on exports can be easily rebated. To start with, at least Section 56(A) of the Excise Act should be extended to a large number of commodities so that duties paid on inputs get credit on the duties payable on the final product. I am glad that the Jha Committee has also recommended this approach.

It is satisfying to find that the Alexander Committee has recommended the continuance of the present pattern of cash assistance for the ensuing year 1978–79. The suggestion for combining duty drawback rate and cash assistance will also be helpful in reducing the workload of disbursing agencies. The premium on import replenishment licences has been going down with the easing of restrictions on imports. With further liberalization the extent of this premium will go down further and the support it provides to calculate profitability on exports will decline. Indian manufactures also suffer from other inbuilt disadvantages such as the high cost of imported machinery and rising project costs. Moreover, in the matter of export finance we are at a great disadvantage inasmuch as most of the competitors from capital-surplus developed countries offer attractive terms of credit. All these and other disadvantages have to be offset. The continuance of incentives thus becomes an important element of export promotion policy.

We have to realize that while government assistance is important exports will ultimately depend upon our own efforts. Exports entail aggressive salesmanship. We have a lot to learn from successful exporting countries like Japan. They have evolved special marketing know-how and created a wide organizational network. They adopt sophisticated sales techniques, undertake advertisement, market survey, etc. We have to adapt ourselves to meet these challenges. In this regard I would like to suggest that exporters should set up offices abroad to deal directly with buyers, feed information to head offices, carry out market intelligence surveys, advertise, provide further sales service to buyers, keep a watch on competitors and undertake a number of similar sales jobs. Government should assist exporters to set up offices, independently or jointly, in foreign markets. In the case of engineering goods, a consortium approach is also indicated, particularly where 'after sales service' is needed.

All efforts towards export promotion would be belittled unless there is corresponding and continuing increase in domestic production. Export is a spontaneous offshoot of industrialization. The export strategy must, therefore, be directly related to production planning by broadening and widening the industrial base, along with sustained efforts for increases in agricultural output which constitutes, in many cases, the basic inputs for export industries. Production should be enlarged to meet growing domestic demand as well as for exports. In this context I feel a sense of great anguish that our efforts are being thwarted by labour unrest and inadequate availability of power.

Equally important is the need to give attention to the importance of marketing techniques. This is an area where in many countries the salesman gives constant feedback about new product development, new methods of packaging, designs, etc. Unfortunately, in this matter the efforts by individual enterprises as well as by institutions like the

Export Promotion Councils is woefully inadequate in relation to the needs and potential. In India the protected home market has lulled us into a sense of complacency and our marketing skill has not been tested adequately in the domestic scene; consequently, the concept of export marketing and the vigour which it requires have not been fully realized. We can learn a lot about this from Japan. In this context it is of utmost importance that representatives of export houses and others undertake more frequent travels abroad and take advantage of the liberalization that is already in force. Each visit by a sales executive can result, for the corporate entity, in a remodelling of its marketing system and production planning for export markets.

As you are all aware, export markets demand production of quality goods. Inspection facilities require strengthening. Greater recourse should be taken to self-inspection and plant quality control, especially for engineering goods. The dependence of industry on government certification should get reduced. This can come about only if quality consciousness develops in the country in a big way. It should be regarded as a national responsibility so that in due course India comes to be identified as an exporter of quality products.

Lately there have been problems in the matter of adherence to delivery schedules. In some cases the production schedules have been disrupted due to strikes or non-availability of power. What we have to realize is that the foreign buyer is not concerned about India's internal problems and therefore serious attention requires to be paid to sticking to delivery schedules. Complaints about delivery schedules should be regarded as being in the nature of warning signals and the economy should be set right so that this problem does not thwart India's export effort.

I have touched upon some issues pertaining to the problems and prospects of exports in a larger context. Before I conclude, I would like to emphasize that production and exports are not the responsibility of any single sector. It calls for a joint effort by the government and entrepreneurs. Cooperation and coordination between all the sectors has to be close. Export is not an end by itself. It is in fact part of the total development for national growth and employment, and must be so regarded. Only if each one of us realizes the responsibility and undertakes the job with dedication and diligence will there be all-round progress and acceleration of exports. A dynamic and forward-looking view has to be taken to realize the possibilities, which are immense. Utmost emphasis has to be laid on proper implementation of export policies and programmes. A coordinated and integrated approach in this matter is the only way to achieve national prosperity

---

Address at the Engineering Export Promotion Council, New Delhi, 9 February 1978.

DOUBLING EXPORTS BY 1990

The subject of the workshop is most appropriate in the context of our present balance of payments situation. While it is not necessary for me to emphasize the importance of this subject, it is surprising that in spite of the recognition of this problem, which has been with us for many years, we do not seem to have done enough to face up to the challenges. I would like to take this opportunity to place before you my perception of the problems and, perhaps, some solutions.

One may ask, why do we need to export? The reason is simple. If we want a high rate of economic growth we cannot do without substantial imports, particularly because we are not self-sufficient in many items required by the country. In fact no country can be self-sufficient in everything. It becomes imperative, therefore, that we must export not merely to balance our trade but also for faster economic development.

Our adverse balance of trade has been continuously rising since 1970, partly because of the substantial rise in oil prices and partly due to our failure to match our exports to the import requirements. It is a matter of concern that in 1985–86 the trade deficit shot up to nearly Rs 8,750 crore and last year it was about a Rs 1,000 crore less. The situation is likely to take a turn for the worse again since this year the conditions created by drought will perforce necessitate larger imports of a variety of goods like edible oils and petroleum products. On the contrary, exports may face a bit of a setback because of the smaller availability of agricultural commodities like cotton, food products and so on. Undobtedly, the situation is very grave and the business community particularly must realize the consequences that may follow.

To achieve an 8 per cent rate of growth in industry imports will have to grow at a rate of nearly 6 per cent in real terms and about 10 per cent in money terms. To finance this import bill, exports will have to increase in real terms at a rate of over 16 per cent per year and, allowing the same rate of inflation as in the international economy, in money terms exports will have to grow at over 20 per cent.

Our past performance has not been encouraging. Last year, exports increased by over 20 per cent but in the previous year there was actually a fall by 6 per cent. On an average, the growth would be about 12–13 per cent or so. This year some exports have been looking up. In cotton textiles, where we have actually been falling short of the quotas assigned to India, for the first time, we have been able to fulfil our quotas and are in a position to export even more. But spasmodic increases in exports do not add up to a reasonable solution to the problems we are facing. What we need is to build up an export capability backed by an appropriate marketing infrastructure to ensure that the growth in exports will be steady and high.

Let us ask ourselves why we have not been able to export in spite of the vast development that has taken place in the last four decades. In countries like Japan and Korea, exports have been growing at a rate of 30 per cent year. Why can we not reach these levels of performance which have been achieved by others? There are, I believe, a variety of reasons, and we have to look at them closely if we are serious about achieving a high rate of growth in exports. Of course, my intention is not to suggest that we should follow the path of Japan or Korea, who are compelled to export because of their small domestic markets. We will have to design our strategy differently as our domestic market is large and exports are, relatively speaking, a smaller activity. Even so, we will have to expand exports to at least 9 per cent of the GNP compared to the present 6 per cent.

We have not been able to build up an adequate export capability because our economic policy framework has been entirely guided by domestic considerations. The industrial licensing system, the MRTP and FERA created conditions in which industry did not achieve an economic scale of output. As a result, the cost of production was high and we were priced out in the international markets. Of course, in the last two years, the government has liberalized policy and it is incumbent on certain industries to instal a minimum capacity rather than a maximum capacity, as was the case earlier. Even so, the present hadicaps need to be recognized and adequate facilities provided for units to grow in size.

Second, our industry has not been able to achieve the same level of productivity as in other countries, even after modernization. Some of the studies made reveal that labour productivity in India is only about a tenth of that in countries like Japan and the USA. This means that in spite of our low wages, labour is more costly. The reason why our productivity is low is that our labour laws provide excessive protection to labour. Undoubtedly, there was a time when labour was exploited by management. Now, it is labour that is exploiting the country.

Third, while in many of the processing industries, efficiency is comparable to industries in most other countries, the basic raw materials supplied by mother industries are costly and as such the final price addressed to the importers becomes inconsistent with the international market conditions. Take, for instance, steel, which is twice as costly in India as in the world market. Our electricity is equally prohibitive and raises the cost of production substantially. The reasons for high prices of steel, electricity, coal, etc. are quite well known and there is no need for me to elaborate on these issues. The basic fact is that there is excessive over-employment and there is need for greater managerial efficiency.

Next, I would like refer to the impact of high interest rates on the cost of production. This issue has been brought to the notice of the government time and again and I must admit that some corrective action has been taken. But the difference between the interest rate here and interest rates in most other countries is so high that our cost of production, particularly in capital heavy industry, is exorbitant. The interest rate has a snowball effect which enters the final price in a magnified way.

I have mentioned the various factors which inflate our cost of production mainly because without becoming competitive we have no chance of forging ahead in the international market. Exports can increase only when exports are profitable. While a large internal market does not push us into exports, a large domestic market also has some special advantages from the point of view of marginal costs.

Lastly, business has not given as much attention to quality as exports would require, largely because of a large protected market within the country where the consumer accepts whatever is produced. I suppose everybody knows that before the war anything made in Japan was considered third class, but today Japanese goods are considered the best. What is really required is an attitudinal change by manufacturers so that we can build the image of a top-quality goods producing country.

It is against this scenario that we have to design our export effort not merely for the next three years, but for the next decade. Today, a large part of exports, nearly 40 per cent, is undertaken by the small-scale sector. The large companies have not got into the export business mainly because many of them were set up as import substitution agencies. But they cannot remain so for all time. It is true that some of the import substitution industries have already turned into export promotion industries. This is so, for instance, of bicycles, sewing machines, fans, refrigerators, even textile machinery. However, a large part of industry still continues to serve the domestic market without reaching out to the much larger, though more competitive, market abroad. The responsibility for the future development of exports lies more with large companies than with small enterprises which have until now assisted the export effort. It is my impression that presently the top ten large companies export only about 6 per cent of their output. Their contribution to exports has undoubtedly to increase. I am laying special emphasis on the role of large companies, and particularly the large houses, because it is they who will have to be in the vanguard if exports have to rise fast enough to meet our import requirements.

As I mentioned briefly earlier, marketing is probably another weak link in our export effort. In present-day international trade, up-to-date information is necessary in order to meet competition from other sources. Japan and Korea have established trading houses with a worldwide marketing network. While we cannot match that effort we have at least to move in that direction in order to be able to capture a part of the market and regain our share in international trade. At present, the only comparable trading houses we have are STC and MMTC which, being in the public sector, have their own limitations. We need ten such trading corporations with a worldwide marketing network in the private sector if we have to catch up with the fast-growing world trade. These can be set up only by the large business houses, either on their own or in collaboration with trading houses abroad. These trading houses could be the vehicle for exports of the manufacture of small and medium-scale industries, which obviously do not have the resources or expertise in export marketing.

I notice that the seminar will later break up into eight sub-groups dealing with different subjects. This is a good strategy. However, I would not like each group to come up with only new demands for incentives from the government. I would like to see each group evolving targets for exports for each commodity. These targets have to be worked out not in overall terms, as we are apt to do, but split up into sub-targets for each unit. Only when the responsibility is fixed on the enterprise will the effort be fruitful.

I am talking in terms of fixing responsibility because so many trade delegations go abroad and when you read their reports they all seem to say there are great prospects for exporting to the countries visited. However, in fact, there is no real follow-up action to pursue the reports. I suggest that every time a delegation goes abroad, its report should be thoroughly discussed in a forum comprising of business and government so that real benefit comes from these visits.

I have deliberately restrained myself from referring to the problems business faces vis-à-vis government. I do not want to underestimate the difficulties but I would like to emphasize more the need for an attitudinal change on the part of business in the context of our national needs. Business has a responsibility towards the government and the people, and to itself if it has to progress and even to survive. Export is a national task to which business must address itself sincerely, in spite of the attraction of the domestic market.

May I also request the government that they must help industry by enabling the installation of the most efficient equipment and technology, as without this, sustained growth of exports will not be possible. Export is a cooperative effort between business and government. It is important that each one knows the difficulties and objectives of the other. I would, therefore, suggest that the government constitute a high-level committee to monitor the progress of foreign trade, assess problems and find instant solutions to keep exports high and growing.

Keynote Address at an Assocham Workshop, New Delhi, 15 October 1987.

BUSINESS MANAGEMENT

ATTAINING MANAGERIAL EXCELLENCE

The subject that I have been asked to speak on is 'Attaining Managerial Excellence'. It is as well that we are clear in our minds as regards the connotations of 'excellence' and 'management'. The very virtues of the English language, which is so rich in expression and which is an excellent medium to bring out nuances in thought, can oftentimes become an obstruction to clarity, if for no other reason than the fact that the same word may mean different things to different people. According to the Oxford Dictionary, while 'excel' means surpass or be pre-eminent, excellence is no more than 'great merit'. The same dictionary defines 'management' as administration, skilful handling, manager or managers of a concern. While going by these meanings, I would suggest that management also covers government administration. Although it has become fashionable nowadays to substitute the word 'management' for the traditional and pedestrian term 'administration', I am inclined to apply the term 'administration' to the management of enterprises as well.

I would request you to keep these prefatory remarks of mine in mind so that you may follow easily the trend and logic of the observations that I will make in the next few minutes. Also, please bear with me if instead of dealing with the immediate day-to-day problems which inundate every factory or company manager today, I refer to some general and fundamental pressures, for it is these pressures which impinge upon day-to-day events.

First, let me refer to the components of the character of our national life. These, of course, are not unknown to you. But in the many preoccupations and difficulties that surround the workaday life, we are apt to forget them or at best look upon them as hindrances. My basic proposition is that the overall environment cannot be dismissed or wished away. But it must become our concern, it must be faced squarely, seen for what it is, and to the extent possible, refashioned and improved by our efforts.

What is the character of our national life? We have a democratic political system and a mixed economy.

I shall not go into the questions which are in the forefront, viz. whether parliamentary democracy should be replaced by the presidential form of government, or the kind of electoral reforms that require to be initiated, or in what manner corruption can be reduced. No doubt, all these issues are important, but to me, of greater significance is the need to ensure a greater understanding of democracy itself among both the classes and the masses.

In parenthesis, let me say that today we think of democracy as if it has been the only kind of government throughout history. Depending upon one's ideology, the private or public sector is thought of as the only efficient agent of growth. A moment's reflection will show that modern democracy and modern methods of production are but a hundred and fifity years old. Modern democracy, unlike direct democracy of ancient days, is representative democracy. The peculiarity of representative democracy is that it ascribes the right of sovereignty to the majority, but entrusts its exercise to the minority. It demands less from the citizens than direct democracy, but more from the representatives. It relies upon the self-confidence of free and equal citizens, at the same time it trusts that they will be modest enough to select their best men and to submit willingly to the rule of their representatives as long as they retain the confidence of the majority. Well, we have seen how in recent years in almost all democracies the very first assumptions have been belied.

Political democracy implies two things. First there should be a substantial degree of equality in the sense that all voters have equal influence over the decisions that affect important aspects of the life of the society. Second, flowing from this, it means that inequalities of wealth or of social rank or of education should not be so sharp as to result in the permanent subordination of some groups of men to others in any of the various spheres of social life, or to create great inequalities in the actual exercise of political rights. It is here that, for one reason or another, distortions have crept in. Even those who accept natural individual differences among men—health, strength, quality of mind, etc.—are unwilling to encourage the criterion of merit as such, and to give it its due place. Whether one likes it or not, since time immemorial all societies which have progressed have had a minority which sets the pace. In traditional or controlled societies, this minority—call it an 'elite' if you like—has no merit other than the fact that it has power sanctioned by custom, or that power has somehow been acquired and the general structure is such that a different set of people cannot acquire it. On the other hand, in a democracy, it is not as if the elite as such should be eliminated. There is, or ought to be, a new mode of elite selection and a new interpretation of the elite. Further, from time to time new elites emerge and even groups of elites emerge which engage themselves in varying degrees of cooperation, competition or even conflict with each other. In other words, a democracy is a type of society in which elites—economic, cultural and political—are 'open' in principle and are recruited from different social and economic strata on the basis of individual merit.

What happens in our country is that merit is frowned upon, either because of a wrong understanding of democracy, or a wrong formulation of policies, or both. So much so, those with merit are even discriminated against, and what is worse, people are anxious to disown responsibility. On the other hand, in an on-going society people will be anxious to assume new responsibilities and earn more, if possible, but in any case would want recognition and status. And this motivation is not only deemed respectable, but also essential. We have, however, reached a stage in our national life when those who might be promoted as officers are unwilling to accept this new rank because often as non-officers they would earn more. This is what is happening in the banks and insurance companies following the distortions in the system of dearness allowance. Our present interest rates are such that in the event that anybody is able to save, the savings go as deposit money, whether in banks or companies, rather than as investment in shares. Entrepreneurs of proven ability are asked not to expand, and if they do expand, they are called all kinds of names. The general atmosphere is one of anti-production, as if greater production itself is a vice.

My plea therefore is that first of all, no effort should be spared by those who can think for themselves to create an environment where enthusiasm and energies are quickened and given opportunity for expression.

As I said earlier, one of the major components of our national life is a mixed economy. This is as it should be for I have always held and still hold that private enterprise by itself cannot do all that is necessary to be done. When I was President of the Federation of Indian Chambers of Commerce and Industry, I had organized, in August 1963 or so, a seminar on the problems of private and public industrial undertakings because I felt that quite a few of the problems confronting enterprises whether in the public or the private sector were common and amenable to solution. One of the main speakers at this seminar was Prof. Edward S. Mason, who for long was Dean of the School of Public Administration at Harvard. After pointing out that a great deal of attention was paid to managerial problems in the USA, particularly at the enterprise level, he opined that where the American economy was weak was essentially management at the national level. On the other hand, according to him, in India management at the national level is relatively good and in the Indian economy a great deal of attention has been paid to aggregative problems. He went on to add that when it came to the level of the enterprise in India, he did not have that impression. I felt inclined then to accept Prof. Mason's judgement because, by and large, my own judgement is similar. However, it is a matter of great regret to me that the position is entirely different today; while I am happy that management at the enterprise level, including that of the public sector, has certainly improved, the overall management of the national economy has lost its elan. It will be unrealistic if the problems of inflation, deceleration in economic activity, plan cuts, power shortage and a host of other such ailments are attributed only to the failure of monsoons, the burdens shouldered on behalf of the refugees from Bangladesh and the subsequent war forced upon us by Pakistan.

But some time or the other, we must face the moment of truth and the truth is that over the years our policies have become restrictive, contradictory and demotivational. There is little or no coordination of the activities of the various ministries; there is an endless debate as to who should produce what, when, where and how. The result is that shortages have got intensified, with the production of wage goods not matching the creation of new income or the addition to existing income. Even today planning techniques are discussed as if we have launched upon planning only now. Planning for what, whom and how still continue to be the major issues, and ponderous statements are made that the economy can achieve the best results possible by using the available resources, limited though they may be, in an efficient manner. Nobody, however, is prepared to conceptualize efficiency, lest it seem that there is a reversal of policy which hitherto, by a strange quirk of sentiment and logic, placed the highest premium on wastages of all kinds.

To my simple way of thinking, the ends and means are clear enough. The objective must necessarily be to remove scarcities and improve the lot of the common man. The agencies to be utilized are many: the public sector; big, medium and small industries in private hands, alongwith a clearance of the woods of official controls which are thick with overgrown trees. Above all, there has to be unequivocal and firm acceptance of a proper scheme of incentives, along with correct pricing of skills and capital. If these are done, the so-called conflict between rapid growth and more equitable incomes for the poor will resolve itself. While I agree that growth itself might not benefit the lowest income groups in the short run, it would be fantastic to believe that social equity can be promoted without growth at all. Growth has to be there, and it can be designed in such a way that it is achieved without losing sight of what is good for the masses. The problems of poverty in India are rooted deeply in the institutional framework. If I may adapt the language of Robert S. McNamara, President of the World Bank, 'To postpone reform on the grounds of political expediency is to invite political extremism. To remain indifferent to social frustration is to foster its growth.'

I have deliberately set my focus on broad national parameters, for, in my opinion, they are extremely relevant to an understanding and appreciation of the working of corporate enterprises. After all, unless there is some general recognition of excellence, excellence itself in any department of life will lose much of its relevance. Of course, excellence like virtue can be its own reward; while it would certainly give subjective satisfaction, it cannot be an effective tool if, as I said earlier, the environment is just not there.

The study of management is very widespread today, and like most subjects in the expansionist period of study, it is defined by sophistication and complexity rather than simplicity. There are many new terms to describe and define the principles and practices of management, and there are the inevitable charts. All of you, I am sure, can draw an excellent organization chart. May I suggest that while such a chart has its usefulness, it cannot be an answer to problems that have a human angle. I suppose in a way the organization chart takes note of human nature to the extent that the structure is pleasing and status-giving. But, on the other hand, no chart can anticipate or provide for the imponderables of human nature. Anyhow, it is up to the top management to give flesh and blood to the generalized objectives and to give to projects that meaning and inspiration which will stimulate all the people working in the company to put in better effort.

Those who are at the top have another special responsibility, which is difficult to shoulder, for it proceeds on the principle that one is expendable. Technically called 'management by exception', the concept centres around the point that the top man must train someone as his deputy who will take over at the right time. It is not unusual to find that while most senior executives are anxious to maintain a flow of managerial trainees at the lower levels of management, they are not anxious to remove themselves from the upper end in order to give more opportunities for promotion of the talent they have created. All the training at the lower level, thus, will only result in creating frustration.

In my opinion, the quality of effort that is made by every one of us to improve ourselves as individuals will provide the critical key to open even the most obdurate door standing in the way of management excellence. This improvement is not only in the area of competence and adding to the stock of professional knowledge; it is much larger and covers the whole gamut of life. In other words, we have to get out of pettiness of all kinds, if for no other reason than that life is too short to be little. Finally, let me end with the wise words of Dr Samuel Johnson: 'Life affords no higher pleasure than that of surmounting difficulties, passing from one step of success to another, forming new wishes and seeing them granted.'

Address at the Calcutta Management Association, Calcutta, 26 February 1975.

MANAGEMENT STRATEGIES TOWARDS FULLER EMPLOYMENT

I am indeed happy to associate myself with this Sixth National Management Convention organized by the All India Management Association in collaboration with the Madras Management Association. The theme of the Convention, 'Management Strategies towards Fuller Employment', is of great significance and considerable debate on this subject has already taken place. A broad approach has been indicated in the Economic Policy Statement of the Janata Party, the Industrial Policy Statement of the government and the sixth five-year plan. Yet, the subject does seem to need further discussion in respect of both the strategies to be adopted and, more important, the manner in which these strategies can be implemented effectively.

The fact that we are confronted with the problem of massive unemployment even after three decades of development is indication enough that there is something grossly wrong somewhere. But before we reject everything that was done in the past and attempt to replace it by something brand new it is worthwhile to question why earlier policies have not entirely succeeded.

It is unfortunate that even after the completion of five five-year plans over 250 million people are subject to utter poverty. As I see it, there are four basic shortcomings in the development strategy: employment was not made the primary objective of development but only its side-effect; inadequate implementation of the time-perspective set out, even though there was no shortfall in financial resources; larger investment was made in sectors which were highly capital intensive; and, possibly the most crucial, population control was lacking or misplaced.

In the past five-year plans the GNP growth has been around 3.5 per cent, about 2 per cent short of the targets set out. If GNP had increased according to expectations, it would by now have been about Rs 15,000 crore, nearly twice the current level. With even a constant distribution pattern, this would have meant doubling of the per capita income in the lower income brackets. Consequently, almost all sections of population would have risen above the poverty line. In fact, if distribution had improved, which was likely, the benefit to people at the lower end of the income spectrum would have been even greater.

The failure of performance was not due to over-ambitious planning. Indeed, many other countries have secured much better results, some even without planning. In countries like Japan and France or Thailand, Brazil, Malaysia and Korea the growth rates have been far in excess of our plan targets. Our failure can be unhesitatingly attributed to the sloppy management of the economy. Programmes planned for five years usually took about eight years to be completed. Unless plan projects are implemented with utmost efficiency, they would fail to give the expected results. Indeed, the sixth plan poses an even greater management challenge because it brings to the forefront the less developed sectors and the less economic-minded people; consequently, the implementation of programmes becomes extremely difficult. You would agree with me that it is far easier to set up an industry with assets of, say, Rs 1 crore, than to establish one thousand small units of Rs 1 lakh each. Multiplication of industries also leads to multiplication of problems. It is far easier to set up an industry than to build up entrepreneurship which poses a whole host of problems such as purchasing, marketing, quality control, transport, etc. This is not an imaginary situation. The experience of most of the state governments has been that the industrial sheds they built did not find worthwhile tenants. The management problems of the sixth plan are colossal and if advance thought is not given to these, the failure is not likely to be any smaller.

The other issue to which I have referred is the concentration of investment in capital heavy industries. For instance, investment in industries in the public sector, which during the plans amounted to about a quarter of the public sector outlay, was in heavy industries like steel, petrochemicals, heavy engineering and heavy electricals. On an average, an investment of Rs 51,000 was required to be made in these industries to create one job. On the contrary, in the consumer goods industries, where the private sector dominates, the investment per man was less than Rs 20,000. Naturally, therefore, the employment potential of the plans was reduced. In saying this, I am not decrying the public sector or heavy industries, but only highlighting the effect of the policies pursued. In fact, perhaps, emphasis on heavy industry was justified in the earlier stages.

The failure of the earlier plans from the point of view of employment has led the new government to almost totally reverse the approach to economic progress. It is dangerous to let the pendulum swing the opposite way. Let me explain why.

We may accept that the capital required per man employed in organized industry is large, and as such its employment potential is comparatively less. On the contrary, the capital per man employed in agriculture, and in cottage, village and tiny industries is small and the employment potential is relatively high. Earlier the Government laid greater emphasis on industrialization which saw the emergence of a number of diverse industries, the benefits of which, while leading to a strong industrial base, did not accrue to all sections of the population equitably. The Janata Government has stressed the development of rural areas through agriculture and village and cottage industries so that employment is maximized in a short time. Such employment, however, is not compatible with a high rate of growth. This is precisely why the sixth plan projects a growth rate of only 4.7 per cent with an outlay which is twice as big as that in the fifth plan.

Personally, I do not think the choices are so clear. It is not as if we have to opt for labour-intensive technology simply to create employment. Neither is it that we have to invest the bulk of our resources in large-scale industry where the surplus per man is high. What is required is a judicious combination of labour-intensive sectors and production-intensive sectors. We should look upon agriculture, tiny and village industries as a source of employment, provided the output per man is at least equal to the wage rate. In large-scale industry, employment cannot be the major consideration; it should be commercial efficiency, which minimizes the cost per unit of output. This enables generation of surplus which can be utilized for capital formation. A proper combination of these two strategies will create fuller employment, on the one hand, and ensure a higher rate of growth, on the other.

The employment potential of agriculture is tremendous and has not been sufficiently explored yet. It is not very well known that in India agriculture employs only about 93 persons per 100 hectares, compared to 222 in Japan and 136 in Egypt. The employment potential of land in our country can be substantially increased by provision of larger irrigation facilities. It is estimated that irrigation of 40 million hectares of land can create job opportunities for nearly 20 million people. Housing is another employment-spinning activity. House construction at the rate of 4 million units a year can create jobs for 30 million workers. These are the areas where development needs to be intensified not merely for the sake of employment but also because they produce basic wage goods like cotton, sugarcane, oil seeds, etc., and the much-needed residential facilities. In fact, the development of agriculture itself would necessitate setting up several large-scale industries like fertilizers, cement, tractors, etc. Furthermore, these investments would create employment through small-scale ancillary industries.

Industrial policy does not quite follow the line of maximum efficiency. The approach seems to be that what can be produced by the cottage industry will not be produced by the small-scale and large-scale sectors; and what can be produced by small-scale industry will not be open to large-scale industry.

It is, in my view, necessary to distinguish between 'what can be produced' and 'what can be economically produced'. This distinction is not usually made and, therefore, the whole question of demarcation of sectors is left absolutely vague. The benefit of larger job opportunities can be completely outweighed by the loss to society by way of higher costs of production. The division of industries among cottage, tiny, small, medium and large industries should be done on the basis of social cost and social benefit. There are, no doubt, a number of areas in which small and cottage industries have a very effective role to play as contributers to production and employment. But any arbitrary political decision on this economic issue is likely to go against the very forces of growth and affect both production and employment. If the cost of production of the small and tiny sectors becomes unreasonably high, the government would have to subsidize them for loss of consumption.

I had mentioned earlier that apart from adopting a correct development strategy it is equally necessary that the programmes that are outlined are implemented with efficiency. Here, management is of paramount importance. In earlier plans, the performance failure was largely due to the fact that the plan programmes were not worked out in sufficient detail so as to be ready for implementation when the plan period started. Only broad targets were indicated; specific proposals which could be put into immediate operation were not framed. I feel that the sixth plan also suffers from this handicap. In fact, the failure in this case will be all the more grave because plan implementation depends upon cooperation from a large number of people, particularly in the rural areas, who are not reputed for their management acumen. It is the responsibility of the government and of the local administration to create the necessary environment and infrastructure to make implementation easier. Basically, I would say that the success in achieving our objective would depend on detailed planning, political will, quick decisions and efficient management.

Before I close, I would like to refer to a problem which may seem quite unrelated to the main theme of the Convention. I had briefly mentioned earlier that the increase in population had greatly diluted the benefits of development. Unfortunately, the issue, for one reason or the other, receive sufficient attention and we may be faced with a very explosive situation in a short while. Whatever the political overtones, population control is an economic necessity. I would go to the extent of suggesting that it should be made compulsory by law to limit the size of the family. For instance, sterilization should be made legally necessary after three children. But before such a law is passed, the government will have to provide medical facilities in different centres all over the country for the implementation of such a policy. I mention this because without population control neither fuller employment nor improvement in the standard of living of the people can be achieved.

Address of the President, COIS, at the inaugural session of the Sixth National Management Convention, Madras, 8 April 1978.

MANAGEMENT PERSPECTIVES

Management studies have, in a very short span of time, expanded rapidly in India. The gain in popularity is, no doubt, attributable to the possibility of a lucrative and prestigious career that it offers. That apart, over the last decade it has helped Indian business in professionalizing the management of their enterprises, filling a void which had been created by the abolition of the managing agency system. Management education, however, though of undisputed quality, has often tended to be academic and not quite suited to the needs of the corporate sector of our country. This is understandable as most of the decision-making techniques that it teaches have been developed and are more applicable to corporate enterprises in the developed world where conditions are different and the information system is highly developed. In India, on the other hand, large information gaps exist which make it difficult to apply the tools and techniques taught in management science.

A lacuna in management education is that it fails to kindle an entrepreneurial spirit. Most students aim at careers in leading business houses rather than at starting out on their own. This is, at one level, understandable as some experience in an established concern is absolutely essential before one can spread one's wings. Management institutes should also have specialized courses for people who have already served for a few years in enterprises so as to familiarize them with the latest techniques, as also to help them become entrepreneurs if they wish. No doubt, the entrepreneurial spirit has to be inherent in a person and cannot be taught, but more persons could be helped to develop the confidence which is so necessary to take risks, as also to recognize that the ability exists. An imaginative course of study could do this.

Management education in India has confined itself to teaching decision-making for corporate enterprises, and the teaching institutions have not concerned themselves with the broader issues of management of other sectors and the national economy. This is important because corporate performance in India, as elsewhere, nowadays is a function of the performance of the entire economy and the activities of the government. The linkages are closer and the impact greater in India because government has a large share in economic activity. It plays a predominant role in the distribution of agro-products; it has a share of over 50 per cent in industry; it controls the distribution of critical industrial raw materials like steel; almost all infrastructure—power, transport, banking, financial institutions—are in its control. Consequently, even if these institutions produce the most efficient managers they would not cure the management malaise which is affecting the entire economy.

Today, the economy is being plagued by two-digit inflation attributed to the rise in oil prices. However, this inflation is a result of a decade of faulty economic policies and inept handling of the problems of the economy. While unrealistic industrial policies have resulted in stagnant capacities, shortages and higher imports, simultaneously, an increasing proportion of the productive activity has passed into the hands of the public sector, siphoning more and more investment in the public sector which has yielded nothing in return. At the same time, the management of government finance has been such that expenditure there is runaway. All these factors have naturally resulted in increasing taxation to feed the mounting government spending which in turn has naturally fuelled the price rise.

Management crisis has become pervasive today. Take the public sector enterprises. The total investment in these enterprises today amounts to over Rs 15,500 crore but returns are non-existent. Nowhere is the management crisis more evident than in the public sector where sometimes the top post remains vacant for long periods or the same person functions as the head of two enterprises. Except for those public sector enterprises which are virtual monopolies in their field, there is hardly any public sector enterprise which shows profits or stands on its own feet. Yet, no attempt is made to even recognize that such a crisis exists, to find out the causes for this lack of performance, or to seek remedies. This, in spite of the fact that the public sector is well protected with all the required finance, price preference in purchases from the government, etc.—privileges which the private corporate sector does not enjoy.

The same is true of infrastructure. Additions to power capacity have been taking place over the years, though slowly, but the rate of utilization continues to fall. No attempt is made to cut down transmission and distribution losses in power generation even though these have been noticed as long back as ten years ago. Today, most states have imposed power-cuts in the range of 40 to 60 per cent. Moreover, there is hardly any push to seek an alternative energy source to oil. Oil prices are bound to rise over the next decade. They are already at $ 35 a barrel and in the coming year oil imports will account for 75 per cent of our exports. We have yet to redefine are industrial priorities, intensify oil exploration at home by roping in the assistance of the private sector, and take steps to utilize energy capacities in other sectors so as to reduce the dependence on oil.

Coal, which is considered an alternative to oil, is in a state of disarray. Coal production has been stagnant at 100 million tons over the last five years. This is in spite of the fact that the very purpose of nationalization was to improve the quality, production and supply of coal, all three of which are in a worse state today than before.

Simultaneously, the corporate sector which could have functioned efficiently has been subject to numerous regulatory measures which have cramped its performance. The government has imposed a large number of production, pricing and distribution controls which have eroded the viability of unity. The result is a low rate of return, affecting profits. This, combined with the high rate of corporate taxation, has significantly reduced the resources available not only for ploughback but also for maintenance and replacement. The spate of sickness in industry which emerged in the seventies was often caused by these factors rather than bad management as asserted by political propagandists. On the other hand, almost all sources of external finance have been severely curtailed. For example, limits have been imposed on the amount and period of public deposits raised by companies; bank finance since nationalization has been severely restricted and increasingly diverted to agriculture, small-scale industry, exports and food procurement; whenever anti-inflationary measure are initiated it is bank credit to industry which has generally been restricted; the financial institutions, on whom dependence has consequently increased, have also imposed stiffer terms and conditions, of which the most pernicious is the convertibility clause. The share market, naturally reacting to the low rates of return, has been continuously dampening. The restriction on inter-corporate investment has siphoned off an important source of finance for investment at a time when project costs have risen so sharply that only a few companies can find the required resources for launching a new project.

The industrial licensing policy has only compounded the problem. Delays in licensing, while project costs rise, have led to giving up many an investment proposal by an aspiring entrepreneur. The MRTP Act is one piece of legislation which has influenced all subsequent policies in a manner which, far from curtailing concentration of economic power, has affected the growth of industry itself. The areas of growth of large houses have slowly closed in; for example, automatic growth in production is banned in areas reserved for the public sector or the small-scale sector, completely ignoring the fact that the small sector's own growth is dependent on the growth of its user sectors, viz. the large-scale sector. And why reserve for the public sector? After all, if more competition is brought in with the public sector its performance would vastly improve. Today, apart from those public sector units which are virtual monopolies, the rest are making losses. Better competition can ensure better quality goods, more efficient operation and better results. The tendency towards monolithic organizations must be avoided at all costs. Then again, take power management in Maharashtra. It is much better than in other states because there is competition between a large private plant and the MSEB plants. This competition is not unhealthy and in periods of crisis, as well as in normal times, these two are in constant touch and interchange expertise and consultants whenever problems arise, proving that the relationship between the private sector, and the public sector even when they are in the same field, can be healthy.

The result of all this has been low investment, stagnant capacity, shortages, inability to compete in the export market, costly imports of even those products, such as paper, cement, edible oil, sugar, for which capacities already exist. The outcome—industrial growth in the last decade has slumped to an average of 4 per cent a year as compared to an average of 8 per cent in the fifties and the sixties and corporate investment is barely Rs 1,663 crore as compared to Rs 2,511 crore in 1974–75. In real terms the fall is even sharper.

Why did these policies and controls come about? And why is it that even such legislation as the IDR Act which had a development bias turn out to be restrictive and anti-growth in effect? I would attribute this to wrong perspective and bad management. The bureaucracy which formulates policies and the administrators who execute them have never had the practical experience of being at the helm of an industrial unit to able to foresee the consequences of policies or bring in greater pragmatism in their execution. Policies are often based on a microview or result from political compulsions and therefore have a total disregard for the needs of economic reality. Thus, the corporate sector may be manned by professional managers but management drawbacks in the other sectors are so pervasive that the result is inefficient utilization of national resources.

How can this management malaise be cured? Taking the public sector enterprises first, a major cause has been faulty policies and political interference. Constant supervision by parliamentarians, who hassle ministers, has slowly resulted in greater centralization of authority.

Every minister and every chief executive of public sector enterprises has tended to keep decision-making in his own hands so as to minimize errors down the line which could draw public attention. This is primarily because our Constitution was handed down to us by the British at a time when so much economic activity in public hands was not anticipated. Consequently, the powers of surveillance by Parliament over the government has extended to the public sector enterprises as well. This has a demoralizing effect. In any decision-making situation one must judge not by individual failures but by the number of good decisions made by any manager. In my opinion, if 50 to 60 per cent of managerial decisions yield good results it is good enough.

Then again, within the public sector one must have a policy of reward and punishment. Reward for good performance and punishment for inefficiency. People must be made accountable and responsible for their performance. Efficiency cannot be taken for granted. Further, the current practice of inducting experts from outside in major positions in a corporation must be replaced by a system which gives opportunities for the personalities within a corporation to grow. Unless an individual is ensured that exceptional performance and talent will get its due reward there will be a lack of sense of belonging and loyalty to the unit. There must be a feeling that the growth of the corporation will automatically mean fulfilment of the ambitions of the individual professionals who work for it. These changes, combined with the policy of greater competition between public sector units, as well as between public and private sector units, and accompanied by more autonomy would ensure greater efficiency in the public sector. The above policies will also enable greater decentralization of authority and, therefore, responsibility, which itself will bring better job satisfaction to those at the lower rungs of decision-making. After all, the same talent seeks jobs in both the public and the private sectors. But those who find jobs in the private sector show better results than their equally talented counterparts in the public sector.

As for the rest of the economy, toning up the management and performance of public enterprises by improving their returns would reduce the pressures on government finance. Simultaneoulsy, controls and regulations should be reduced to the minimum so that the government machinery is put to better use in areas such as education, by toning up administration and improving the working of infrastructure. Unfortunately, government efforts are at present dissipated in formulating and administering more and more controls on an already over-regulated and disciplined sector of the economy. If these efforts were diverted to improving the law and order situation and disciplining labour, especially in the public sector, economic activity would proceed more smoothly and with less disruptions, resulting in better growth all-round.

The performance of the private sector, despite having to face many hurdles, is quite commendable. For example, while the public sector in 1977–78 made a loss of Rs 14 crore on an investment of Rs 11,400 crore, the 1,650 medium and large public limited companies are estimated to have made an after-tax profit of Rs 328 crore on total capital employed of Rs 11,479 crore. The better return is not entirely due to the fact that the private sector, by and large, is engaged in lines where the capital-output ratio is favourable. It will be wrong to ignore the contribution of good management. In this connection, I may refer to the unnecessary controversy created about family business. This controversy is totally irrelevant both in the historical context and in terms of our social milieu. Today, the Board of Directors of any company comprises of professional directors as well as representatives from the government and financial institutions. Moreover, quite a few scions of eminent business houses are technocrats with formal management training. It would be unfair to deny them an opportunity merely because they belong to a large house. In fact, they are likely to show better results and need to be doubly encouraged because they have the twin advantages of their technical knowledge and the wisdom and guidance of their experienced elders. Besides, since they belong to a family business, personal involvement is bound to be greater. Moreover, current policies require a minimum contribution of 20 per cent from a promoter, if he is covered by the MRTP Act or where the project cost exceeds Rs 25 crore. No individual or group of unrelated individuals would be willing to risk such large amounts unless they belong to the same family. The tirade against family business is thus absolutely illogical and inconsistent. Further, identification with family interests does give the member of the family a sense of identity and belonging, and a sense of continuity to the corporate entity. Even though finance management theories may treat the corporate entity as an entity distinct from the shareholders, the employees, etc., the fact remains that those who work for the enterprise cannot have a sense of emotional belonging to an inanimate entity.

Today, a large chunk of management time is rather wastefully devoted to fulfilling the technicalities of the various pieces of legislation and policies which affect the corporate sector. This is not all. Getting clearances under various policies, sanctions for loans, etc., consume both time and energy. When will the powers-that-be realize that time is valuable and that it is not only a business cost but also a social cost?

Let me conclude, as I began, by saying that with the direct involvement of government in economic activity through pervasive laws, regulations and rules pertaining to the establishment and operation of enterprises in the private sector, a new dimension has been thrown up to management techniques. Proper management of the economy at the macro level is an essential prerequisite for the successful management of tens and thousands of enterprises at the micro and individual levels. There is another aspect which has came painfully to the fore. Even as the State has launched upon planning or programming, and emphasis is not lacking on a long-term perspective, the fact of the matter is that, especially in democratic societies with periodic general elections, changes do come about from time to time in the centre of power, so much so that the government of the day tends to get overwhelmed by short-term considerations. This enhances uncertainty about the future, and enterprises are unable to implement longer-term policies on account of revision of laws and enactment of fresh legislation. Nevertheless, the management of business enterprises cannot afford to neglect the future, and therefore, must do all that is possible to overcome existing and potential constraints on growth through an adaptive decision-making approach.

One final word and I am done. Those who are in the private sector must develop a comprehensive and coherent business stand in relation to government and put an end to the ambiguous double talk of the 'We want competition—not in our industry, but outside' variety. Unless we are clear in our own minds about our role and status, nobody else is going to accord us the prestige that we seek. I have no doubt that even though the task of management is becoming more difficult and complex, this in itself must be looked upon as a challenge to our skills. We must sharpen them and develop the skills of all those who are associated with the management structure at different levels.

Address at Bangalore Management Association, Bangalore, 16 July 1980.

MANAGEMENT APPROACH TO PRODUCTIVITY

Ever since man invented the wheel and thereby commenced designing tools to improve output, he has had no choice but to be deeply concerned about productivity. Productivity, in essence, simply means how efficient we are in utilizing our means of production to achieve a given output. Indeed, the time-honoured concept of productivity has been the output of workers in relation to a set of machines and production parameters.

However, in a modern complex world, such as we live in, this definition is far too simplistic in that it does not take into account the many volatile and complex variables which have an intimate inter-relationship with productivity. For example, productivity does not merely hinge on men or machines, it also revolves around investment of capital, the use of energy, and indeed the entire socio-economic system prevailing at a particular place or country. I would, therefore, at the outset define productivity as optimizing the complex inter-relationship of inputs such as capital, labour, energy, machines and raw materials, so as to achieve the ideal mix in a given set of socio-economic conditions. In short, there cannot be one correct solution applicable to all conditions in all places, the test of our skill and ability utilizing the optimum mix, so as to achieve the ideal output.

Essentially, productivity is a ratio of different inputs to output and with this in mind, I would like to examine the concept of productivity in relation to: (i) Capital, (ii) Labour, (iii) Machines and (iv) Energy—with particular reference to the socio-economic conditions prevailing in the textile industry in India in relation to other countries in the world. A few years ago, the World Bank constituted a study team to investigate the textile industry in our country. Briefly, barring a few exceptions, the report talked of the apallingly bad conditions of work in factories, extremely low machine/labour output and generally unsatisfactory quality of the finished product. As a case in point, it was stated that the average production per spindle in India is about 40 per cent as compared to other countries. Productivity per operative in automatic weaving in Hongkong was about 280 per cent higher than the comparable Indian figure; for non-automatic powerloom weaving the productivity per operative was estimated to be about 6.5 times greater.

The clear conclusion that can be drawn from these figures is that the Indian textile industry suffers from the economic malady of very low output per machine and operative as compared to even Asian countries, let alone the industrially advanced countries of the West. This is a situation which should be of the deepest concern to all of us, particularly as the textile industry is one of the oldest industries in the organized sector and has had a tradition of reasonably efficient management, besides the good fortune of tremendous inputs of entrepreneurial innovation. What, then, has gone wrong and why are we, by and large, in so unhappy a situation? Suppose imports were freely permitted in India, would we, in fact, be able to compete effectively with foreign countries in quality and in price?

It is worth bearing in mind, in this connection, that barring a few mills, the bulk of the industry basically exports grey goods and that too with incentives, and is unable to effectively compete in regard to more sophisticated fabrics requiring high quality standards. I venture to submit that the crux of the problem lies in the following three areas, all of which hinge on the concept I had earlier mentioned of optimum blend of scarce inputs to achieve an ideal mix.

The first, and possibly the most important, is the apathy of the industry modernizing. It is worth noting that a large number of looms in the organized sector are non-automatic and are likely to be so even in the year 2000; this needs to be compared with the era of shuttle-less weaving that has been introduced not only in western countries, but even in Fourth World countries in Africa and Asia. Again, the bulk of spinning, from the blow room onwards, has out-dated technology and design, and can only contribute to low production, even when compared to other countries in Asia. In processing, we largely rely on obsolete technology, which is inefficient in the use of energy. This alarming situation has largely been the product of availability of cheap and abundant manpower, relatively cheap energy and a sheltered market which required relatively small runs. Given these factors, clearly, concentration would be more on the cost of raw materials rather than on increasing the productivity of men and machines by major capital investment.

In recent years, this position has radically changed in that the increasing cost of labour has made it a scarce resource and energy represents a vital cost factor. It is heartening to note that with the soft loan schemes now available to the textile industry, a number of mills are modernizing their productive machinery. Even so, I submit that what we are doing is not enough, because a large part of the indigenously manufactured machinery that is available is of obsolete design and it is of vital importance that the latest technology is made available to the industry without the crippling impact of a massive customs duty, which in itself renders it uneconomical to instal.

Second, over the years the textile industry has developed work practices which are prodigal in the use of labour. Looking back over my association with the industry spanning nearly half a century, the reason is very clear: labour was cheap and it was easy to employ additional men to maximize output. In those days we never thought of optimizing output, that is the relationship between the number of men and production, but worked instead on the theory that the machine should produce the maximum it can irrespective of the labour complement. With this concept in mind, the industry, which by its very nature is labour-intensive, has become more and more so over the years and the attitude that prevailed in the 1930s, of putting more men on the job so as to maximize machine output, still continues. As a consequence, most textile mills carry large numbers of unproductive workers who have not been properly trained for the jobs they have to do; neither has any systematic study of workload or work assignments been undertaken in many individual mills, so as to optimize the relationship between men, machine hours and output.

In a situation of a high labour complement, most of us resort to the plea that it is not possible to reduce manpower because the trade unions will not permit it. I submit that we need also to examine whether or not the overall condition of operations in mills are conducive to the reduction of men For example, if the number of operatives in a loom shed or in a ring frame department has to be reduced, the end breaks must be correspondingly cut down by proper process control; otherwise, the result would be counter-productive.

Again, tremendous effort needs to be made in training workers in the requisite skills and, in the case of men who are surplus, in retraining them in alternative occupations. In the socio-economic conditions prevailing in the country today, we cannot have a policy of 'hire' and 'fire' and getting rid of a large number of workmen at one stroke. We must address our minds, our energies and our skills to starting a meaningful dialogue with the representatives of the workmen, taking the help of the government in order to evolve an optimal mix of process conditions, machinery maintenance schedules, operative hours in relation to machine output and ensuring that the labour thus rendered surplus will be absorbed elsewhere over a period of time. It is of paramount importance that we are not lax in enforcing discipline. There are, indeed, very few textile mills where there is not a certain degree of what I would term, 'loafing on the job' and 'feather-bedding'. I know of certain mills where workers are outside their departments in canteens, rest-rooms, or elsewhere, for about 30 per cent of their work time, and having enjoyed this privilege over many years, now consider it their right! Unless we take urgent steps to rectify such situations, we will never be able to optimize productivity, irrespective of any other measures we may seek to implement.

Another factor contributing to poor productivity is absenteeism. In many textile mills, workers are drawn from rural areas and they have strong roots in their villages. They have definite social and work obligations in the places from where they come, necessitating their going back for harvesting or for marriages. The heavy exodus of workers from mills during the marriage and harvest seasons results in mills facing the dilemma of either stopping the machines or augmenting the number of men so as to keep production running. If the machines stop, production and profitability suffer. On the other hand, if additional men are recruited, they may not be sufficiently trained to perform the tasks required of them; if they have the requisite skills, then there is the attendant problem of adding to the labour strength. Regrettably, there does not appear to be an easy solution to this complex problem, but I would suggest that one of the means of tackling it would be for managements, by relying on past experience, to delineate the precise periods when the maximum absenteeism is likely to occur and to ensure that trained workers are available in lower occupations to meet the requirements of more skilled jobs.

The third major area is the poor maintenance of our machinery. The World Bank team found that in many of the mills they visited, the condition of the machinery was extremely bad and was not conducive to productivity or quality. Here again, looking back over many years, the reasons are not far to seek. Expenditure on spares and stores was often seen as an avoidable cost, which in times of lean profits, had to be drastically curtailed. At the same time, there was a need to increase output, as a result of which, given the age of the machinery, its utilization factor and lack of expenditure on vitally important spare parts of good quality, the condition of machines steadily deteriorated. We have also been prone to taking short-cuts in the maintenance of machines and using poorly trained maintenance staff, all of which eventually results in the machine performing badly.

Taking these factors into account, that is, relatively low capital expenditure, a high labour complement and poor machinery maintenance, the conclusion is irresistible—that unless they revamp their approach to the management of productivity, many mills will not be able to withstand the winds of effective competition both nationally and internationally. Following the approach of the 1930s towards productivity, in my view, is one of the main reasons for so many mills going sick and for the inability of the industry, by and large, to compete even with developing countries in producing fabrics of high international standards.

For such a complex set of problems, there can be no simple panacea. The essence of what we have to do lies essentially in our determination, indeed, our will, to achieve internationally accepted standards of productivity. Leaving aside the problems of obtaining the best machines and the latest technology, we need to give intense thought and attention to improving productivity in the existing environment. Research associations like ATIRA, BTRA, SITRA and NTRA have done tremendous work in this field, both in relation to specifically designed productivity studies and in compiling inter-firm comparisons. A glance at the data reveals very high differences even amongst mills with the same machinery. Unfortunately, the results of these studies are not given the attention they deserve either by the top management or by operativ-level management and the studies themselves all too frequently become subjects for debate and not guidelines for meaningful, action-oriented solutions. Speaking again from personal experience, I found that in one of the mills with which I am associated, it was only 15 per cent of the machines in one particular department which were causing poor results; once this aspect was pinpointed, intensive action was initiated with a view to improving their condition. In a few months, productivity in that department showed a steep rise.

I recently looked at an international study comparing the productivity of the best mills in the USA and some Western European countries, measured by picks per operative hour on conventional looms on 40s/40s polyester cotton shirting. Interestingly, the USA was far ahead of the others, with the UK at the lower end of the spectrum, while West Germany was the best among European countries. Transposed with this study was the average age of textile machinery, which revealed that the equipment in the USA was not significantly newer than a Germany and the UK. Clearly, therefore, factors other than the age of equipment have had a role to play, resulting in the best mills in the USA having the highest productivity without a higher level of modernization. The principal factors contributing higher productivity in the USA, according to this international study, revolved around machine efficiency and operative conditions in relation to labour utilization and working methods. I think we too need to look at our own mills in relation to these factors and both top management and operative-level management must satisfy themselves that conditions are optimum; if they are not, then strenuous effort should be made to bring them up to the required level.

The same concept applies to workers. The traditional method of training has been for the men to pick up skills on the job and by acting in higher occupations. This procedure was adequate in times when technology was simple, but in an age of increasing sophistication, definite efforts have to be made by managements to ensure that the skills of the operatives are sufficiently upgraded so as to cope with the requirements of the machinery on which they work. Equally, maintenance needs increase in geometric proportion to the technological level of the equipment. Here again, I would stress that what is required is not to train large bodies of workers, but to effectively isolate those who are particularly weak and arrange for their skills to be upgraded. Training should be directed at specific areas of deficiency and should not just be a slogan, resulting in dissipation of effort and money.

The textile industry is a heavy consumer of energy, both in terms of power and of steam. I recently visited the International Textile Machinery Exhibition at Hanover and was extremely impressed by the tremendous strides being made in the industrially advanced countries of the West in reducing energy consumption and re-cycling waste energy so as to conserve this scarce resource. We have a great deal of work to do in this field and unless we increase the productivity of energy, in the years to come, we may well find ourselves in the same vicious cycle as with redundant labour.

Finally, I would like to dwell on a subject to which, in my view, more attention needs to be given and that is productivity of management. Ultimately, the ideal mix of scarce resources to output which constitutes productivity has to be put together by the management and it is the productivity of management which, in the final analysis, represents the touchstone of success or failure.

Management in the textile industry has largely been of a conservative nature and has followed time-honoured concepts in evaluating performance and optimizing it. However, with intense competition, both nationally and internationally, and the demands of modern technology, our concepts of management have to undergo a radical change. While we should not be swept overboard by western styles of managing textile mills, we could usefully profit from their experience in operations research and in computer applications. Many of us in India seem to have a deep-rooted apprehension that computers are not really productive and that they can best be utilized for fairly simple calculations involved in pay-roll accounting, invoicing and other work of a similar nature. In fact, micro-processors and computers can play a very dynamic role in helping management to obtain the right information so as to optimize productivity.

Most mills have fairly established costing systems, which are updated once every six months or once every year, and the costs, by and large, are accurate. This system, however, is a static model which needs to be changed to suit a dynamic world. Mills today are faced with the twin problems of inflation and the need for some amount of capital investment or alterations to machines to make them more efficient. In these circumstances, one of the crucial requirements of operative-level management is the ability to see the effect of a change in one cost variable on others, and the total effect on productivity. For example, if a fuel efficient device is incorporated on some machine, then the operating manager would like to know how this would affect the cost of individual products and the total overall cost. Similarly, a change in cotton mixing would affect a whole series of production variables, which cannot be quickly highlighted in the present static costing system. Another aspect which merits consideration is that different fabric qualities require varying numbers of spindles per loom and the opportunity costs of running heavier fabrics, which need more spindles, as compared to lighter fabrics, which require less spindles, thereby diverting some spindleage for sale of yarn in the open market, needs to be carefully evaluated when planning the optimal use of the productive capacity of the mill. I would stress that each one of these aspects can be examined by manual methods, but would require a considerable amount of clerical time, whereas the essence of the problem is quick information. A computer/micro-processor would, in my opinion, represent an ideal choice.

Again, colour matching in most mills is basically left to the dyeing chemist who selects the recipes through a process of trial and error and eventually arrives at what he considers to be an optimal solution. In recent years, there have been tremendous strides in other countries in the use of computers in this field and I am glad to say that at least one research association in India, within my knowledge, has done commendable work in computerized colour matching. Here, again, the essence of the matter is that with increasing costs, the optimal mix of scarce resources to achieve ideal productivity can be obtained by using computers to broaden the range of options before management and reduce the unnecessary, repetitive, monotonous clerical tasks that have to be undertaken for the options to be formulated.

The third field is inventory control. Money represents a productive asset and should not be blocked in unproductive inventory. Most mills are familiar with modern concepts of material management and purchasing, yet, inventory continues to pile up and attract attendant costs. What is required is careful analysis of lead times, requirements of material and other factors. This information, if properly programmed on a micro-processor, can readily be obtained with pinpoint accuracy so that the operating management of the mill does not have to rely on guesswork to optimize inventory levels in relation to production.

Most operating managements formulate their production programmes with regard to the requirements of the market and the machine capacities that are available and blend these so as to arrive at an optimal mix. This is a regular exercise and although most of us take it in our stride, I would like to draw attention to the fact that in reality what we are doing is exceedingly complex, when one bears in mind the very large number of machines in a textile mill and the enormous number of options in products that are available. A tool that is being successfully used in many advanced countries is that of linear programming, where the available machine capacities are fed into a computer along with the available list of products and an optimal solution is provided for the management's consideration. I am not suggesting that the computer can do the work of the management, but it gives the management a much wider range of options to utilize production capacities in relation to the market requirements that can be achieved by simple manual methods.

Yet another application of computers is the use of electronic sensors on certain key machines, which are linked to a micro-processor that shows on an illuminated console the performance of the machines during the working period. This enables the operating management to see very clearly how each machine operates and take remedial steps on the basis of the defects outlined by the micro-processor.

To sum up, therefore, in my opinion, in the same way as the groundwork for the textile industry in India was laid during the early part of this century, we will have to review the policies we have followed with regard to productivity in evaluating the requirements for the next twenty years. Productivity, for the reasons I have mentioned, cannot merely be a slogan, but must instead be a system optimizing scarce resources like capital, men, machines, material and energy. How we achieve the best mix, in an ever-changing matrix of volatile elements, will be the acid test of the productivity of the management. How best to optimize the productivity of the management, keeping in view the constraints that exist in our country and the socio-economic conditions that prevail, is indeed a dilemma that confronts all of us. May I say, as a parting thought, that optimizing the use of these elements of scarce resources also represents a challenge and, indeed, our hope for the future.

Keynote Address at the conference organized by the Indian Association for Productivity, Quality and Reliability, Calcutta, 21 November 1980.

INDUSTRIAL RELATIONS

PUBLIC SECTOR, JOINT SECTOR AND LABOUR MANAGEMENT PROBLEMS

It has been my good fortune to have participated in many symposiums, seminars and conferences, not only in India, but in several countries—developed and developing. I can without hesitation say that the symposium in which I am participating today is a unique one in many ways. The conveners are all Members of Parliament, and they belong to different political parties. All of them are desirous of spreading socialist education even though, because of their differing political persuasions, they cannot be unanimous in their views on either the means of achieving socialism or the content of socialism.

In any event, I believe there is need for an attempt at reformulating all ideologies and philosophies in terms appropriate to the latter half of the twentieth century. In addition, I believe that the ideologies and philosophies must be relevant to the Indian situation. Years ago, when I was a student, we used to have a paper called Indian Economics. Till recently, I held the view that this appellation 'Indian economics' was somewhat odd on the analogy that we cannot have, say, Indian physics or Indian chemistry. With age sometimes wisdom dawns, and I now appreciate how necessary it is to study economic organizations and laws in the national context. I, therefore, submit that the members of your institute should consider the changing configurations in international politics as much as developments at the national level in India. This will help bring into focus contemporary problems, and help give a better lead to socialist education.

It would be worthwhile to look back at the origins of socialist philosophy. There is no denying that Karl Marx made an immense contribution to thinking. He lifted the natural sympathy of human beings for the underdog to a social science. He based his conclusions on his investigations in Britain in the early days of the Industrial Revolution. It was a stupendous effort. He found men in desperate poverty despite the advancement of science, unparalleled in the history of the world then. The middle classes, having succeeded in enfranchizing themselves economically, were indifferent to the lot of the factory workers who constituted the helpless flotsam and jetsam of society. The working classes were without education and without any voice in politics or in the management of political affairs. Against this background, Marx envisaged the unfolding of a drama which, according to him, was inevitable—viz. the growing enslavement and degradation of workers; society at length finding the anarchy of capitalistic production intolerable; the seizing of political control by the proletariat; the eradication of class distinctions: and the disappearance of individual struggle for existence.

History since Marx, however, has recorded a different tale. I shall not narrate it except to point out that everywhere the more serious thinkers are probing to find a more comprehensive and consistent view of life. There is considerable convergence in purposes and aims in respect of all worthwhile matters, whether it is the growth rate, distribution of incomes, educational opportunity, or social welfare. The American hamburger, the Chinese duck and the Russian salad are boldly listed in the same menu card for the world to take note.

One fundamental point which strikes me is that, contrary to the apprehensions of the socialist thinkers, the conditions of the working class have improved phenomenally. This is not fortuitous. It reflects more than a basic change in production processes. Indeed, it shows how societies and individuals can change for the better, think in larger and longer terms, and bring about an identity of interests of different elements. Marx, in my view, was too much of a pessimist. Professor Galbraith has observed, 'production has eliminated the more acute tensions associated with inequality. And it has become evident to conservatives and liberals alike that increasing aggregate output is an alternative to distribution and even to reduction in inequality . . . . Our increased concern about production in modern times would be remarkable in itself. But it has also pre-empted the field once occupied by those who disputed over who should have less and who should have more.' Technically, socialism by itself is merely a question of methodology.

I was wondering whether it was at all possible to define socialism, and have come to the conclusion that all that can be done is to describe socialism. I feel that socialism, like democracy, is a way of life. It has mainly to do with economic and other relationships that exist between a man and his fellow men. In concrete terms, socialism must mean the promotion of economic, political and social justice. Detailed regulations will not produce the desired results, even as market forces cannot. The only 'invisible' hand that will operate effectively is a change in attitude. And such change can only be stimulated through the method of emphasizing ideals and thoughts, not by decrying them, much less by drowning every issue in the turgid waters of egotistical or ideological calculations.

I have taken more time than I intended in my general observations. I have indulged in these observations in the hope that my views and suggestions on the specific issues relating to labour management problems, the place of the proposed joint sector in our economic life, and how best the public sector can contribute in the fullest measure to our economic development, will be better understood.

Taking labour management problems first, I do not agree with the traditional view that there has always to be a conflict between management and workers. This approach is largely responsible for the present unsatisfactory situation in the public and private sectors as well as in government services.

It is unfortunate that there are a number of cases of go-slow and illegal strikes even in public enterprises. One would have thought that labour would look upon at least these enterprises as national organizations and therefore refrain from adopting an unreasonable attitude. What is more distressing is that labour leaders who claim to be socialists to the core do not appreciate that they have to go out of the way to ensure discipline in public sector enterprises for their successful operation. There is the sophisticated argument that in a mixed economy like ours, public sector enterprises are not really people's enterprises. Such sophistication, I am afraid, does less than justice to the intelligence of the public and does greater disservice to the cause of socialism. Has the trade union leadership developed a vested interest of its own? Or, could it be that it has not woken up to the reality of the change that has taken place in the national economy ?

It is also erroneous to think that the working class will grow dangerously apathetic to their own interests unless presented with starkly opposed alternatives. Today, anyone who is employed, at whatever level, has as many obligations to discharge as the so-called richer classes. The factory and other workers in India have already risen to the level of the middle class. This class accounts for only a small proportion of the population, and in the present conditions in India any rise in its standard of living can only be at the cost of the aspirations of the poorer and weaker sections. Having said this, I feel that the present system of dealing with disputes between labour and management has to be improved upon. Even those who oppose the Industrial Relations Commissions, as suggested by the National Commission on Labour, are agreed on the point. The executive-appointed adjudication machinery must be replaced by a more independent machinery.

In the field of industrial relations, as elsewhere, attitudes have to change. The management tends to look upon every demand of labour as unreasonable, and this is not merely due to occupational proclivity. Not a day passes when the trade unions do not make out how the workers are being exploited, even when the labour force is no longer the weaker section. It is in a position to coerce not only management but society as a whole. Once again, the tested dictum is applicable—it is good to have the strength of a giant but the strength should be used wisely.

Coming to the joint sector, it is unfortunate that already much misunderstanding has been generated, in most part deliberately engineered by some vested interests. It has come to be propagated that the private sector is anxious to get hold of more public funds, and the best way of doing this would be through a joint sector. If the private sector in India has to depend upon public funds, it is because the levels of taxation do not encourage enough savings.You cannot have it both ways. You cannot have heavy taxation and ask industry to generate its own funds. You cannot impose price controls and expect surpluses to be created for expansion. You cannot have regulations on the expansion of enterprises and criticize these enterprises for not being willing to expand. This is, to say the least, a childish attitude.

I feel that the joint sector can play a useful role if we start on the assumption of mutual trust, and on the premise that such a sector can hopefully combine the plus-points of both the public and the private sectors, and reduce to a minimum the minus-points? To my way of thinking, while the private sector is, by and large, efficient, we have not been able to devise a system of social accountability for this sector. On the other hand, the concept of public sector is posited on public accountability, and efficiency is expected to be a by-product. As a matter of fact, so far, we have not been able to evolve realistic guidelines in respect of accountability to Parliament by public sector enterprises. Nevertheless, I am convinced that if Members of Parliament exercise some self-restraint and refuse to discuss in Parliament the individual names and detailed operations of these enterprises, it will be for the good.

Perhaps, it is not adequately appreciated that while running an enterprise, hundreds of decisions have to be taken. Not all decisions can prove to be correct in retrospect. Consequently, it will be more than unfair if decisions are viewed in the light of hindsight, and decision-makers are suspected of inefficiency or malafide intent. I, therefore, plead for greater understanding of the running of enterprises. If efficiency and social accountability can be combined in the joint sector, is it not worthwhile to experiment with it? The fields in which this sector can operate need not be reduced to a rigid formula.

The joint sector, thus, reflects a confluence of two factors—public control and private efficiency. This philosophy itself should be a good index for framing an approach to the joint sector. I have expressed myself on a number of occasions on this subject, and I sincerely feel that if the joint sector is to give worthwhile results, it has to combine management by private enterprise with a view to promoting efficiency and control by the government for ensuring public accountability. I hope that a viable approach will evolve which will not only permit, but even induce, private sector companies to participate in the joint sector in a manner that will help them make their contribution in the field in which they are best equipped, viz. management. The private sector has to be induced because the present administrative procedures and tax laws make inter-corporate investment difficult or unattractive. These matters should be objectively considered so as to make the joint sector concept a dynamic strategy of future industrial development.

Sometimes I feel that the public sector has been more sinned against than sinning. Those in charge of the management of public sector enterprises are extremely vulnerable. Moreover, the management of these enterprises are asked to fulfil contrary objectives. For example, they are asked to set the pace for development without any consistent personnel policy; and to contribute to the exchequer without following a profits policy. I can cite a number of other contradictions. What I have said will, I think, indicate my thinking on the subject.

In our economy, the public sector has come to acquire a very dominant position, and it is in the interest of everyone to see that the public sector has been well demarcated by the Industrial Policy Resolution and, in actual practice, been made to conform to the requirements of growth. There is a certain economic logic which governs the distribution of industrial activity among public, joint and private sectors. Even within the private sector, considerations of efficiency and growth dictate the distribution of industries among small, medium and large. If this economic logic is violated, the costs of production go up, surpluses for future investment have to be reduced and growth becomes attenuated. We have had experience of such misallocation of resources in the past. Such mistakes are often difficult to be noticed or understood, particularly when the market for products is protected and competition is absent. In such circumstances special responsibility devolves both on the planners and the policy-makers to ensure that industrial development conforms to such conditions as would have prevailed in a competitive and efficient economy. It is these factors which should govern our pattern of industrialization. If, as a country, we have to progress fast, be able to enter the export markets, generate surpluses for investment and particularly create opportunities for bringing the large numbers of unemployed and underemployed people into the productive stream, the policy emphasis has necessarily to be on competitive economic efficiency which is possible only when the different industries are operated under economically viable forms of organization.

The futile controversy over private sector, public sector and joint sector has gone on for too long. I am afraid politicians have kept alive this controversy, some in good faith, and some others, to put it bluntly, for ulterior motives. There is, however, a common trait in the family of politicians—to be suspicious of each sector for one reason or another. As they are in positions of power, decision-making is delayed and action for development is stayed. The victim, unfortunately, is the poor man. His lot is in no way better or improved by the daily sermons of some political dignitary or the other, that administrators must change their thinking habits, businessmen and industrialists must reorient their attitudes, students must be conscious of their good fortune, so on and so forth. I suppose all of us can improve ourselves all the time. This applies equally to politicians. If only they would cease to believe that rhetorical exhortations and hypocrisy are the necessary tools of politics, immense good will accrue to the country. Moreover, if they analyse problems in a more mature way and take note of the complexity of human nature, worthwhile solutions can be found. While man is not an entirely selfish creature, he is not entirely unselfish either. Often, the quality of selfishness takes the form of acquisitiveness, and acquisitiveness can manifest itself in many ways, good and bad. It may be the desire to earn more money, acquire more knowledge or gain more political power. If this instinct becomes either too obsessive or if what is acquired is misused, the consequences may be anti-social. The crux of the matter is that having accepted democracy and a mixed economy, every sector, whether it is public, private or joint, must be allowed to function and succeed. Otherwise, we will get into a situation where Nero was found fiddling when Rome was burning. We, as a nation, have to travel a long way on the path of economic development and social welfare. It is futile to lose ourselves in verbiage and dogma. So long as all political parties and all sections of the public agree to find agreement without sacrificing principles, and are willing to suspend disbelief in one another, the future of the country will always be bright.

Address at a national symposium sponsored by the Institute for Socialist Education, New Delhi, 11 August 1973.

INDUSTRIAL DISCIPLINE AND INDUSTRIAL RELATIONS

When some members of the Committee of your Association met me to invite me to be the guest speaker at this seminar, I felt privileged and readily consented. Later, I must confess that I began to entertain doubts as to whether the subject matter of the seminar, 'Disciplinary Proceedings', was really my field of competence. Yet, I felt that I could learn by associating myself with the seminar, and I have also ventured to trust that disciplinary proceedings will not be instituted against me if I were to talk to you on industrial discipline and industrial relations in the wider context of economic development and with reference to the economic crisis through which we passing.

With shortages of essential commodities and an unprecedented rise in prices, the present time is hard for the people. These are hard days for authority also. The current fashion is to question the authority in the home, in educational institutions, in the factory, in the trade union and in the State. And such authority as subsists is unsure; it behaves, alternatively, with reticence and extreme caution, or with overconfidence and niggling formalism. Two other contrary but natural phenomena in the circumstances are as follows. It is those who are relatively well off in industrial employment and whose wages are related to the cost of living index who are strident in the demand for rise in emoluments, while the large mass of the people are bearing the brunt with the customary Indian patience. The government, which has acquired for itself additional powers to take over property without payment of compensation and control and regulate economic activity in the minutest detail, has allowed itself to be weakened by labour legislation, to which I shall revert later. In fine, there is a decline in moral standards both in politics and in economic organization. The rules of the game are not observed, there is neither deference nor conviction. The conventions of discipline have grown weaker, and the mainspring of individual and group action from obedience to command is just narrow self-interest. I would even say that today society needs protection from the irresponsible action of organized groups of workers.

I may mention that as a member of the National Commission on Labour which dealt with important matters covering the entire field of industrial relations and labour legislation, I was able to get better insight into the laws and practices pertaining to labour affairs. You may recall that this Commission was appointed in 1966 and its Report was submitted in August 1969. The Chairman, Dr Gajendra Gadkar, former Chief Justice of the Supreme Court, brought to bear in our internal discussions not only his keen understanding of the broad sweep of labour problems, but also a vibrant feeling that law courts are human institutions and that laws can be a fertile source of both inspiration and perversion. My own limited and practical experience fully endorsed this approach. The Commission's Report reflected many wise compromises on the part of the representatives of both employers and workers. I should have thought, therefore, that the government would have taken action to constitute Industrial Relations Commissions at the centre and in the states, as recommended by the National Commission on Labour. These Commissions, in our judgement, would be judicial bodies with a structure entirely different from the existing tribunals and courts, which have not inspired sufficient confidence in the minds of employers and workers alike. We envisaged that the Industrial Relations Commissions would take up industrial disputes *suo moto* and not engage themselves with issues only when they are directed to do so by the government. Although about three years have elapsed, follow-up action on these recommendations has not so far been taken up. There is still some hope that the government will not completely bury the Report, because the other day the Union Labour Minister, Shri Raghunatha Reddy, informed Parliament that an Industrial Relations Bill would soon be introduced in Parliament.

Be that as it may, I wish to urge that legislative and other provisions, whether in the field of labour or industry, should serve the national objectives of establishing a just society and of achieving orderly and speedy economic development. These objectives have come to be compendiously called 'democratic socialism'. As may be expected, democratic socialism is interpreted differently by different people. But on one point there can be no disagreement, viz. better living conditions among the people as a whole can be brought about only through economic growth. However, the term 'economic growth' itself refers to a whole family of concepts with somewhat different meanings. Either it can be defined in terms of increase in the total flow of total economic output; or improvement in the output per worker; or increase in consumption per head; or increase in personal welfare; or change in the economic structure, i.e. the degree of urbanization, level of manufacturing output, extent of literacy, ratio of capital to labour, etc. Each of these definitions of economic growth has its own use, technically speaking. It is safe to conclude that laymen would like to group them together, rather than separately.

Simple and logical as this popular sentiment may seem, it is not usually realized that economic growth has a number of costs. One, current leisure must be sacrificed for current work. Two, current consumption of goods and services must be sacrificed in favour of savings and investment. And, three, apart from inherent instability or uncertainties of economic growth in our country which is dominated by agriculture and where agriculture in turn depends upon the monsoon, there are also certain external factors, such as the international monetary crisis, world energy shortage, etc.

It is in this wider context that the whole gamut of questions related to labour must be viewed. Such facts as are not very agreeable to one party or the other cannot be wished away, nor can we ignore what has come to be called 'a revolution of expectations'. We have to reconcile, on the one hand, the demands of organized labour and of politically conscious workers, and, on the other hand, the existence of substantial numbers of unemployed and under-employed in both urban and rural areas. This is, to say the least, a very serious dilemma.

At the risk of sounding pedantic and even being misunderstood, I wish to make certain postulates here which have to be recognized both by employers and workers. Incidentally, today, government is the biggest employer. The government at the centre and in the states, local bodies, departmental and non-departmental undertakings together employ 10 million workers as against less than 6 million in private industry.

First, both the groups must not only desire and demand the fruits of a modern economic system, but learn the much more complicated relationship between inputs, efficiency and outputs. I must add here that this recognition has to permeate the thinking of our legislators and government as well. More than anybody else, perhaps the policy-makers have to understand the discipline involved and the cost of economic growth.

Second, the effective organization of an industrial enterprise, or for that matter any enterprise, presupposes a hierarchy, a cadre. In this view of things, an industrial enterprise, though primarily a collective endeavour, calls for division of work on a certain recognized and recognizable basis. The top management has to function as a coordinator of men, materials and finance to produce and distribute goods and services. It has to discharge several obligations to the employees, customs, and investors in the community of which it is a part, as well as to the State. Similarly, the middle management has its own responsibilities to fulfil. Foremen and supervisors too have to perform special duties. In a sense, all those in management at different levels have the obligation to run their enterprises efficiently and successfully. Responsibility presupposes power. Without the necessary authority, responsibility cannot be effectively shouldered. Without obligations, authority degenerates into coercive power. It is, therefore, incumbent on both management and labour to observe some norms in respect of their rights and obligations in order to ensure the smooth and effective functioning of enterprises. Unfortunately, however, discipline has come to be identified not so much with freedom or with restraint as with subservience. This is a hangover of our past political dependance. At the same time, there is a sharp reaction which equates indiscipline with heroism and inefficency with social purpose. The whole attitude to work is thus affected. If an industrial worker in a factory is a perpetrator of indiscipline, he is a victim of such indiscipline in his daily life, when he travels by bus or by train or when he goes to buy his daily necessities in the market. This same industrial worker and his family are put to needless inconvenience when there is a strike in the railways or in other pubic utilities.

Third, it is no more than jumping on the bandwagon if the protection of law is sought by well-paid employees like engineers, pilots, doctors and others, on the ground that they are covered by the term 'workmen' as defined in the Industrial Disputes Act. It is equally unfair if those who are employed in hospitals, educational institutions and other public bodies desire to be protected by this legislation. I do not mean to suggest that all of them should not have job protection and a machinery to redress their grievances. Such a machinery, in my view, has to be different from that which takes care of industrial labour.

It is in this wider context that the whole gamut of disciplinary proceedings must be considered. I do not wish to deal with the disciplinary procedures of a domestic enquiry, which cover matters like formal complaint, preliminary investigation, holding of an enquiry, suspension pending enquiry, findings of the enquiry officer, etc. Perhaps, it is not widely known that in very few countries workers enjoy as much job security as they do in India. In 1962, the International Labour Organization attempted to evolve an international instrument for ensuring job security of workers. In India, however, cases of termination of employment have been the subject matter of judicial enquiry and decision since 1947, and in all cases where workers are dismissed or discharged arbitrarily, they have been either reinstated or paid compensation. Even a minor technical flaw in a department enquiry may result in the reinstatement of a workman who may otherwise be guilty of misconduct. The Industrial Disputes Act has been further modified so as to enable a dismissed or discharged worker to raise an industrial dispute even when his case is not sponsored by other workmen or a union. By another subsequent amendment, a labour court can substitute its own judgement in the case of discharge or dismissal of a workman even if the management has already followed a strict procedural enquiry. This is not all. The employers' right to terminate redundant workmen has been severely restricted. The decision for such retrenchment, as also the basis of selection of the persons to be retrenched, have often been subject to scrutiny by labour courts. Despite what some critics may say, industrial workers in our country have an amplitude of job security which is not enjoyed by their counterparts elsewhere.

In one sense, this over-protection of jobs is understandable. When there are so many unemployed, a job is more than a privilege; it is a means to life itself. Life is sacred in a democratic society. In a community where employment is so difficult to get, a job is also sacred. It is most unfortunate that this privilege can be misused with the result that a husband and wife in India can more easily part company than an employer and employee. My attitude to good labour relations has always been that it is worthwhile for the employer to give a little more to labour than what he thinks is justifiable, on the one hand, and on the other hand, it is in the interest of labour to accept a little less that what they think is their due. Only with such an attitude on the part of employers and employees can there be lasting peace and good relations.

My final submission is that the exercise of irresponsible power, no matter by whom, is dangerous to individual freedom and to democratic society as a whole. Laws and procedures are no substitute for personal responsibility and disciplined private action. We have a choice between accepting inroads to freedom or risking the advance towards a fully democratic and just society.

Address at the Labour Law Association, Delhi, 15 September 1973.

INDUSTRIAL RELATIONS : SOME KEY DEVELOPMENTS

In my talk this afternoon, I propose first to review what I consider to be some key developments around the world, particularly those with a bearing on the theme of your conference. And then, I shall proceed to deal with the Indian situation. Finally, I shall offer some suggestions towards resolving the present unsatisfactory situation on the industrial relations front, which forms part of the general economic milieu.

First of all, I wish to set out my assumption, which is that the industrial relations spectrum is influenced by forces outside the spectrum. A whole complex of economic and political issues, not to speak of new thinking on these issues, require to be looked into, if we are to understand correctly the problem of industrial relations in our contemporary world. I shall exclude the centrally controlled from this review because information about what is happening in these economies is meagre. On the other hand, we have quite a few studies on the problems which beset democratic countries, developed and developing. There is now a 'new inflation' abroad resulting from the behaviour of different economic groups. Although modern governments have acquired enormous powers with a view to directing and regulating their respective economies, they are apparently helpless when faced with the problem of persistently rising prices. The causes of the 'new inflation' are many and differ from country to country. Prices have been rising in economies which are bursting at their seams. The position is no different, as may naturally be expected, in economies which are afflicted by shortages. Conventional theories do not give an adequate explanation in that they make the mistake in particular of seeking a purely economic explanation instead of an economic-cum-socio-political one.

Let us take a look at the world labour movement. Till not long ago, this movement was intended to help the poorer sections throughout the world. It was reinforced by the Marxist ideology with its clarion call, 'Workers of the world unite. You have nothing to lose but your chains.' Good or bad, nationalism has triumphed. Workers in every country wish to improve their lot even if it means transferring hardships to poor people in the developing nations. This is not all. There is a trend among trade unions to protect and promote the interests of their members without regard for the health of even their national economy. The sectional structure of trade unions has led to sectional wage bargaining. The objective is not to gain a larger share of the national product for the work force as a whole. This kind of sectional bargaining, pursued without regard to its effects on production and prices, has led to a vicious spiral of inflation with money wages chasing prices and without any real gain. Such inflationary development, which has become a global phenomenon, spells expropriation for the old-age pensioner, untold suffering for the unemployed, and is a real impediment to the policy of multiplying employment opportunities. These consequences are manifest in different degrees in almost all economies; their pervasiveness and influence depending upon the degree of industrial organization as well as the general level of economic strength already attained in the respective countries.

There is also a diplomacy of violence—open or veiled—on the part of the different economic groups and sub-groups in each nation. Everyone is desperately anxious to maximize his gains and minimize his losses. Political parties freely indulge in fishing in troubled waters. Governments resort to preventive action by way of limiting the crisis so that the prevailing system-wise stability—such as it is—is not greatly endangered. Notwithstanding all the sophistication that has developed in the management of political and economic affairs, the general picture is a mix of violence and appeasement. Thus, there coexist, to put it in political terms, the Chamberlain technique of appeasement and the Dulles technique of brinkmanship. So much so, in politics as well as in economics, the theory of crisis management has attained a respectable academic position, and learned discussions take place about the content of this theory.

As I see it, over the years, political and other theories have become so preoccupied with the question of the inter-relationship between the State or government and the individual that the place of society as such has been relegated to a back seat. There has been a continuing debate between democracy versus communism, individualism versus collectivism, and competition versus cooperation. The facts of life also reveal the need for such preoccupation, in that Fascism brought about the Second World War, and thereafter the USSR as a centrally controlled economy emerged as an important factor. Mao's China also began to obtrude on the world scene in no uncertain fashion. Meanwhile, industrialization gathered further momentum in the developed countries; in the developing countries too industrial programmes got underway. This meant the loosening of tradition and family ties and greater concentration on individual effort and welfare. Thus, theory and practice combined to neglect the concept of a stable society as the nexus for individual wellbeing as much as for decent politics.

There has, however, been no dearth of arguments about bringing about social changes, or as the votaries would have it, a 'fundamental social change'. These votaries always speak in terms of the common man and the under-privileged sections even though they do not obviously belong to these categories. When changes are peacefully effected, they are opposed to them on the ground that they are meagre. The interpretation is put forward that the changes under contemplation or that have been effected are but a device for postponing the date of 'fundamental social change', whatever that means. The thought cannot escape the student of contemporary affairs that the advocates of great change perhaps do not want any change.

There is yet another development which is relevant to note—the marked change that has taken place in the relative positions of the triumvirate that exists in a democratic political system as well as in industrial relations. In the political field we have the three principal institutions of the executive, the legislature and the judiciary. The tripartite approach was to maintain an equilibrium between these institutions. Checks and balances were implicit to prevent the aggrandizement of any one institution at the expense of the others. With the growth in the functions of the government in modern society, there is no denying that the executive has an edge over the legislature and the judiciary in terms of power and influence. Similarly, in industrial relations, the respective roles of the three parties, namely, employers, workers and government, have changed. With the growth of the public sector and nationalization of industries, the government is also an employer, and the interests of the government as an employer is no different from the interests of employers in the private sector. Consequently, doubts are raised about the impartiality of government. Over and above this, it should be noted that industrial labour has developed into a political force. Even while economic literature and political pamphlets abound in discussions about the superior economic strength of monopolies, oligopolies and other enterprises, in reality the management of these enterprises have been, and could be, disciplined by sovereign national governments. On the other hand, it is next to impossible to enforce discipline on trade unions. This is evident from the way strikes are resorted to. The government of the day is almost helpless in enforcing the law against illegal strikes, and more often than not, if some action under law is taken it is subsequently cancelled or withdrawn.

I have set out the position as obtaining in many countries, and it is nor different from ours. Whether this is comforting or not is certainly an open question. Nor do I wish to appeal to you to take comfort in the fact that there are difficulties in every country. I have no doubt that it would be disastrous if we in India do not make special efforts to improve the situation. We do not have the accumulated strength of the developed countries to withstand adverse movements which erode our economic viability. The recent oil crisis has more than an economic dimension for us. 'Oil politics' may well go hand-in-hand with geopolitics and the consequences in the short run will upset the power equation in the Indian subcontinent. Already, we hear about the developed countries making 'arrangements' with the oil-producing Arab countries to get their oil supplies. These arrangements range from a long-term understanding about the price payable for oil to military assistance of different kinds.

No doubt, we are in a vulnerable position, and not merely because of the hike in oil prices. During the past two years our economy has been suffering from inflation as well as shortages. It is not as if such a situation has not arisen in the past. The point is that the situation has moved to a qualitatively new plane of both economic and political importance. Inasmuch as developed countries have their own domestic problems, it will be unrealistic to expect them to help us in a big way. Moreover, it is undignified for a large country like India, which is also fortunately endowed with natural resources, to unduly depend on external assistance which is not essentially commercial in character. In other words, we have to become self-reliant in terms of paying for our import requirements.

Basically, therefore, the question revolves around the capacity to make our economy viable. As a businessman, I appreciate the place and role of finance in the growth process of an enterprise and of the economy as a whole. At the same time, I attach greater importance to human endeavour to make the best use of resources including finance or capital. This is certainly not to say that if there is enough supply of capital, then everything else looks after itself. The accumulation of capital is as much a result as a cause of economic growth and cannot be regarded as the determining factor. I, therefore, eschew both the capital fund and wage fund theories as outmoded. We have to look for new laws for growth, and these will be found, I think, by activising resources, human and material, so that they effectively get into the mainstream of the production process.

If I may, I would like to digress for a moment, to emphasize that there is no substitute for work or for honesty. This has to be inculcated in the minds of all groups, economic and political. What is more, practices must conform with professions. Otherwise, moral precepts, however well-founded, will lose their validity, and what is worse, disillusionment will spread and our very body politic will be in danger of disruption. Already, the by-elections have hoisted the storm signals. I, for one, earnestly trust and hope that Prime Minister Smt. Indira Gandhi, will take note of these signals and stem the rot in our political and economic affairs. I must confess that I am a great believer in a strong government, by which I mean a government which undertakes its primary duty of governing in the interest of the people without fear or favour. If there is no such government in a large country like India, one shudders to think of the consequences. Not only would we have to bid goodbye to economic growth but also to the democratic values and hopes that we, as a nation, cherish.

Who can in this day and age deny that social and economic justice must reach all sections of the population? Who can deny that those who work should be paid handsome remuneration, proportionate to their output? Who does not want that economic opportunities should be multiplied so that the curse of unemployment and poverty can be removed? If we are to go ahead towards realizing these desirable objectives, then it stands to reason that all the parties concerned, i.e. government, managements and workers, should go beyond their traditional stances and approaches. One tradition, though of recent origin, that has somehow to be overcome, is the compulsion to go to other countries for assistance. We have done it for food; now we are anxious to procure oil supplies on concessional terms. Such instances can be multiplied. In my opinion, we have not realized the strength that we possess in our resources—physical and human. The missing link is the will to action, and the will to withstand hardships for a while. I am, however, confident that this missing link will be found, and that we as a nation will meet new challenges.

The challenge of our growing import bill should be met not by cutting down imports, which is a negative action, but through a more positive approach of increasing our exports of all items, traditional and others. The international markets are ready to buy as much as we can sell of commodities like sugar, coffee, textiles, engineering goods, chemical products. A step-up in exports will mean lower domestic availability and even a rise in prices. In a situation which is already marked by rising prices and shortages any further movement in this direction would create hardship. No nation can forge ahead without undergoing hardships. The government of the day should be able to convince the people that hardships are being borne by every section of society according to its enduring capacity. Similarly, the government should not hesitate to enforce laws which are enacted through the

Parliament and state governments. If the laws are unrealistic, they must be changed as speedily as possible. So long as the laws are there, it is the duty of the government to enforce them, whoever the offenders might be—business managements, trade union leaders, or public figures. Trade union leaders, on their part, should look to the interests of the nation as a whole. If they cooperate with managements in the programmes of greater production, it is with the nation they are cooperating. If this view is taken there should be no objection to working seven days a week or cutting down on wastages. It is not the managements that would benefit but the nation as a whole. Managements too, whether in the public or the private sector, must learn to appreciate that management is an art that should not be confused with management techniques. Mere knowledge of sophisticated behavioural science will not make a dent in the fast deteriorating labour relations. Management essentially is leadership and a commonsensical method of handling men. Leadership, in essence, is a blend of many qualities such as courage, will power, knowledge, judgement, and flexibility of mind. One kind of knowledge that managements cannot but possess is that of men, how they can be motivated to work harder and more cheerfully.

I have covered a wide ground, and I hope I have been able to place before you the fact that we are passing through a 'watershed' phase, and how, more than any other time, today there is great need for wisdom and resolution. A historical perspective is only useful to the extent that it provides a useful corrective for remedial action. Let us look upon the challenges as opportunities for positive and joint action instead of thinking in terms of narrow and sectional interests. On this note I close my talk.

Luncheon address at the Industrial Relations Conference organized by All India Organization of Employers, New Delhi, 25 January 1974.

ROLE OF EMPLOYERS AND TRADE UNIONS IN ECONOMIC DEVELOPMENT

'Service Above Self' is the Rotary motto, and I believe that if this spirit permeates all walks of national life, everyone will be better off. I congratulate you for the selection of the topic 'Role of Employers and Trade Unions in Economic Development', which of late has evoked considerable discussion. These discussions have brought out the different aspects in varying degrees of emphasis—such emphasis, of course, depending upon different approaches. To my mind, the development process is a social phenomenon conditioned by inter-human relations and socio-economic institutions. It must thus be seen in a special light and certain factors must be taken into account for meaningful role-orientation of individuals and groups. A clear understanding of the economic framework and the growth perspective naturally becomes a paramount necessity, particularly in the wake of the new economic programme that has been set in motion after the declaration of Emergency in June last year.

The issues affecting economic development are comprehensive and multi-faceted and, in view of the time constraint, it shall not be possible for me to do justice to them all. I, therefore, propose to place before you certain ideas that are backed by my association with industry spanning a period of more than three decades.

What are the tasks and challenges that confront us today as we embark on a renewed process of development and nation-building? The first challenge is to achieve sustained levels of economic growth in order to provide a solid material base for wider enjoyment of the fruits of growth and social justice. Vigorous and dynamic economic growth is the basic condition for the attainment of acceptable living standards for the masses. Unless we can, by cooperative effort, achieve the capacity for self-sustaining growth and for generating higher incomes from increased output of goods and services, there is no prospect of reducing or eliminating the blight of poverty that afflicts the vast majority. Unfortunately, growth rates in the last few years have been disappointingly low and only now the economy seems to be back on the rails. The scourge of inflation with its deleterious effects on savings and income distribution has been a major unsettling force. Besides, a sense of overall indiscipline was eating into the vitals of the economy. As a result, the economy was going downhill, society was becoming inchoate and the polity was disturbed. The task of primary importance in the years to come, therefore, is to remove the constraints on more dynamic growth. Self-sustaining growth requires effective marshalling of national resources and more rational use of our plentiful human resources. It requires the development of skills so as to ensure the availability of indigenous manpower for development. And above all, it requires the promotion of structural, social, psychological and economic changes in all sectors so as to ensure more balanced development.

The second challenge is to create a larger measure of social justice, which is not secondary or incidental to economic development. On the contrary, it is what growth and development are about. In my view, patterns of growth and strategies for development are to be judged by the increase they bring about in the national product and the reduction of inequalities.

There are many dimensions to the problem of inequality: there are inequalities between those who earn adequate and steady incomes from their work and those who do not; inequalities between rural and urban; inequalities between different regions of the country; so on and so forth. To some extent, these inequalities are the legacy of not only a more recent but a distant past. To a possibly larger extent, they are due to the imbalances that have resulted from a somewhat conventional approach to development. The identification of development with large-scale, mainly urban-based, projects has led to the emergence of a small and relatively well-off minority of wage earners. But it has barely contributed to improving the living standards of the masses in the urban and rural areas. As I have already said, greater social justice therefore requires the creation of proper and more equal opportunities—opportunities for more people to secure jobs at adequate levels of remuneration and opportunities for the entire population to participate in planning and implementing development policies.

If I have gone into a somewhat detailed presentation of the current challenges, it is only with the idea of making the perspective clear. Only thus will it be possible for both managements and labour to better appreciate their responsibility, for development and nation-building call for a measure of sacrifice and discipline, a higher sense of responsibility on the part of all individuals and social groups.

The Emergency and the 20-Point Programme have not only provided a point of departure from the past taken-for-granted attitudes, but have also equipped the nation with a new frame of reference whereby individual actions can be judged and suitably readjusted to meet the present challenges, economic and others. However, in various ways and to a varying extent, our ability to achieve the objectives set out in the Programme depends on the cooperative and uninhibited efforts of each section of our society. The basic problem before all of us no doubt, is that the policies for social and economic development reflect our basic commitment to a pattern of social change and economic progress which provide full scope for individual initiative and participation.

In this view of things, what is the role of employers, workers and trade unions and how do we bring about their full participation and commitment? It must be frankly accepted that traditional attitudes are not going to be of much help. New demands call for new responses. We are not alone in our quest. Virtually all countries, developing and developed, are grappling with the problem of adapting institutions and procedures to completely new situations created by profound structural and technological changes and by evolution in social values, attitude and mores.

The most important obligation which both partners—labour and management—owe to the nation in its accelerated process of development relates to the maintenance of harmonious industrial relations, thereby ensuring peaceful and smooth functioning of industries. Strict industrial discipline has to be observed since there is no substitute for it. Unless absolutely unavoidable, there is no room for strikes or lock-outs. There might be occasions when genuine grievances of workers are ignored by managements and absence of a timely solution might result in work stoppages. It is, therefore, our primary obligation to evolve a system whereby corrective measures are adopted well before an issue gets out of hand. There is hardly any problem which cannot be resolved through rational dialogue.

It must be borne in mind that a development strategy aimed at growth and social justice requires much greater use of labour and the rational use of scarce capital. The extent to which employers will be able and prepared to use more labour will depend on their ability to deal with personnel management, labour relations and other social issues which arise from the existence of a labour force which is often unfamiliar with the pace, discipline and hazards of an industrial environment no less than with the technical production and marketing aspects of management. Another area where employers have to initiate purposive action is the educational and informative aspects of factory operations and management. I am convinced that a wide range of educational and practical measures are essential to eliminate the social prejudices which have developed in industry over the last few years. Unless the systems and procedures for resolving differences and conflicts by rational dialogue are widely accepted and the partners in the dialogue are sufficiently responsive to the needs and aspirations of a modern society, there will always be the serious danger of a breakdown of the orderly conduct of industry. The needs of conflicting interests and the consequent class war is really and finally out. It is the convergence and confluence of interests which has to be constantly understood and material attitudes fashioned accordingly.

Our trade union friends have an invaluable, indispensable role to play in the processes of industrialization and economic development. They owe it to society that they educate and inform the workers of the benefits they will derive from development, as well as the sacrifices and changes that development calls for. Trade unions can have a modernizing influence on workers and provide an institutional framework in which all workers, in whatever sectors, benefit from and contribute to build a nationwide movement of solidarity for the poor and the dispossessed who have been by-passed by the process of development.

Based on my own experience, I feel that trade unions must fulfil two essential conditions if they are to play to the full their vital and indispensable role in development. Trade unions must be free. It is everyday experience that a union which becomes the tool of others loses its value as the authentic voice of workers. More often than not, they play to the tune of those who are but remotely connected with workers and are totally ignorant of the interests of workers. Second, trade unions must be strong. It is no secret that the trade union movement in our country has been enfeebled by inter-union rivalries and dissensions. For instance, the limited experience that we have of the working of Shop and Joint Councils brings into sharp focus the problems arising out of the multiplicity of unions and inter-union rivalry. Trade unions, therefore, have not only to accept full commitment to the schemes, but also narrow down their ideological differences. After all, a higher level of production is not a sectarian issue. It is a national commitment and an economic compulsion. The problems of multiplicity of unions and inter-union rivalry can only be resolved by the trade unions themselves. Trade union unity imposed from above is as self-defeating as it is inhibiting on their freedom of action. The National Labour Commission a few years ago made several useful recommendations to avoid and settle any disputes which may occur in spite of the best efforts of employers and trade unions.

One area where labour and management have to narrow down their sectional interests for realizing the goal of economic growth is the development of bipartitism. A view widely shared now is that the existing machinery for the settlement of industrial disputes, whatever merits it may be credited with, has failed, in so far as the concerned parties have not developed the right type of attitudes and behaviour patterns so necessary for the uninterrupted functioning of industries. Too much reliance on adjudicated awards has not put the brakes on the emergence of rational and responsible action norms; further, a tendency has grown to look to a third party for all solutions. Third-party solutions and their willing acceptance is no substitute for bipartite solutions and collective bargaining. No doubt, there are many hurdles. But efforts have to be constantly made to create an atmosphere in which the dark clouds of mistrust, misunderstanding and hatred are dispelled. Admittedly, inter- and intra-union rivalry and multiplicity of unions have been the biggest obstacles. Serious thought should therefore be given to the evolution of a system whereby only one union operates in a unit and, if possible, in one industry. This might sound utopian and may take generations to come about. Yet, attempts in this direction are worth making.

I have very briefly put before you what employers and unions can do to promote the interest of economic development. It is my conviction that a given series of successful responses to successive challenges is a real manifestation of growth, and to achieve this, both management and labour have to stop looking inward. Workers have to seriously review their attitudes towards sharing the gains of production. Likewise, employers have to appreciate that traditional methods of management and the running of industries are anachronistic in the changed techno-socio circumstances. Not only the need to separate ownership from management but also infusing management with social awareness are of paramount importance.

In the end, I would again stress that the concept that labour and employer must necessarily have conflict is outmoded. The world today has advanced not only industrially but socially from the times of Karl Marx. Numerically, organized labour and employers constitute a very small percentage of the total population. Neither employers nor labour has any right to exploit the consumer and, therefore, they have to work together in the interest of the country as a whole.

Address at a seminar organized by Shri Ram Centre of Industrial Relations and Human Resources, New Delhi, 4 November 1976.

WORKERS' PARTICIPATION IN MANAGEMENT

I am indeed thankful to the Employers' Association of Rajasthan and the State Productivity Council for inviting me to participate in this seminar. Many speakers have already touched upon the various aspects of workers' participation in management. I, therefore, propose to limit my observations to what I personally consider basic to the success of any participatory management scheme.

The Prime Minister's 20-Point Programme and the Emergency in the country undoubtedly provide the backdrop to our discussions today. We live in a period of major change, a period in which intensive efforts are being made in all walks of life to establish a secure basis for industrial peace and growth and to thus ensure millions better conditions of existence. The compulsions of development being what they are, a new approach to the problems arising in the field of labour and social policy is obviously a necessity. The participation gap has been the bane of our economic and social life. Many a problem could have been avoided had the people at large accepted a fair share of the burdens of development. To the extent that workers' participation in management serves to achieve the objective of deeper involvement of workers in the economics of an establishment, it is most welcome.

Desirable as the objective appears to be, there is need for better understanding of the idea. Without going into the concept and definitions, I will come straight to the issues involved in the acceptance and working of any scheme whereby workers become a partner in management. According to me, to take a rounded view of management and a simplistic view of associating employees with it, is both unrealistic and confusing. Management encompasses a gamut of activities ranging from the arrangement of finances to the ultimate sale of products. While, on the one hand, it is the repository of the expectations of those who invest, it has equally to watch over the interests of the software of the establishment. Management, therefore, is naturally distributed between different levels of management and a degree of control is exercised at each level, the highest resting with the Board of Directors.

This is one side of the industrial spectrum. The other side is constituted by workers. Gone are the days when labour could be treated as a mere commodity. We have travelled too far and too fast, and today the concept is entirely different, sometimes so different as not to draw any difference between management and workers. I venture to put forward the proposition that the interests of workers and of management may be accepted as identical only if the workers themselves do not feel that they are different from management. I hope, while saying so, that I shall not be misunderstood or misconstrued. There has often appeared to me an inherent conflict between the interests of shareholders and the demand-pull of workers.

To my mind, there is need to understand the real nature of shareholding, since much of the controversy has emanated from lack of it. A return to a shareholding public is looked upon with a frown. But an objective analysis of the economics of production will convince us that what is generally termed as profit is nothing more than the cost of finance or the return on investment. All those who put up capital in a venture do expect and deserve, a payment for not only forgoing their immediate consumption needs but also for taking the risk. Much of finance today comes from financial institutions and even from international transfer of capital. We pay a cost for it. To attach any stigma to such payment of cost, to me, is not fair.

Let me add a word of caution here. It would be wrong to attempt to see in differences the seeds of class struggle. I do not think that in a democracy and economic system like ours, there is any place for class consciousness or struggle. As a matter of fact, the present Emergency is aimed at curbing any such tendencies that might have crept into our body politic. Yet, striking a balance between the pulls and pressures on the gains of industry has been an important concern of planners and economists. It would, therefore, be puerile to pursue an idea without examining its chances of smooth sail, and I feel we should do it now.

I have referred to this management-organization only to highlight the true nature of managerial functions, since any scheme of participative management would require a decision as to at what level of management participation of workers is to be accepted. I submit that we study the whole idea from a somewhat unconventional angle. Let it be shorn of all sensationalism and let us be absolutely objective in our approach. To my mind, for the success of any participatory scheme, a degree of commonality of interest is a must. This commonality can best be found in increased production and productivity. Unless workers look at the economics of production as any shareholder would, the participation would only be superficial and lead to those very ailments which the scheme is intended to remove. Merely sitting on the Board of Directors or in Management Committees would not serve any purpose. The concept of trusteeship sounds very nice to the ears and evokes sophisticated emotions. But the hard fact of life is that the investing public has a larger stake in any establishment than those who join when everything is set for production. We should, therefore, start workers' participation by making them participate in equity shares. A particular year's bonus may be paid in the form of shares.

Participation at this level would have a number of advantages. First, there would be better appreciation of the functional organization of the establishment. Second, with workers' shareholding, the confidence gap as regards financial arrangements would disappear, and workers would have better access to the information they so eagerly wish to have. The ever present scepticism about the *modus operandi* of management will not be there.

I am really worried about the suspicions and doubts that are generally entertained by both sides. Any participatory scheme is bound to fall flat if it cannot remove these doubts and create an atmosphere of confidence. The real test, therefore, of workers' participation in management, is the degree to which each partner can shed his inhibitions and approach production problems in a spirit of give-and-take and cooperation. Hence my suggestion for equity participation by workers. This would not only help create an atmosphere of trust, but would help remove impediments in the way of introducing incentive schemes, and much of the controversy that surrounds 'the sharing of the gains of productivity' will melt away on its own.

I am quite conscious of the implications of my suggestion and the kind of responses it will evoke. I do not, however, even for a moment, suggest that we wait till such time as the idea gets accepted. A beginning can be made either by activating the already existing Works Committees or by setting up Joint Consultative Committees. It is not my intention here to spell out the functions which these committees or councils should be entrusted with. The responsibility rests with both managements as well as workers. Managements must see that they are not unnecessarily conservative about passing on information to workers, and trade unions have to ensure that their multiplicity and rivalries do not result in bogged-down discussions.

I have a suggestion to make here. We already have some experience of the work of Joint Management Councils. It would be a worthwhile exercise if the participants present here probed the reasons for their failure. Absence of commitment apart, my own feeling is that these Councils are loaded with terms of reference which are beyond their will to discharge. More often than not, they become forums for horse-trading. Or they come to be regarded as the antithesis of trade union functions and objectives. This might be one of the reasons that in a number of Scandinavian and West European countries, which have been pioneers in initiating workers' participation in management schemes, the whole idea is being abandoned. What is, therefore, of paramount importance is that the workers recognize the role they must play to impart health to our economy, with or without participation. The happenings in England are a creation of inward-looking trade unions and a pointer to the fact that self-interest pursued beyond a point is a self-defeating exercise. Their wage demands undoubtedly have gone far ahead of the gains of the economy, and the Labour government has been forced not only to place restraints on wage increases, but also to think in terms of throwing open the reserved sectors to private entrepreneurship. We need not, and should not, repeat past mistakes.

I would like to add a note of caution, before I close. A number of economic, political and social problems have arisen today because we have tended to pursue certain high-sounding ideas and cliches without examining their practicability. It must not be forgotten that what is right in principle may not always be so in practice, and unfulfilled expectations and promises are as bad as their creation. Much of our suffering is undoubtedly on account of the 'expectations explosion'. I, therefore, implore the participants here to thoroughly examine the pros and cons of the participatory scheme and then formulaté practical guidelines. It is not that I am against such a scheme. As a matter of fact, I have experience of about four decades of the scheme in my own concern, where an elected worker-member sits on the Board of Directors. I am, however, a born debater and have always accepted scepticism as a source of enlightenment.

Address at a seminar in Jaipur.

IMPACT OF THE NEW ECONOMIC POLICY ON LABOUR AND INDUSTRIAL RELATIONS

It gives me great pleasure to welcome you all to this national seminar on 'Impact of the New Economic Policy on Labour and Industrial Relations' organized by the Shri Ram Centre in collaboration with the International Labour Organization. This seminar was earlier scheduled to be held from 13 to 15 January 1993, but had to be postponed keeping in view the suggestions from several quarters. Many participants felt that by postponing the seminar by a couple of months, i.e. after the budget proposals are presented in February 1993, it would be better able to review the entire package of reform measures—both old and new.

The seminar has been designed so as to provide sufficient time for deliberations, especially in the syndicate groups. The participants would not only get an opportunity to put forward their views on various issues but will also benefit from the response of others. In the process, something pragmatic will no doubt emerge. Unlike other seminars, which are usually of a tripartite nature, the present seminar has a large participation of academicians. It is hoped that the views of the concerned parties will be reviewed by the academicians for working out alternatives within a theoretical frame. The right alternatives could then be chosen and acted upon through the process of consultation.

While the broad theme of the seminar is 'Impact of the New Economic Policy on Labour and Industrial Relations', four important thrust areas have been chosen as sub-themes for in-depth discussion. In the course of the deliberations, other important aspects having a bearing on the sub-themes can also be taken up. The objective is to undertake a review of the reform measures already initiated and to evaluate the present status of their implementation. The objective is also to assess what new measures need to be taken and identify the areas in which a broad consensus exists.

As one who has been associated with the country's industrial development for long, I have been pursuing the course of the reform measures with great interest. As I understand it, at the heart of the present programme for economic reform is the desire for integration of the Indian economy with the world economy on a broad front. The expectations are that such an integration would contribute to higher growth as has happened in several other countries of the world. The new policy obviously assumes that India from now on, in increasing measure, will have to compete with the rest of the world—for markets, for investments, for technology.

These are developments of historic importance and it is clear that every aspect of our industrial life, including industrial relations and human resource management, will need to undergo changes if things are to succeed. The first thing that comes to mind is the necessity of having a well-thought-out industrial relations policy as well as institutional arrangements for putting it into practice. On the industrial relations front India has had so many stalemates for so many years that we would now have to quickly go about clearing the cobwebs. Workers, entrepreneurs, investors, all will have to know where matters stand regarding the various pending legislations. While healthy debate is the most necessary part of the democratic process there is no doubt that sooner or later clear-cut decisions on certain over-riding matters will have to be taken.

A second area of crucial importance is our ability to absorb new technology. This means that the human resource development and industrial relations of an organization will have to be such that it can make continual improvements in technology without getting derailed and without facing breakdowns of the human system. A certain flexibility will have to exist on the shop-floor and the workers will have to be kept well-trained. If there are redundancies, the need for retraining is going to be more urgent than ever. Above all, there will have to be a higher degree of participation of all concerned at various levels so that the organization can forge a common will and convert it into material gains.

A lot of well-deserved attention is being paid to the issue of developing an exit policy. There is no doubt that we should have an exit policy and that it should have a human face. Yet, I cannot help feeling that the redundancy of workers here and there and their redeployment is not so much the issue as is the general discipline of those who are at work, who are not threatened by redundancy, who have no danger even of becoming obsolete.

Many great men have remarked that Indians, while superbly gifted in so many ways and a match for anyone in the world, tend to show a disheartening lack of discipline when it comes to organized endeavour. I am afraid this is all too true of the situation in the industrial domain. The shortcomings that one notices when one compares our industry to the successful industrial cultures of the world are not lack of intelligence, or technique, or even money, but the phenomenon of indiscipline multiplied a thousand-fold, over and over, until our efforts are reduced to a level where they have neither the effectivity nor the force to compete on the global plane.

Nowhere is this problem of indiscipline reflected more than in the quality and cost of our products. As is well known, our reputation for quality in the world markets is not high. Our human and industrial relations systems will have to be such that they stimulate a dynamic improvement in costs and quality rather than be a hindrance to it. Unless this is done our share in global trade is bound to remain poor irrespective of the changes we make in our economic policy.

What is most encouraging in the present scenario is the fact that many trade union leaders are also thinking of ways of boosting the country's economy in the quickest possible time. They recognize that only better economic health can raise the standard of living of the masses and provide more employment. It is also being better understood that the struggle for higher material gains is important but that such gains can ultimately come only through higher productivity, and that if this linkage is broken, then no industry can survive in a globalized context.

Of late, there has also been greater emphasis on bipartitism. The trade unions are considered mature enough and strong enough to negotiate directly with managements. The government has also been encouraging such direct negotiation as the trade unions no longer need its continual intervention. As a result, in many of the industries, bipartite agreements, including five-yearly wage agreements, have been signed, resulting in industrial peace. Let us hope that in the coming years, such trends will continue.

Finally, it has to be well understood that managements now have to lead their companies more conscientiously than ever before. In order to command respect and regard, one has to elevate one's values in life and set an example for others. As I said, discipline is at the root of all success. India demonstrated a very high level of discipline during her freedom struggle. Let us demonstrate the same once again in our struggle for economic freedom.

Welcome address at a national seminar at Shri Ram Centre for Industrial Relations and Human Resources, New Delhi, 13 April 1993.